0

Other books by Arthur Faram:

La Merica

Ancient Signposts

ISBN-13: 978-0-578-71432-5

Published by The Foundation Press

Edited by Elite Authors

The

Ancients

Secrets of the Old World

by

Arthur Faram

Dedicated to my wife and children

Who have supported me through it all.

Introduction

You are about to enter into a world where knowledge, spirituality, and science come together in a way only the ancients and a few protectors of the ancient ways are aware of. A world that steps outside the norm and brings to you ancient knowledge and spirituality combined in ways practiced by the ancients. These are ways taught and passed down from the early days of creation.

For millennia ancient information has been available to those who had the resources to access it. Recently there have been research tools developed, such as Google, Google Earth, and other sites, which have allowed individuals to travel the entire world and perform research in places where they would have never had access before.

With the recent technology boom, much of this previously hidden and ignored information is becoming available to the academic community. This book will go back in time and visit many of the artifacts and geoglyphs around the world to present an updated and more complete picture of man's ancient history and spirituality. The main theme of the book is to reveal the true nature of ancient beliefs and practices and to expose many secrets that have been hidden from the general public. While reading this book, you will be exposed to two concepts of belief systems, "religion" and "spirituality." The concept of religion is a modern concept adopted by many academics to explain various modern belief systems. (See Brent Nongri's paper "Dislodging 'Embedded' Religion," quoted in Chapter 1.) It is difficult for one who has not been exposed to ancient spirituality to understand that the original concept of spirituality has been replaced by a structured ceremony called religion. From ancient times until recently there was no religion. Spirituality is an individual concept of everyday living and communing with our environment and God. It requires no organization, as the individual is one with and in constant contact with the eternal force that many call God.

Much of the history written here you will see for the first time. That is because this history was not available until the discovery of the ancient science of geoglyphology. Since the discovery of geoglyphology in 2003, many of the physical discoveries made possible have been intentionally removed or altered by some unknown entity. This is presumably to hide the fact that there once existed an ancient technology and belief system rivaling our own.

The beliefs and science mentioned in this book have been handed down through the ages to various cultures, some secret and some public. The cultures practicing the ancient science of geoglyphology are the same cultures which practiced the ancient spiritual ways that can be traced back tens of thousands of years to ancient Japan. This knowledge can be tracked by following the symbols used by the ancients, from their beginnings to modern days. I warn you against trying to follow cultures by name. Names change, but cultural and spiritual symbols do not. "Follow the symbols, not the names".

For centuries man has known that there had to be a worldwide culture. There are too many objects, such as pyramids, dolmans, petroglyphs, and symbols that span the world with their presence to believe otherwise. However, there has been an absence of academic support that would tie them all together. The discovery of geoglyphology places us one step closer to understanding our ancient past.

Ancient Japanese documents, ancient Japanese symbols, Vedic and other surviving texts from the ancient periods all tell a story that has been handed down for millennia, and for the most part hidden from or ignored by the public. Although these geoglyphs and other important discoveries should be heralded by scientists, the academic world has been slow to pick up on the new discoveries being published around the world.

In ancient times there was a harmonious and symbiotic mix of philosophy and spirituality. In modern times these disciplines were separated into science, philosophy and religion. This separation has not served us well. There have been more lives lost in the name of religion than for any other modern reason. Hopefully after you read this book, it will become clear that we once lived in a harmonious world community of spirituality rather than fighting each other over whose religion is better or who can build the bigger bomb. The ancient spirituality was a way of life, not a religion, lived under respect for our environment and all living things. The ancient way was to live as a spiritual being rather than as a member of a recently developed, man-made, organized religion.

In the book there will be references to ancient spiritualism. These references are not made to change anyone's ideas about their religion. That is a personal choice, but the choice should be an informed one. The reason spiritual beliefs are even mentioned here is because our research has shown that the cultures who used the ancient technology revealed in the book were the same ones who followed the ancient spirituality. That spirituality consisted of a personal communication with cosmic energy, God, and the practice of goodwill and love. This is the belief system taught to us by our ancient teachers and adopted by many ancient and modern cultures. Many times, due to persecution by less informed groups, the ancients went underground when their culture was in danger of being disassociated from the truth.

Some areas of study do not interface with science at all, such as theology, history, ethics, and more. This doesn't mean that each of these areas never interact with science. Still, the point is some issues lie outside the scope of science but can still be rationally evaluated and counted as knowledge.

As the philosopher of science Nicholas Rescer put it, "Science does not have exclusive rights to 'knowledge'; its province is far narrower than that of human intellectualism in general. Even among the 'modes of knowledge,' science represents only one among others...But there are other areas of human experience—

areas wholly outside the province of science—in which we have cognitive interest."

"There is knowledge outside science."

Author's Note:

It would be very difficult to understand the history discussed in this book without first understanding the ancient science of geoglyphology. Geoglyphology has been used and handed down through secret societies for tens of thousands of years. The facts that "Stone Age man" was able to project lines across thousands of miles, and connect to their objective with little or no error, is in total opposition to current teachings. This would suggest that a higher technological capability existed either in or alongside ancient cultures. Before proceeding, please read Narrative P for a complete description of geoglyphology.

Once you have read Narrative P please visit Narrative Q for a look at a survey of the Sterling Castle, Scotland, geoglyph. This geoglyph is provided as a sample of perfection in a geoglyphological survey.

What follows in the book is a history documenting the trail left by the ancients in perpetuating and protecting these ancient truths.

Table of Contents

Chapter 1
Ancient Influences

Much of what we are today, as a world community, is the result of an original concept of civility, spirituality, and love, which was taught to man millennia ago and passed down through time. Unfortunately, this pattern of world peace and civility has been interrupted by various outside influences that would make the world over into their idea of normalcy. These disruptive influences have had a horrific effect on the world peace and harmony that once existed. Throughout time various groups and persons have corrupted these ancient teachings through self-indulgence, greed, and the intentional destruction of ancient wisdom.

Scholars and philosophers have been trying to pin down the concept of a worldwide social network for millennia. Most know that a pattern of world commonality is there, but they are tied by their academic allegiances to a pattern of peer pressure that leads to the rehashing of old ideas rather than striking out in new directions. The deterioration of the original teachings is easy to imagine when you take into account all the thousands of years of self-serving conflict, both politically and spiritually, which has fractured the original concept of man living in peace as one people.

At this point in time, explorers that represent the close-knit community of lettered scholars are slow to recognize or research the discoveries made by persons outside the academic community. This also holds true of discoveries made from inside the community, if that information threatens previous concepts.

It is understandable that before a discovery is accepted by the academic community, they must insure that the initial information expressed in a new discovery is accurate. The process by which this information is vetted is called peer review.

Peer review is the evaluation of work by persons with similar competences to the producer of the work (peers). This process functions as a form of self-regulation by qualified members of a profession within the relevant field. Peer review methods are used to maintain quality standards, improve performance, and provide credibility. In academia, scholarly peer review is often used to determine an academic paper's suitability for publication and can be categorized by the type of activity and by the field or profession in which the activity occurs.

One problem is that researchers tend to research areas with which they are comfortable or familiar. Academically, those who stray outside the structured road of acceptable protocols are chastised for leaving the accepted standard. This type of structured thinking and research can only lead to selective disclosure of any new discoveries and the rehashing of old ideas.

But what happens if the new discovery is so radically different than any current field of study? Where does the discoverer of such radical information go for vetting of his or her new discovery? Is there a clearing house for new discoveries to be presented and dispersed for examination? If there were, could such an organization exist without being threatened by scholastic, political, or religious influences?

There are several interests around the world that have attempted to maintain the teachings of old as they were passed down to us from our ancient ancestors. Several have been successful; several exist in a slightly modified atmosphere of truth. Some have maintained the spiritual
aspects of the old teachings but have also bowed to the political, religious, and peer pressures of their environment.

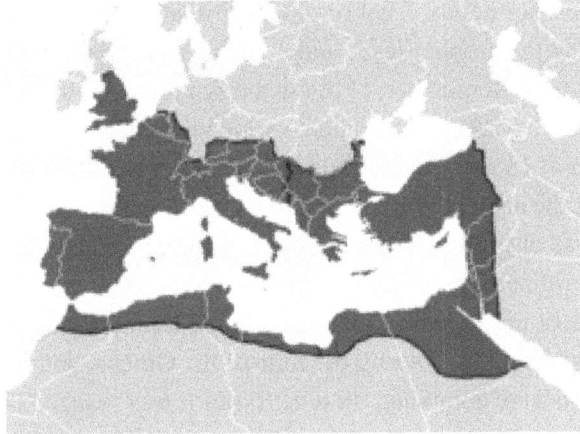

Roman and Byzantine (East Roman) Empires, ca. 400 CE

Many spiritual practitioners exist in a highly modified or even corrupt form of beliefs that includes politics, corrupted spirituality, and greed. The image above shows the two Roman Empires, east and west. The west was Christian, and the east was Orthodox Christian. Orthodox means original. Merriam-Webster explains,

"An orthodox religious belief or interpretation is one handed down by a church's founders or leaders. When capitalized, as in Orthodox Judaism, Orthodox refers to a branch within a larger religious organization that claims to honor the religion's original or traditional beliefs. The steadfast holding of established belief, as seen in religious orthodoxy, is apparent also in other kinds of orthodox behavior."

Orthodox Christianity retains much of that spirituality today. The Eastern Orthodoxy originally practiced the Coptic ways taught by Jesus. They bowed under the pressure of Rome and amended their outward appearance to appease the Roman church. Just the word orthodox is a clue to the relationship that existed at the time Christian orthodoxy was formed. In order for there to be an orthodox, there must be an unorthodox. That original spirituality is known as Coptic, as taught by the prophet Jesus and many prophets before him under various names. Remember, "Follow the symbols, not the names."

In the perfect world, there would be no need for politics or greed. But of course we do not live in a perfect world. However, by practicing the ancient ways taught to us by our ancient ancestors, we can begin to change our world to more closely resemble the paradise we were originally given by our creator.

Most fail to realize that our original teachers taught wisdom, love, and philosophy. During the time of the Greeks, both philosophy and science were combined. In older times it was realized that there can be no science without recognizing the spiritual aspects of all we do. Down through time this noble concept was affected by the many agendas instilled by its detractors. We have not always been prey to our hedonistic desires. Society in general has been influenced by outside forces that exist to use us for their own designs. Ancient documents tell us that man lived on the earth in a state of peace and grace much longer than the relatively short time we have been subjected to the sins of our forefathers. By destroying our history, our detractors remove any measuring stick with which to judge our current situation. We were not born to suffer but came here to live in a state of peace and love and learning.

It is this ancient spirituality that is mentioned throughout this book. The old teachings have been carried down through time on the shoulders of some very brave men and women so that when it is again the accepted norm, the earth will return to its former glory.

A Convergence between Religion and Science

The following passage is taken from the book *Kami no Daikeirin*, by Koya Okada, narration by Dennis Mitchamson.

> "Religion (Christianity) had absolute power in Western Europe during the Middle Ages. Scientific truth was also hushed up when presented in regard to religion. Big

changes began in the sixteenth century with the appearance of Copernicus and Galileo.

In the nineteenth century there was a leap forward by science which completely changed its views. A self-satisfied science had deluded itself in having gotten to the point of knowing everything about the universe. However, in the twentieth century the absolute authority that science seemed to have obtained began to waver due to quantum mechanics. The reason for this was that the fact of a borderline between matter and what is immaterial, which up to then had been a religious matter, was acknowledged precisely by way of quantum mechanics.

The existence of "the beyond" became a subject for research. Scientists in the West carried out research on telepathy and the mechanism of communication with the spirit world.

Professor Charles H. Townes, who was an expert in the modern physics sector, stated the following in his conclusion that there would soon be a convergence between science and religion: [Author's note: Little did Townes realize that when he made this statement about science and spirituality, they were already once combined.]

"Religion and science are too similar to a large extent. As long as they don't arbitrarily lock themselves up in their own domain, they should, sooner or later, converge in clear fashion."

I'm convinced that such a convergence is inevitable. The reasoning is that religion and science are the demonstration of the efforts made by people to understand Great Nature (the Universe) and their need to decisively tackle the question regarding its essence. The one who in the religious world made use of the thesis by Professor Townes was Master Kotama Okada.

The same Master Okada predicted that, thanks to the progress made by physics, we would enter in the realm of a matter divided up into extremely tiny parts, i.e., a realm full of completely invisible infinitesimal particles.

In recent times a great deal of attention was given to the fact that a "top quark" was finally identified in the research center of the American Fermilab laboratory. This discovery led to a successive thesis. In other words, the confirmation of the existence of a top quark forced important scientists to tackle a new and difficult subject related to the existence of virtual particles. It was undoubtedly the attack on the nature of the theory concerning elementary particles that brought about the outburst by the well-known American critic J. Lipton, who exclaimed, "Tinier and tinier particles keep emerging one after another. There's no end to them!"

Master Kotama Okada had already carried out research on the subject from the beginning of the 1960s, passing from atoms to the realm of elementary particles. He foresaw that the realm of the "void" would be reached in the end, which was something that the science of quantum mechanics had been unable to grasp. He insisted on stating that religion and science are ultimately a oneness.

I think so too. Isn't it true that the discovery of the Higgs Boson particle was followed by the discovery of the ectoplasm already foreseen by Master Kotama? Furthermore, the same master had already explained that within ectoplasm there are astral particles which themselves contain other particles. Rather than material, these last particles are of a spiritual nature.

The most advanced part of quantum mechanics is by now on the threshold of the spiritual realm. There have even appeared researchers who have concluded "something conscious created all the things in this world" and that moreover there is a gigantic spiritual realm behind this "something conscious." Some scientists have already widened the range of their studies on the world of the beyond which has so far been a matter reserved to religion. Religion and science are re-converging."

The following is an excerpt from "Dislodging 'Embedded' Religion: A Brief Note on a Scholarly Trope," a paper presented by Brent Nongbri of Yale University's Department of Religious Studies in 2019. It expresses so well our lack of understanding in that the "spirituality" of the ancients was not a religion but a way of life.

Abstract: Scholars of ancient cultures are increasingly speaking of the "embeddedness" of ancient religion—arguing that the practices modern investigators group under the heading of "religion" did not compose a well-defined category in antiquity; instead, they claim that "religion was embedded" in other aspects of ancient culture. These writers use this notion of "embeddedness" to help us see that categories post-Enlightenment [*] thinkers often regard as distinct (such as politics, economics, and religion) largely overlapped in antiquity. The trope of "embedded religion" can, however, also produce the false impression that religion is a descriptive concept rather than a re-descriptive concept for ancient cultures (i.e., that there really is something "out there" in antiquity called "Roman religion" or "Mesopotamian religion," which scholars are simply describing rather than creating). By allowing this slippage between descriptive and re-descriptive uses of "religion," the rhetoric of "embedded religion" exacerbates the very problem it is meant to solve…

[*Merriam-Webster's defines the Enlightenment as "a philosophical movement of the eighteenth century, characterized by belief in the power of human reason and by "innovations" in political, religious, and educational doctrine."]

The Applicability of Religion as an Analytical Category for Antiquity

To see this difficulty more clearly, we must cast a quick glance to recent developments in the historicizing of the category of religion. In modern conversation, both academic and popular, the word "religion" generally means something like "the belief in and worship of a superhuman controlling power, especially a personal God or gods," and "a religion" generally means something like "a particular system of faith and worship."

The Christianizing assumptions of such definitions have not escaped the notice of most of the scholars of ancient history who employ the trope of embedded religion. Indeed, the whole idea of the components of religion being "embedded in ancient society" seeks to address this problem of an overly Christianized concept of religion. What a growing number of historians and anthropologists have recognized, and what I want to emphasize here, is that the very category of religion is itself a Christian phenomenon. In a short but trenchant article, Werner Cohn described a similar problem in the study of modern "non-Western" cultures, noting that many anthropological studies contain "an error in reasoning" that "consists of an unacknowledged and apparently unrecognized switch of meaning for the term 'religion' in the middle of the argument" (1967:73). When I speak of what "religion means," I have in mind the later work of Ludwig Wittgenstein, as is expressed in Section I.43 of the Philosophical Investigations:

"For a large class of cases—though not for all—in which we employ the word 'meaning' (Bedeutung), it can be defined thus: the meaning of a word is its use in the language (Gebrauch in der Sprache)" (1953 [2001]:18). I draw these definitions from *The New Oxford Dictionary of English*, a dictionary of "current English." For the editorial philosophy of the dictionary, see the Preface and Introduction to the work (Pearsall 1998: vii–xviii).

While the use of a standard dictionary definition may seem naive, I stress again that my interest is not whether the definition is "accurate" in corresponding to some "real thing" out there in the world; I just want to get a sense of how people use the word. Some classical scholars are coming to acknowledge this point as well. For example, Jason P. Davies has recently written, "It may well be that the very idea of religion as a category is in itself misinformed and simply a further legacy of Christianity" (2004:7). If we take seriously Wittgenstein's notion that the meaning of a term is in its use, we scholars of religious studies and students of antiquity still write as though religion was a universal human characteristic, present at all times and in all cultures, but this trend is changing. The past few years have seen a number of studies convincingly arguing that the analytical category of religion, and the carving up of the world into different religions, is a relatively recent development that can be traced to intra-Christian debates, Enlightenment, intellectuals, and colonial encounters in the seventeenth and eighteenth centuries.

This trend has led some scholars to argue that the term religion ought to have a completely re-descriptive use. The most forceful articulation of this kind of viewpoint is Jonathan Z. Smith's oft-quoted statement from *Imagining Religion* (1982). After observing that humans have been imagining deities for their entire history, he notes that humanity "has had only the last few centuries in which to imagine religion." He goes on to conclude: "Religion is solely the creation of the scholar's study. It is created for the scholar's analytic purposes by his imaginative acts of comparison and generalization. Religion has no independent existence apart from the academy. He could state the meaning of religion even more bluntly: Religion is simply something that looks sort of like modern Protestant Christianity. Many of the debates about whether this or that -ism (Confucianism, Marxism, etc.) is "really a religion" boil down to the question of whether they are sufficiently similar to modern Protestant Christianity. Even some relatively recent historians of the field of comparative religion simply assume the universality of religion. [Author's note: This problem has been exemplified and exacerbated by the past Christian practice of labeling anyone who is not Christian as pagans and savages.]

Consider these comments from the renowned historian Eric J. Sharpe: "Religion is simply there as an identifiable factor of human experience" (1986:318). "To define religion is, then, far less important than to possess the ability to recognize it when we come across it" (1983:47). Thus the answer to Robert Segal's incredulous rhetorical question, "Are we to believe that modern theorists have been unaware that their vocabularies are their creation and not part of the lingo of the cultures to which those vocabularies have been applied?" See, for example, Harrison (1990), Asad (1993:27–54), Smith (2004:179–196), and Chidester (1996). For the later development of the "world religions" model that currently dominates academic and popular thought, see Masuzawa (2005). Interestingly, two scholars who view the category of religion as emerging earlier than the Enlightenment (in the fourth century CE, though still as the result of Christian debates) both describe the process as the "dis-embedding" of religion. See Schwartz (2001:179, 289) and Boyarin (2004:11, 27, 202). Smith has elsewhere sharpened this point:

"I take it we can agree that the term 'religion' is not an empirical category. It is a second-order abstraction. The statement is provocative in the best sense of the term, but it requires some modification for application to modern cultures. Tomoko Masuzawa has perceptively noted that as one reflects back on these consequential sentences nearly two decades later, they seem not so much an overstatement as a case of not having said enough. It lacks a necessary complementing thesis, or at least some statement of the incontrovertible fact that, much as 'religion' is an imaginative invention originating in the academy, it has thoroughly permeated and saturated our quotidian (nonacademic) discourses in such a way that the reality-effect of this theoretical abstraction is not in the least confined to the life of the academy. (2000:126) Although academics (along with colonial administrators, missionaries, native informants, and others) did participate in the invention of religion for their own purposes, people have since claimed the resulting religions as their own, thus enfleshing the category in a way that Smith's dictum seems not to acknowledge. On the other hand, this nuancing of Smith's position is decidedly not necessary for those who study pre-Enlightenment cultures. While it is possible to speak of theorizing about religion in general, it is impossible to 'do it' or 'believe it' or be normative or descriptive with respect to it" (1988:233).

Richard King provides an especially clear example of this phenomenon of indigenous people becoming representatives of "imagined communities" in his discussion of Vivekānanda and Hinduism (1999:93–98, 207). Objections to this assertion usually claim that some group in antiquity can be called "a religion" in the modern sense. Wilfred Cantwell Smith, for example, appears at several points to claim that the third-century figure Mani self-consciously invented a religion out of whole cloth (1963:92–98, 128). The matter appears to me to be considerably more complicated. Both Mani's followers and outside observers in antiquity seemed to regard what modern scholarship calls "Manicheanism" as simply a variant way of being Christian. We learn from Augustine that Mani claimed to be "an apostle of Jesus Christ" (Manichaeus apostolus Iesu Christi providentia dei patris) in the opening of his "Fundamental Epistle" (see Augustine's *Against the Epistle of Manichaeus 5*; the edition cited here is that of Joseph Zycha [1891]). The author known as Ambrosiaster regarded the Manicheans as Christian heretics.

(Brown 1969:98). Furthermore, Peter Brown notes that the persecution of the Manicheans in 287 CE was "a persecution of a group regarded as indistinguishable from the Christians of the Sassanian Empire" (1969:95). Similar claims are sometimes made regarding ancient Islam as a religion in the modern sense of the term, but I am skeptical here as well. Ancient Christian authors wrote of B. Nongbri / *Numen* 55 (2008) 440–460 447 can stand "as is" for those who are concerned with ancient cultures, for the data of the ancient historian cannot lay claim to an identity produced by scholarship. *Religion cannot be a descriptive category for ancient cultures…*

Although academics (along with colonial administrators, missionaries, native informants, and others) did participate in the invention of religion for their own purposes, people have since claimed the resulting religions as their own, thus enfleshing the category in a way that Smith's dictum seems not to acknowledge. On the other hand, this nuancing of Smith's position is decidedly not necessary for those who study pre-Enlightenment cultures. His statement can stand "as is" for those who are concerned with ancient cultures, *for the data of the ancient historian cannot lay claim to an identity produced by scholarship.*"

Japan, the birthplace of ancient spirituality

There are few places on earth, that are currently accessible, whose historical documents have not been destroyed or corrupted by outsiders. One such place is Japan. The only country that has subdued Japan is the United States in WWII. Fortunately the United States had no desire to destroy the history of Japan. It has been said that; "The easiest way to conquer a people is to destroy their history." This erases any reference point with which to judge the current administration.

According to hitherto established theories from the world of archaeology, Japan should be a place of a relatively new civilization. This is how it has been regarded in the past. Nevertheless, in recent times ancient artifacts have been turning up all over Japan that dispute these long-supported ideas.

In the book *Takeuchi Documents I*, Kosaka Wado writes, In Japan there exists the world's oldest documentation of the history of earth and mankind, which has been conscientiously noted down.

It is the Takeuchi documentation which I am introducing in this book. Around two thousand years ago, Takeuchi (Heguri) Matori passed down this documentation (rewritten from the original text in a mixture of ideograms and Japanese "kana" alphabets) to the Koso Kotaijingu (Great Imperial Ancestor Shrine) in the municipality of North Ibaraki, Isohara. It had been written on the basis of Divine Era characters before being brought up to date.

An amazingly complete authentic history is recorded in it. The imperial family came to earth from another heavenly body. A world government was established in

Japan with heavenly emperors ruling the world. Saintly people such as Moses, Jesus, Mohammed, Shakyamuni, Confucius, and Lao Tse were born from the descendants of the five races, who had branched off from Japan and returned to undergo spiritual training.

This may seem absurd when measured by current teachings, but the truth of a super-ancient civilization is meticulously written down in the Takeuchi and other documentation around the world. Unfortunately these writings are considered myths by much of academia. However, as time passes, more and more of the so-called myths are being proved to be true. This book will further validate that much that we regard as myths are in fact true.

Kosaka Wado, author of the book *The Takeuchi Documents*
The Takeuchi Documents, Records of an Ultra-ancient People

There are ancient documents describing the creation of the universe, the descent of godlike humans (divine beings) onto earth, and the development of mankind. These ancient documents are known as the Takenouchi documents, and they have been handed down through the lineage of the Takenouchi family, the head of the family being the chief priest of the Koso Kotai Jingu shrine. These documents purportedly give the true history of mankind, a history drastically different from what we have been taught.

It is a grave mistake to assume our current civilization is at the highest stage of development ever experienced in human history. The history of mankind has been a constant struggle with catastrophic phenomena known as *Tenpenchii.* (Apocalypses). More than one hundred tenpenchii have occurred up until the present time, and these have been vividly described in the Takenouchi documents.

The Takenouchi documents state that the legendary civilizations of Mu and Atlantis truly existed. These civilizations were destroyed during tenpenchii. The existence of such civilizations is substantiated not only by the Takenouchi documents but also by the existence of ancient relics and buildings around the world that cannot be constructed even with today's technology. The Takenouchi documents contain the true history of Japan, its influence on the ancient world, and the lineage of the first gods, the Sumera-Mikoto. Modern religion would teach that it is blasphemous to even think of more than one god. The ancients teach that the gods were but a part of the cosmic family of habitants. This commonality is ruled by quantum laws (God) that unite the physical galactic family into one by their very nature of being. Therefore, if that is true, all beings emanate from the same cosmic energy and are but one small part of this marvel we call the cosmos.

The Takenouchi documents refer to not only written documents but also to sacred treasures and artifacts. The written record covers the genealogy of gods, many different types of divine characters, ancient maps, the genealogy of the Takenouchi family and the history of mankind. This is indeed an astronomical work. Few documents of this type of chronicle can be found anywhere else in the world. Two that come to mind are the *Mahabharata* and *Ramayana* of the Vedic culture. Japan has always taught their past as history rather than myths. This is because they are in documented touch with their past, as opposed to those who's history has been intentionally destroyed by their conquerors. Besides the documents there are sacred treasures and articles that are essential to gaining an understanding of the history of gods. These articles have been preserved in the Koso Kotai Jingu shrine.

It would be difficult to accept Japan as the advocate of many spiritual cultures, including the acceptance of Jesus, unless it is understood that the spiritual teachings of the Sumera-Mikoto have been passed down from ancient Japan to Jesus and other prophets of the world. Along the way many groups and individuals have manipulated these teachings to further their own agenda, but the basic concepts and understandings have remained intact through many dedicated and secret protectors.

The Takenouchi family has been preserving the documents secretly as treasures "to be returned to the Sumera-Mikoto (gods) when the time is right." In fact, the Takenouchi family record tells of some family members who sacrificed their lives to protect the sacred treasures from influential people. The person who disclosed the Takenouchi documents after such a long period of time was Takenouchi Kiyomaro (1880–1965), grandson of the sixty-sixth generation. The timing of the disclosure was dictated in the documents. The disclosure of the Takenouchi documents has ramifications for the history of all nations.

The following is taken from the book *Takeuchi Documents IV*, by Michiyo Miwa, dialogue by Dennis Mitchamson.

The historical events that appear in Takeuchi documentation go back millions of years. [Author's note: The earth is 4.5 billion years old.] I imagine that many people have doubts about its contents. This may be because the descriptions found in the *Kojiki* and *Nihonshoki* books, which are commonly considered to be Japan's most ancient texts, exclude the history preceding the Joko Era, whilst Takeuchi documentation describes a period long before such a time. Nevertheless, it is a matter of fact that many of the things contained in Takeuchi documentation match up with the contents of acknowledged historical texts such as the Bible.

Takeuchi documentation describes how "the cataclysms that took place at the time of the Heavenly Emperor Amehi no Motohi no Himiinushi Mihikaru Amatsu Hitsugiame no Sumera-Mikoto in the third generation of the Joko Era was such that the whole of the earth was turned into a sea of mud. Three hundred ninety-seven members from the imperial family downward boarded spaceships and left for the heavenly realm of Hidama (Solar Sphere Realm), thus escaping from the great cataclysms." In other words, they fled to another planet.

Let's try and compare this historical fact with *Kojiki* contents. Unfortunately, the history ranging from the first generation of the Heavenly God Era to the third generation of the Joko Era is totally excluded in it. This is to say that Ameno Minaka Nushi Kami Mihikaru Sumera-Mikoto, who was the emperor in the fourth generation of the Joko Era, appears at the beginning of the *Kojiki*. Furthermore, whilst people like Adam and Eve do not make their appearance in the *Kojiki*, the name Yoiropa Adamu-Ivuhi Akahito Mesotai (female pioneer of the red race) appears in Takeuchi documentation.

Adamu-Ivuhi is indicated as the younger brother of Emperor Ameno Minaka Nushi Kami Mihikaru Sumera-Mikoto of the second generation of the Joko Era, who sent them to Mesopotamia, a region situated between the Tigris and Euphrates Rivers. The children of the Japanese emperor thus correspond to the Adam and Eve who appear in the Bible.

The names Seth, Abel and Cain, which are written among the names of Adam and Eve's children in the Old Testament's Genesis, appear in Takeuchi documentation:

"During the reign of the Emperor Kuni no Tokotachi (Mihikaru Amatsu Hitsugiame) Sumera-Mikoto, the emperor departed from the Afri Isawa seashore and descended on Gondar, where the kings Sekki, Abel and Cain offered him the bouquets of flowers that they had brought with them."

Japanese Influence in the Indus Valley

"A variety of rice plants has existed in Japan right from the beginning. The situation regarding rice harvesting in ancient times is becoming clear thanks to research into the presence of plant opal spreading throughout the world. The fact that plant opal has been found among the ruins of the Indus civilization is particularly interesting. The Indus civilization has always been considered one of the oldest-known civilizations. (The Indus Valley is in Pakistan.)

"It has always been believed that the Indus civilization was a wheat-based civilization. However, even though no trace of rice harvesting has been found from that period, rice plant opals have been discovered in the baked bricks that were used for building a town. This could be decisive proof as to the existence of rice harvesting at the time of the Indus civilization.

"After discovering extremely ancient Japanese characters amongst the characters carved on cylindrical seals found among the ruins of the Indus civilization, Mr. Takahashi Yoshinori, who was researching into ancient writing, deciphered these characters and translated them as "Inotsutohanaare" (life is eternal). They were variations of the Toyokoni characters that can be found in Takeuchi documentation. This connection between Japan and the Indus civilization is inexplicable when only having a modern perception of history." Kosaka Wado, author of *Takeuchi Documents I–IV*.)

The Geoglyphic Territories

Geoglyphs have been used around the world for at least thirty-two thousand years. It is most certain that they have been used longer, but dating has not yet been accomplished on megaliths and geoglyphs constructed before 31,000 BCE. Currently the oldest dated geoglyphs are the Bosnian pyramids, which, when a geoglyphological survey is applied, outline perfectly what we now call Europe. (See Narrative A.)

Although territories change over time, due to apocolypses and other turmoil, the major points these geoglyphs use do not change. This would tend to indicate that some ancient civilization mapped out the earth using these particularly important points and used them repeatedly down through time. This is important, because it makes it easier to locate the geoglyphological end points of newly surveyed geoglyphs.

As geoglyphs around the world point out, new districts were formed, most conforming to the shape of the continents and islands of the earth. These territories are self-validating. Even though the geoglyphs describe territories around the world, the territories they outline fit together like a giant puzzle.

According to the Takenouchi documents of Japan, a technologically advanced society joined man over three hundred thousand years ago. At that time man was already on the earth in a primitive form. The Sumera-Mikoto, as they were called, began the task of educating mankind all over the earth. According to the Takenouchi documents, this was accomplished with the aid of flying machines that traveled the world. These flying vehicles were called Ameno-Ukifuni.

In the Takeuchi Documents I, by Kosako Wado, we read:

The name of the first heavenly emperor in the Joko Era was Amehi no Motoashikabikimi　Nushi. "Nihon" (日本, Japan), which means "Originating Land of the Sun" (日の本の国, Hi no

Moto no Kuni, translated presently as Land of the Rising Sun), came from this. Gods of the five colors, red, blue, white, black, and yellow, were born among the sons and daughters of this first heavenly emperor of the Joko Era.

These sixteen children of the emperor were sent to every part of the world as pioneers of the five color races in the time of Tsukuri no Shikiyorozuo Sumera-Mikoto, second-generation emperor of the Joko Era. Adamu-Ivuhi was sent as a king of the people (民 王, Mesotai) to the region of Mesopotamia, where he established the Sumerian civilization. The kings of Tamiara and Miyoi (Atlantis and Mu continents) were also sent. King Ame Eda Hiuke Ebiros was the one who became the ancestor pioneer of Native Americans. Furthermore, the heavenly emperor visited Cairo in Egypt and Ethiopia.

As the heavenly emperors in Japan were visitors from a high-level dimension who reigned from a central position, they represented a point of reference for the five colors of humans living on earth.

Twenty-First Generation of the Joko Era

People famous throughout the world, as saintly men, make their appearance in records of the Fukiaezu and Kanyamato generations found in the ultimate part of the Takeuchi documents. The lineup is impressive: Moses, Shakyamuni, Confucius, Mencius, Lao-tse, Jesus, Mohammed, Fu his, and Shin Nung. All of them were holy men who were active at a turning point in history. It is commonly agreed that there are time gaps in the lives of all these people, [who are] called holy world masters. Since in each holy man's case these time gaps correspond to a period prior to the commencement of their regular activity, it is clear that they relate to a training period. Where and what they did in it has been a complete mystery. Takeuchi documentation enables us to fill up the time gaps in what has hitherto consisted of a mystery. The Takeuchi Documents account for the missing time in the life of Jesus between his 12th and 29th birthdays. As many other holy men before him, he traveled to Britain, Tibet and Japan as a learning process in his ministry.

According to Takeuchi documentation, these men visited Japan and studied there before returning to their native lands. At that time, going to Japan and studying in what was the world center most likely meant being able to acquire the highest knowledge. This is why many holy masters took advantage of the various opportunities they had and made every effort to go abroad and study in Japan.

[Author's note: The Gospels and the Koran are not the writings of the prophets themselves but were penned after their deaths during periods of great political turmoil and influence.]

Ancient Symbols

As mentioned before, names change, but symbols remain the same for people practicing a certain culture. In this book we will reference the symbols passed down from antiquity to today in order to follow the ancient spiritualists.

Figure 4.6. From left to right: the Japanese chrysanthemum, symbol of the Emperor and of the World-Emperor in the Takenouchi Documents; the "Royal Escutcheon of Mu" from Churchward's book; Sakai's Sun Cross.

Kosaka Wado - *The Takeuchi Documents*

The chrysanthemum is still used by Japan as a royal symbol. That symbol can also be seen down through time entwined in the designs and symbols of Japanese royalty and followers of ancient spirituality.

The two most common symbols that have been used from antiquity down to modern times are the four- and eight-sided cross symbols. These and other symbols appear repeatedly in the art and symbols of the cultures that practiced and handed down the teachings of the ancients.

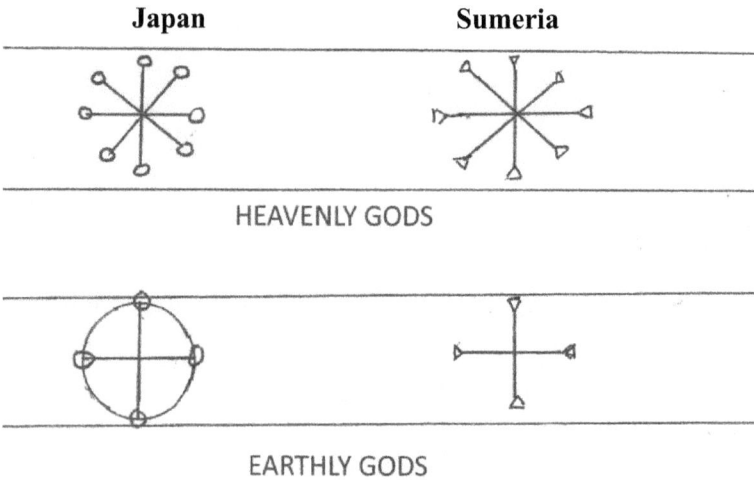

Japan	Sumeria

HEAVENLY GODS

EARTHLY GODS

The Faram Research Foundation

The Eight-Spoked Symbol Reserved for Heavenly Gods or Events

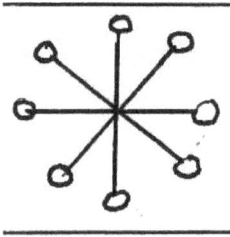 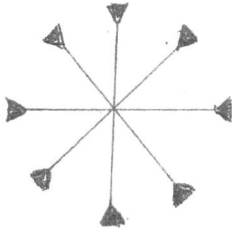 

Ancient Japan   **Ancient Sumerian**   **Buddhist**

The Faram Research Foundation

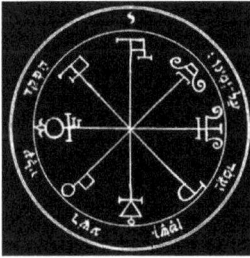  

King Solomon   **Coptic**   **Byzantine**

The Faram Research Foundation

The Four-Spoked Symbol Depicts an earthly Lord or Prophet

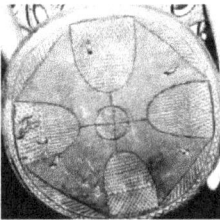  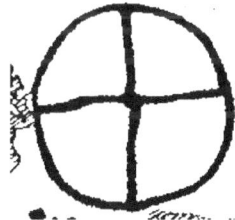

Nigeria   **Mound Culture (USA)**   **Celtic**

AncientOrigins.net

This particular petroglyph contains many interesting and informative symbols. Just as the eight-sided cross denotes a heavenly god and the four-sided cross denotes an earthly god or lord, so the spiral that starts with a right stroke, as these do, denotes a heavenly god or event, and a spiral starting with a left stroke denotes an earthly god or event.

In addition the turtle, seen here, and the snake (not pictured) were ancient sacred symbols. These symbols were given a negative connotation by later religions in hope that it would steer people away from the ancient spirituality. In fact, most ancient sacred symbol have been given a negative connotation by modern religions and societies.

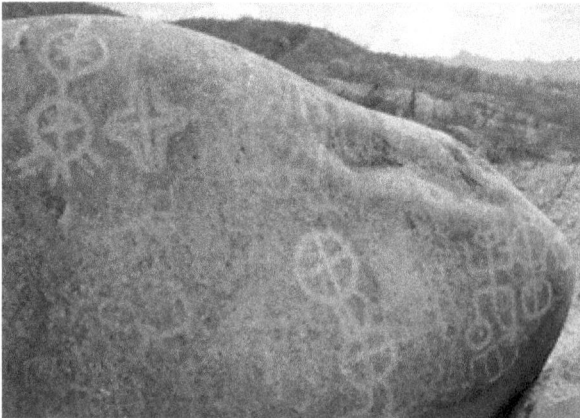

AncientOrigins.net

Peru

Peruvian petroglyphs show the four-sided cross with a circle, a four-sided cross with a halo, and an eight-sided cross. These same symbols can be seen down through time both before and after the date of this site.

Ancient Greek coin with four-sided cross

Notice the four dots, which elevate this to an eight-sided cross

Ireland

These stones show the Irish culture's Coptic past and their Christian conversion.

Mosaic, Chichen Itza, Mexico

Chumash Cave, Santa Barbara, California

SUMERIAN

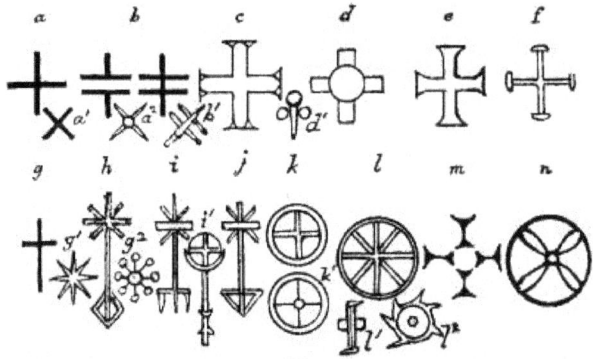

HITTITE OR CATTI

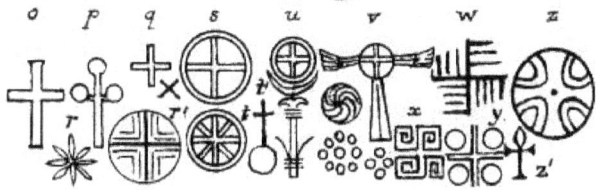

KHASSI OR CASSI

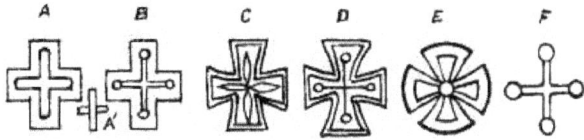

TROJAN & EGYPTIAN & PHŒNICIAN

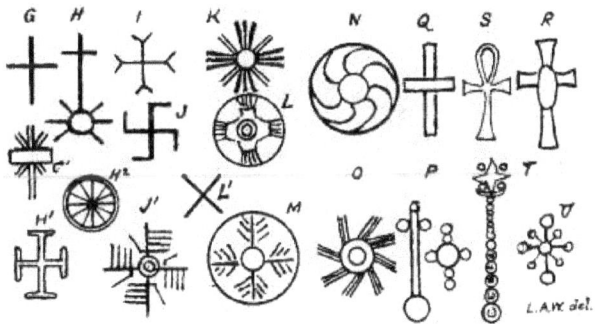

Praveen Mohan

Ancient Symbols Down Through Time

Preah Vihear temple with four-sided cross, Cambodia, ca. 900 CE

Puma Punku, Bolivia, ca. 600 CE

End Chapter 1

Chapter 2
Evidence of a Worldwide Culture

The following chapter is presented to remind the reader that humans and their teachers have been on earth much longer than we have been taught. The earth is 4.5 billion years old. During human development the human species has been subjected to many worldwide cataclysms. These catastrophes leave behind small groups of humans that, apparently with help from outside sources, begin another cycle of expanding their knowledge and technology.

Until we accept the concept that man is much older and has been assisted by technology not yet explained, it will be much harder to acknowledge the overwhelming evidence of man's existence on the earth for tens of thousands of years.

The following images of stone walls and pyramids are included as just one illustration of the overwhelming evidence that intelligent beings have existed as a network on this planet for much longer, and with skills that modern man is once again approaching.

Some of the stones in these ancient walls weigh upward of two hundred tons. They were fitted together with such precision that even a piece of paper cannot be inserted between them. How were these stones moved? Many scholars believe that they were made weightless by some ancient technology and then moved. Others believe that, on some of the walls, the stone was made liquid by some cold process, possibly harmonics, and then poured into place.

Ancient Stone Walls

AncientOrigins.com

Peru

Tripadvisor.com

Peru

Masuda, Japan

Russia

Cuzco, Peru

Easter Island

Ollantambo, Peru

Pyramids are used here to show that there was once a worldwide technology in earths past history. The civilizations that built these pyramids had advanced knowledge that we are unable to duplicate even today. There are thousands more examples of pyramids, but only a few will be shown here.

The convincing evidence that there was a worldwide phenomenon of pyramids is the fact that they were built on every continent on earth. There are many opinions as to why the pyramids were built. But the fact remains that they were built. This could not be a coincidence, as many share common traits, such as a precise orientation due north. Another trait is that the geoglyphological edges of the pyramids form a geoglyph that, when surveyed, points to other specific geographic points, used over and over for millennia. These points, when outlined by the radial end points of the geoglyph, form territories or point out places that were important to the builders of the pyramids.

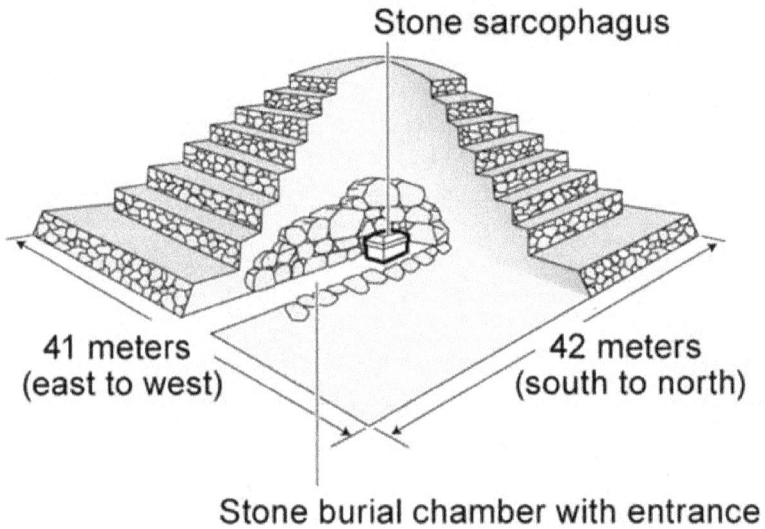

Stone sarcophagus

41 meters (east to west)

42 meters (south to north)

Stone burial chamber with entrance

Google

Japanese Pyramid

Guimar, Pyramids - Canary Islands

Indonesia

Indonesia

Bosnia

53

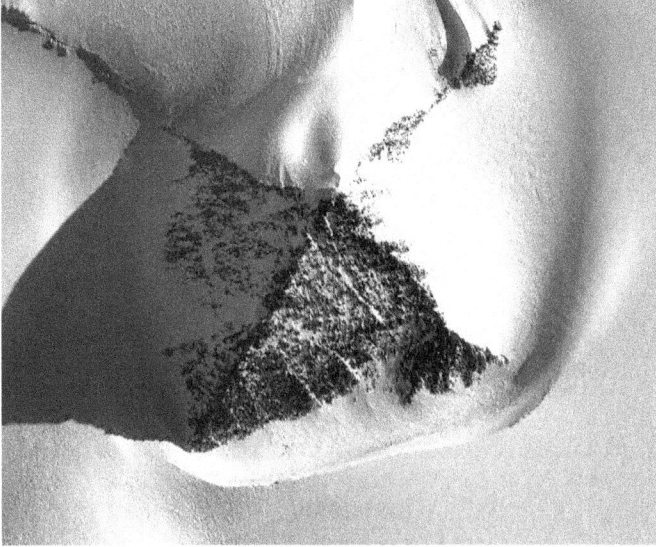

Antarctica

Ji'an, China

Guatemala

Sicily

Mexico

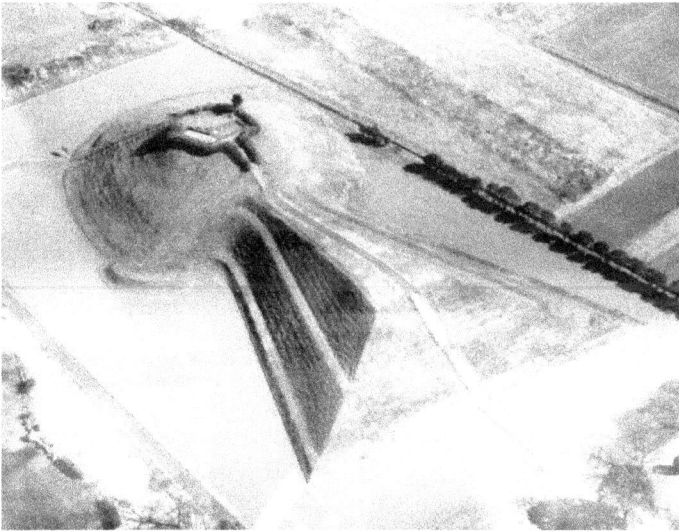

Japan

End Chapter 2

Mesopotamia

Wikipedia Commons

Mesopotamia is where the ideal world created by the original teachers (gods), the Sumera-Mikoto of Japan, began to fall apart. The Sumera-Mikoto and their teachings had existed around the world for thousands of years. It was in Mesopotamia where the fallen angels, mentioned in the Bible and other texts, decided that they would rather enjoy the riches of the world rather than the sanctity of love and peace in the heavens. Mesopotamia is where the Anunnaki first joined mankind and spread their self-centered concepts of greed and control.

The abundance of water in Mesopotamia created a great natural richness, to such a point that, according to the Bible, paradise was located there. The Neolithic period quickly reached a great level of development in Mesopotamia with important urban settlements like Eridu or Uruk (3750 CE).

It was here where the fallen angels (Anunnaki) introduced a complex system of writing called cuneiform which begin the current phase of recorded history. The Anunnaki were eventually defeated by the armies of Sargon, king of the Akkadians (Akkad). Unfortunately their defeat did not erase them from the earth but simply scattered them to practice their evil deeds on a wider scope.

Image Credit: Google
The Savior

The website "History on the Net" explains,

> Sargon, King of Akkad, reigned from 2334 to 2279 BCE. From humble beginnings, he rose to great power, conquering Mesopotamia and parts of Iran, Turkey, and Syria. Not only did he establish the post-Anunnaki empire, but he kept it operating smoothly with the innovative use of Akkadian bureaucrats installed in every conquered city. Akkadians, who spoke a Semitic language, originated in northern Mesopotamia, while Sumerians held the south. Sargon became the first person in history to create an empire ruling over a multiethnic people. Sargon became a legendary figure; for thousands of years, Mesopotamians told heroic, epic tales of Sargon the Great and the Akkadian golden age. The Akkadians spoke the Semitic language of Jesus, Aramaic. **("Sargon the Great, the Akkadian Emperor," History on the Net, 2000–2019, Salem Media)**

From this time two important cultures coexisted: the Assyrians (Assur) to the north and the Babylonians (Babylon) to the south. Each one evolved in a different way, but both ended up being dominated by warrior nations who arrived from the east: the Persians, Medes, and Achaemenids.

End Chapter 3

Chapter 4
The Ancient Symbols

Ancient Spirituality

The spirituality practiced by the ancients and taught by many heavenly prophets down through history was preserved and handed down by many cultures. The ancient spirituality spoken of here is the ancient belief that love conquers all and that every living thing on earth is connected in some way, each having an effect on the other. A few examples of cultures that have retained this ancient philosophy are the Buddhists, Tibetan monks, Native Americans, transcendentalists, and many other cultures that believe in the ancient ways.

The Ancient Symbols

The next chapter uses symbols to show the unbroken connection between the cultures that handed down the teachings of the ancients. This chapter will also familiarize the reader with the various symbols to look for.

"Follow the Symbols, Not the Names"

The preceding quote was coined to remind researchers that the names of cultures change over time. However, there has been a chain of unbroken continuity in the symbols handed down from the ancient Sumera-Mikoto to the cultures adhering to the ancient teachings. This continuity enables the researcher to follow history as it travels through time. These same cultures, and their associates, are responsible for the geoglyphs and pyramids created down through history.

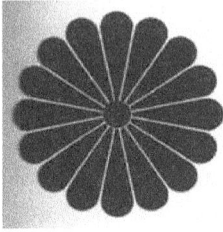 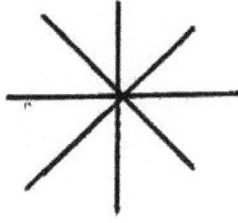 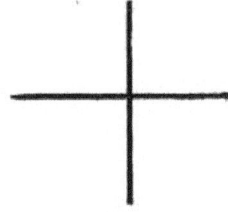

Chrysanthemum	Eight-pointed star	Four-pointed star
Royal status	Heavenly God	Earthly Lord or event

Japan—ca. 300,000 BCE

The three symbols shown above are the most significant symbols passed down from the ancient Japanese. These symbols appear in cultures from the time of the Sumera-Mikoto to today. The three symbols all originated in ancient Japan. The eight-pointed star is associated with a heavenly god, and the four-pointed star is associated with an earthly prophet or teacher.

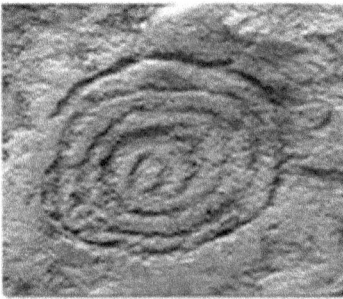 

Heavenly Event	**Earthly Event**

The spirals in the preceding image denote a heavenly god or event and an earthly god or event. They are the right and left spirals. The one denoting a heavenly event begins with a right stroke. The spiral denoting an earthly event begins with a left stroke.

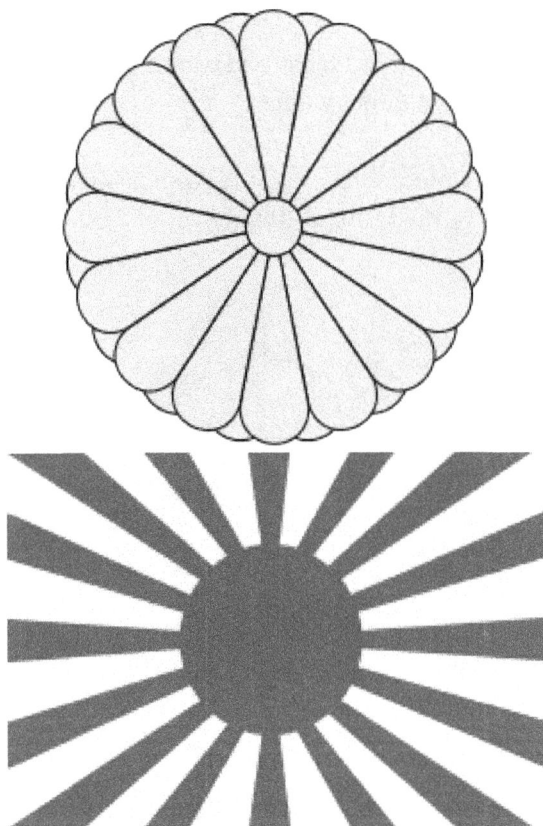

The chrysanthemum is the imperial symbol of the Sumera-Mikoto and Japan. The mom/mum symbol has long been a symbol of authority. This was the symbol of the ancient gods, the Sumera-Mikoto, who united all mankind into a harmonious world. The mum symbol was also adopted by the Anunnaki in order to imitate the true gods. They appear in Anunnaki images as a wristband. The mum is still the royal symbol of the originators, Japan.

People who display the ancient symbols, especially the four- and eight-sided crosses, know of their importance and display them discreetly in their daily lives. You will seldom notice them until you become aware of their significance. It is amazing how many are hidden in plain sight. The sunburst is also an ancient sacred symbol which originated in ancient Japan. This symbol, among others, has been handed down even to this today and can be seen in petroglyphs and in other forms down through time.

European Coins Commemorating the Appearance of Airships Bearing the Official Royal Seal of Japan

Pinterest.com
European coin, 1656 CE

Pinterest.com
French coin, seventeenth century CE
Translation: "Overwhelmed again and again"

The four-sided cross combined with the sun symbol
Hopi, United States

The four-sided cross at Tiwanaku, Peru

In the previous image, as is the case in many displays of the ancient cross symbols, you see the four- and eight-sided crosses combined. Here the four-sided cross is obvious, while the square makes up the additional four points of the eight-pointed star. This symbol is common in the southwestern United States.

Eight-Sided Crosses in Architecture

Eight-sided cross and sunburst

Eight Sided Crosses in a Ceiling

Eastern Orthodox Church
Four and eight-sided crosses on ceiling and chandelier

Tapestry

The Pazyryk carpet with four- and eight-pointed stars

According to the e-magazine *Ancient Origins*, the Pazyryk carpet is the oldest known example of a carpet in existence today. Discovered in a state of almost perfect preservation, it was pulled from a royal tomb in the Pazyryk Valley of Siberia, Russia, and has been dated to around the fifth century BCE.

Just to emphasize the importance of the eight and four pointed star take a look at the new Space Force Flag which was released as we were going to press.

UNITED STATES SPACE FORCE
M M X I X

End Chapter 4

It would be difficult to accept that ancient cultures could have a direct influence on modern history unless an unbroken continuity of the original teachings could be established. This chapter outlines the path, although not the only possible path, the ancient knowledge originally taught by the Sumera-Mikoto followed in order to reach the current protectors of the truth. At the beginning of each section are symbols that tie each culture to the ones preceding it. Symbols displayed in art, pottery, petroglyphs, and geoglyphs are the primary ways to track the practitioners of the ancient knowledge, since most written records have either been hidden or destroyed. "Follow the symbols, not the names."

At the top of each section will be a sacred symbol which each successive culture used. These symbols are the tools we will use to track the practitioners of the ancient spirituality.

In ancient times history was passed down orally. Therefore there is little record of history prior to the cuneiform writing developed in Mesopotamia ca. 4000 BCE. Although ancient man left little in the way of writings, he did leave some things that showed he had access to a high level of technology. In chapter 2 we were presented with unexplained monolithic structures such as great stone walls and pyramids. Other ancient artifacts further indicate that ancient man was much more sophisticated than we are led to believe, or that he had help from an outside source. These ancient accomplishments come in many forms, such as pyramids, mounds, rock designs on the ground (geoglyphs), and the orientation of walls of ancient cities. If the walls of an ancient structure are not parallel, it is most likely a geoglyphological structure.

Another form of historical documentation was petroglyphs. By following scientifically dated symbols on a historical timeline, the followers of the ancient spirituality and the builders of the geoglyphs can be determined. Five of the current practitioners of the original teachings are the Buddhists, Hindus, Tibetans, Native Americans, Freemasons, and Transcendentalists.

It is important to follow the sacred symbols, because the cultures that use them are following the ancient teachings. However, a few "religions," as opposed to spiritualists, have incorporated these symbols into their theology in order to mimic the true spirituality. The true test here is to apply the old adage, **"They will be known by their deeds."**

The following is a list of post Ice Age cultures down through time that practiced and protected the ancient teachings. The list is not all inclusive.

SUMERA-MIKOTO AND AINU—Millennia ago, Japan
THRACIANS—ca. 10,000 BCE, Bulgaria, Romania, and Turkey
SUMERIANS—Post-10,000 BCE, Mesopotamia (excludes the Anunnaki)
CELTS/BEAKER PEOPLE—ca. 4500 BCE, Europe
ASSYRIANS—ca. 2500 BCE, Mesopotamia and eastern Mediterranean
HEBREWS—ca. 2500 BCE, Mesopotamia and eastern Mediterranean
MAYA—ca. 1800–250 BCE, Pre-classical Period only, Mesoamerica
HITTITES—ca. 1600 BCE, Anatolia (Turkey)
VEDICS—ca. 1500 BCE, India
HEBREW EGYPTIANS—ca. 1450 BCE, Egypt (excludes the Pharaonic culture)
PHOENICIANS—ca. 1200 BCE, eastern Mediterranean
ETRUSCANS—ca. 750 BCE, Northern Italy

INDUS—ca. 500 BCE, Indus Valley, Pakistan

HINDUS—ca. 500 BCE, India

BUDDHISTS—ca. 450 BCE, India

DAOISTS—ca. 221 BCE, China

PORTUGUESE—ca. 300 BCE, Portugal (previously known as the Etruscans)

COPTICS—ca. 1 CE, Mediterranean

BYZANTINES—ca. 45 CE, also known as Orthodox (original) Christians

ORTHODOX CHURCHES—ca. 450 CE, Middle East

TIBET—ca. 500 CE, Himalayan Mountains, Tibet

NATIVE AMERICANS—Pre-Columbian, United States

TEMPLARS—ca. 1118 CE, Europe and North America

FREEMASONS—ca. 1450 CE, Scotland

TRANSCENDENTALISTS—ca. 1830 CE, United States

Details of the Participating Cultures

The Thracians—ca. 10,000 BCE

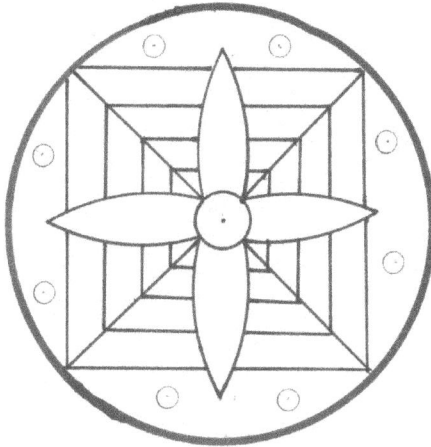

The Faram Research Foundation
Ancient Thracian symbol
Incorporating the four- and eight-pointed symbols, as well as the pyramid.

Google

Thracia grew to occupy all of what is now Bulgaria. Much of the Thracian culture and beliefs spilled over into Anatolia (Turkey).

The prehistoric remains in Thrace are not of great number in comparison to Anatolia. But there is enough to place the oldest inhabited cave in Turkey at Yarimburgaz, which dates back to about four hundred thousand years ago. The mound at Hocacesme near the ancient town of Ainos has provided some rich findings from the Neolithic and Chalcolithic Ages. It is well worth mentioning the number of megaliths (dolmens) found in the Istranca Mountains and in the vicinity of the district of Lalapaşa.

Dolmen

Dolmens in their various forms are seen around the world on every continent. They were constructed by the ancients to enhance meditation and communication with the cosmos (God). The weight of the stones bearing down on the earth creates a piezoelectric effect by amplifying the micro-electric forces emanating from earth. By placing one's self within the dolmen's confines, humans can take advantage of this amplifying effect during meditation. Meditating within or on the top of a conical or pyramid-shaped mountain will have the same effect.

Archaeological evidence indicates that the Balkans was populated well before the Neolithic Period, during the New Stone Age, about ten thousand years ago. At the dawn of recorded history, two Indo-European peoples dominated the area: the Illyrians to the west and the Thracians to the east of the great historical divide defined by the Morava and Vardar river valleys. The Thracians were advanced in metalworking and in horsemanship. They intermingled with the Greeks and gave them the Dionysian and Orphean cultures, which later became so important in classical Greek literature. The Illyrians were more exclusive, their mountainous terrain keeping them separate from the Greeks and Thracians.

Thracian society was tribal in structure, with little inclination toward political cohesion. The Thracians professed individuality and self-reliance, virtues taught by the ancients. Unity was only achieved through external pressure.

The Hindu—India, ca. 5000 BCE

The sun **Four and eight-sided cross** **Spiral**

The sun and cross symbols were originally handed down from the Sumera-Mikoto of Japan. The left-handed spiral signifies a prophet or lord, as opposed to the right-handed spiral, which signifies God. These same symbols appear in many Native American petroglyphs. This particular spiral starts with a left movement and therefore indicates an earthly event. God appears as the ohm (God) symbol in the center of this particular Hindu spiral. As indicated here, the symbols were perpetuated by the enlightened, down through time.

The Vedas are the sacred scriptures of Hinduism and are regarded as one of the oldest "spiritual" texts in the world. Thought to have been composed at least 3,500 years ago, the Vedas are a collection of hymns, magical incantations, dramatic mythological accounts, and sacred formulas for enlightenment. As has been the case throughout most of history, modern man has tried to lump ancient spiritualism into the category called religion. The ways of the ancients were a way of life and philosophy rather than the more modern concept of organized religion.

While it is not entirely clear who wrote the Vedas, the focus has been traditionally placed on the message rather than on the messenger. Some believe that the Vedas were given directly to the sages from God and then passed down by word of mouth until they were finally codified and written down several hundred years later. Others, on the other hand, believe that the Vedas were revealed by the sages themselves.

Public Domain

Generally speaking, the Vedas are composed of Hindu spiritual knowledge that can be applied to all aspects of life. The word "Veda" itself means wisdom, knowledge, or vision, and the social, legal, and spiritual customs laid out in the ancient text continue to have an influence on the lives of Hindu believers today.

While the Vedas are best known as a source of spiritual knowledge, they are also significant for the material knowledge they contain. The Vedas are recognized as having made a significant contribution to modern knowledge and science.

For example, in the field of mathematics, the concepts of zero and infinity, as well as the decimal system, have been found in the Vedas. Moreover, some of the material knowledge from the Vedas has been confirmed by modern science. These include Vedic cosmology and the use of mantras to enhance the overall well-being of an individual.

The Hindu Shatkona

Hind Ustov says, the Shatkona, or six-pointed star, is composed of two interlocking triangles. The upper stands for Shiva, or male energy, and the lower for Shakti, or female energy. The union gives birth to Sana Kumara, whose sacred number is six. Many would associate this symbol with the Jewish religion. In reality it is another ancient symbol displayed by believers of the ancient teachings.

The Hindu Sacred Texts about Human Origins

In *Ancient Origins* (2013), April Holloway writes, "Hinduism goes back to 5000 BCE and is a compilation of many diverse traditions passed down prior to being called Hinduism." This is in contrast to what we call 'religion,' which is relatively modern.

"The Hindu main bodies of texts are referred to as the Veda, the Upanishads, and the Bhagavad Gita. There are many different

Hindu creation stories. However, references to a first world or universe won't be found. Also, though the belief in one god is common, Hindu texts consider all deities to be extensions of this god."

The Beaker People—ca. 4700 BCE

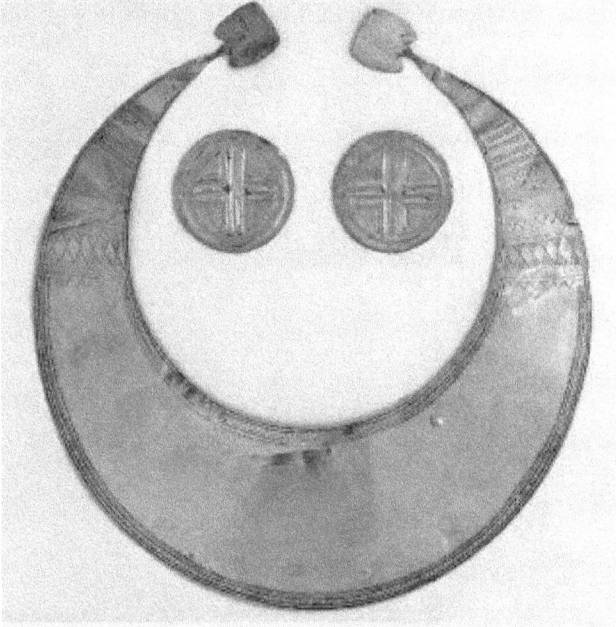

Beaker Burial Goods

The four-sided cross indicates that the wearer was a holy
man/woman or prophet.

In *Ancient Origins* (2018), we learn:

    In one of his new papers, David Reich, a professor of
genetics at Harvard University, and a cast of dozens of collaborators
charted the spread of an ancient culture known by its stylized bell-
shaped pots, the so-called bell beaker phenomenon. This culture first
spread between Iberia and central Europe beginning about 4,700
years ago. By analyzing DNA from several hundred samples of
human bones, Reich's team shows that only the ideas—not the
people who originated them—made the move initially. That's
because the genes of the Iberian population (Celts) remain distinct

from those of the central Europeans who adopted the characteristic pots and other artifacts.

But the story changes when the Bell Beaker culture expanded to Britain ca. 4700 BCE. This period brought migrants who almost completely supplanted the island's existing inhabitants. These were the mysterious people who built Stonehenge. Within a few hundred years, there was a sudden change in the population of Britain. Says Reich, "It was almost a complete replacement."

For archeologists, these and other findings from the study of ancient DNA are "absolutely mind-blowing," says archaeologist Barry Cunliffe, a professor emeritus at the University of Oxford. "They are going to upset people, but that is part of the excitement of it."

The Celts, once a cohesive culture, eventually split into two factions, the Hallstatt and the La Tene cultures. The La Tene culture, from Iberia, is the culture we normally associate with the Celts. The Hallstatt culture is what we now know as Germany.

The Bell Beaker culture, ca. 4500 BCE

About 4500 BCE an influx of migrants settled in Britain. These newcomers have been called the Beaker People because of the shape of the pottery vessels so often found in their round barrow graves.

Examples of Beaker Pottary

The "corded" design is what the Beaker Pottary is known for. This same design appears on Native North American pottary. The Beaker People were the first metal-smiths in Britain, working first in copper and gold and later in bronze, hence the name Bronze Age.

Cardium Pottery Ornamentation

Cardium culture pottery, Europe, ca. 6000 BCE

Based on the similarities in their ceramics, the Cardium culture of Europe could have been the originators of the Beaker pottery in Britain.

Spirituality

As if in keeping with later Celtic rituals, barrow graves were generally filled with grave goods, indicating the importance of the deceased and a belief in some type of afterlife. Some of the goods included in barrows were pottery jars, golden buckles, bronze daggers, cups, necklaces, and scepters in various stones and precious materials. The other main areas of Bronze Age focus were stone circles. Although geometric circles may have been erected earlier, the major circle-building era was during the Bronze Age.

The largest-ever study on ancient DNA has shown that Britain was changed forever by the arrival of the Beaker People. A wave of migrants about 4,500 years ago brought with them new customs, new burial practices, and beautiful, distinctive bell-shaped pottery. Since it recorded history that the Celts occupied all of Europe in ancient times, it would be safe to assume that the Beaker People were first-generation Celts.

The Celts—ca. 2900 BCE

Celtic cross

Around 2900 BCE the Celts, as we know them, split into two cultures, the Hallstatt and the La Tene. At that time they had spread over much of the Alpine region and the areas in France and Spain. Excavations have revealed rich tombs of the chieftains and royal classes. Evidence discovered in these tombs points to trade with all the classical Mediterranean civilizations.

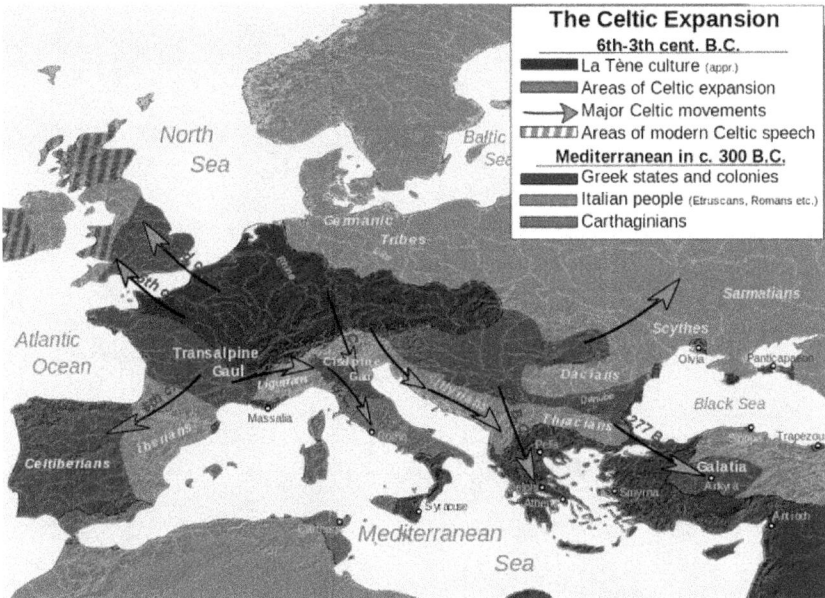

The Celtic Expansion
6th-3th cent. B.C.
La Tène culture (appr.)
Areas of Celtic expansion
Major Celtic movements
Areas of modern Celtic speech
Mediterranean in c. 300 B.C.
Greek states and colonies
Italian people (Etruscans, Romans etc.)
Carthaginians

Google

The Celtic empire, ca. 500 BCE

Varianty hrnčířských značek z raně středověkých hradišť v severozápadních Čechách. Podle Z. Váni.

Kimberly Borchardt

Ancient Celtic symbols taken from Slavic pottery found on hill forts in the Czech Republic

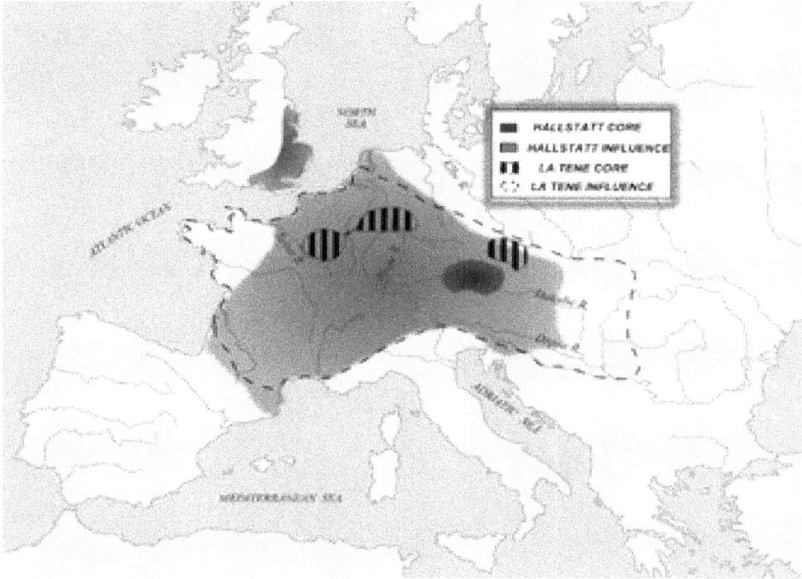

Origins of the Hallstatt and La Tene Celtic cultures

The striped areas, representing the La Tene culture, who would eventually range from western Britain to Russia. The La Tene Celts are the culture we currently identify as the Celts. The Hallstatt culture eventually condensed to occupy what we now know as Germany and became known as the Saxons.

Six of seven Celtic nations
Scotland ▌Ireland ░Isle of Man ▌Wales ░Cornwall ▌Brittany
Google

There were seven Celtic nations (Iberian Galicia is the missing seventh territory on the map). The Celtic culture is one of many who adopted the ancient spiritualism taught and handed down to them by the ancients. The Greeks and Romans portray the Celts as barbaric. Unfortunately, there are no written Celtic texts to defend this accusation. This is one of the drawbacks of passing history orally. Archaeology has proven that these people were not the barbarians they were accused of being but that their society was one of spirituality and was superior in the areas of metalworking. Political entities label other groups as savages and barbarians in order to make it more palatable for their armies to go to war against them.

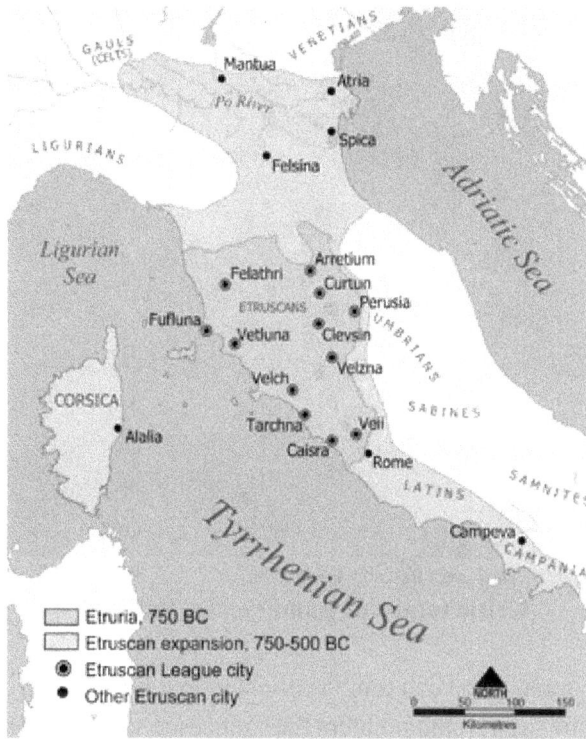

Google

Tuscany, ca. 750 BCE

Circa 800–300 BCE both the Etruscans and the Celts fought together against what was then the Roman Republic. Both the Celts and Etruscans had been handed down the technology for constructing geoglyphs. The following is a survey of one of the Celtic cemeteries purposely constructed to form a geoglyph outlining the territory the Celts claimed at the time.

Google Earth – The Faram Research Foundation
Celtic tombs at Banditaccia, Italy

Notice the entrance to each tomb is oriented in a different direction. These are the geoglyphic pointers the Celts used to designate their territory through geoglyphology.

Celtic tombs, Banditaccia, Italy

As can be seen, the tombs are not unlike the Celtic tombs in Britain.

Celtic tombs in Etruria, Italy

Celtic Banditaccia tomb bearings

This image shows the bearings, in degrees, of the straight lines and lineal entrances in and around the tombs.

Geoglyphic radials from the Banditaccia tombs

Based on this geoglyphic survey, it is apparent that the Celts in Etruria claimed territory in Western Europe, the northern shore of the Mediterranean, including Turkey, England, and its islands. Based on the evidence that the Celts and Etruscans were close allies, it is easier to understand why a coalition of Celts and Etruscans may have been the sea people who attempted to capture the southern and eastern shores of the Mediterranean ca. 1200–900 BCE.

It is obvious that this and other geoglyphs show that there was travel between Europe and the Americas millennia before Columbus. This geoglyph lines up with the historical accounts and other geoglyphs of the Celts in Europe. Based on this information, and the fact that the geoglyphological protocols have been met, it would be difficult to believe that the Banditaccia geoglyphic territory was not correct.

The Etruscans, later called the Portuguese, held claim to the Americas from the southern tip of South America to basically where the United States and Canadian border currently exists. Circa 300 BCE the Etruscans and the Celts moved from Etruria to Portugal and Galicia, respectively. During the Iberian war against the Moors (ca. 700–1492 CE), the Templars (Celts), the Portuguese, and Spain fought together to win back Iberia. It was during this period of collaboration that the Americas were divided among the three powers. North America was deeded to the Templars, Mesoamerica was deeded to Spain, and Portugal retained South America. The Celts, Templars, Etruscans, Portuguese, Phoenicians, and their spiritual predecessors had access to the Americas long before this.

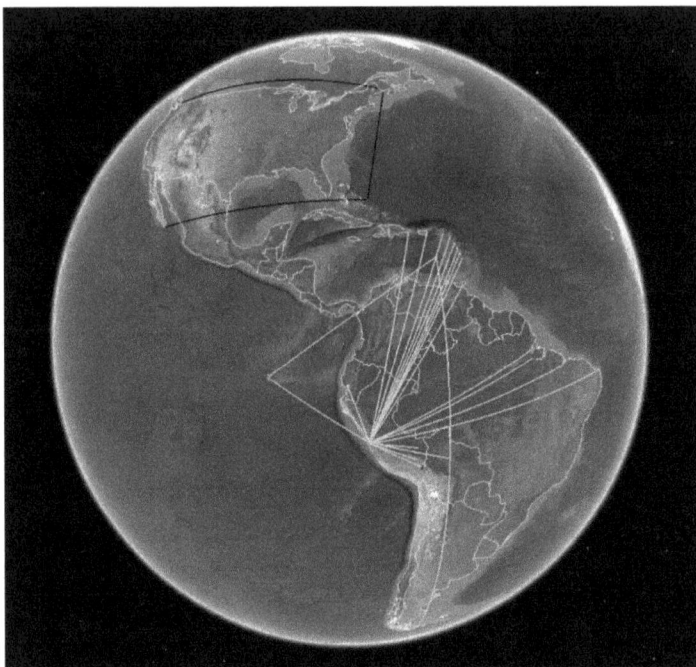

A map showing the territories deeded by Portugal, ca. 1450

In the previous image, the Templar territory appears in black lines, the Spanish territory (Mesoamerica) in red lines, and the Portuguese territory (South America) in magenta.

As described in the book *La Merica* (2013), Christopher Columbus was held on retainer for six years by Spain while they waited for the war with the Moors to end. The true reason for the voyage of Columbus was to construct geoglyphs in the Caribbean outlining and claiming the territories given to Spain by Portugal. (See Narrative O.)

Unfortunately, when Spain came to Mesoamerica, their search for gold took them north into the Templar/Freemason territory, as well as down the west coast of South America. Portugal managed to retain control of the east coast of South America and what is now called Brazil. The incursion of Spain into the western third of North American territory was resolved by the Mexican–American War.

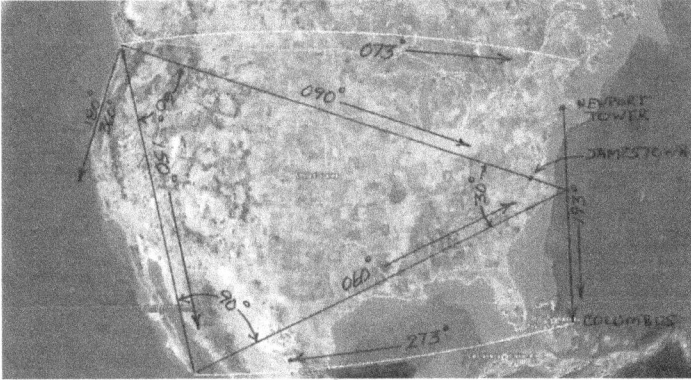

Google Earth – The Faram Research Foundation

Territory owned by the Templars/Celts, ca. 1450 CE

(The outside black and yellow lines. See Narrative N for the full story.)

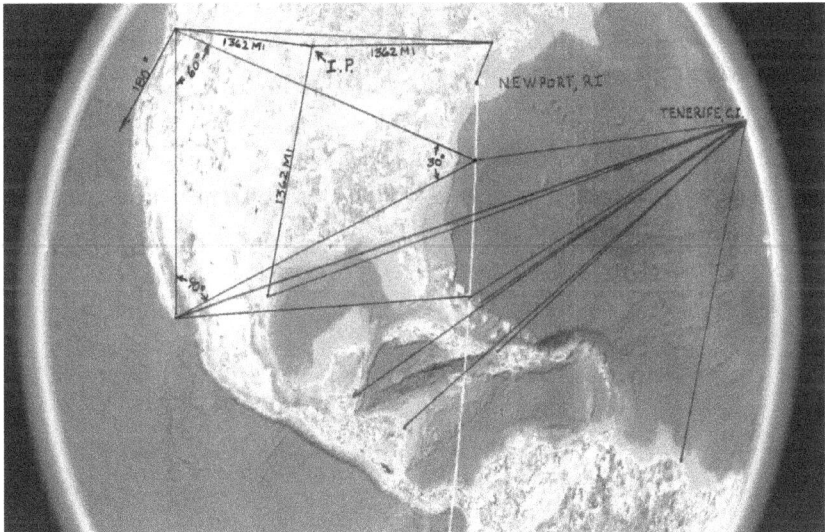

Google Earth – The Faram Research Foundation

The Tenerife pyramids geoglyphic extensions, validating the deeding of North America by the Portuguese to the Celts/Templars/Freemasons

The Guimar, Canary Islands, pyramids were constructed by the Portuguese ca. 1822 CE to validate their gift of North America to the Templars ca. 1400 CE. The lines pointing to Central America and South America denote countries to which Portugal gave independence ca. 1822 CE. The Canary Islands were turned over to Spain shortly thereafter.

Pharaonic Egypt—ca. 2920 BCE

Amun, Father of the Gods

In *Ancient Origins*, Aleksa Vuckovic writes, "Amun was one of the most important gods of the Egyptian pantheon—'The Lord of Truth, Father of the Gods, Maker of Men, Creator of all Animals, Lord of Things that Are, Creator of the Staff of Life.' Translated as 'Hidden One,' Amun was one of the Ogdoad, the eight primeval deities of the Hermopolis, and at the time the chief Theban god.

Elias Rovielo
Relief of the god Amun-Min, Luxor Museum, Egypt

"As the importance of Amun grew and his cult spread, he gained the form of Amun-Ra in the New Kingdom. This combined him with Ra, the sun god, and he became the chief deity, the king of the gods and the creator of the world and its inhabitants. At one period during the New Kingdom, Amun became so emphasized, he overshadowed the other gods. His usual depiction is in human form."

The history of Amun sounds much like the history of the Anunnaki god Anu, leader of the fallen angels. The Anunnaki flourished in Mesopotamia at approximately the same time as the pharaohs of Egypt. Our research has found little to show that neither the Anunnaki nor the Pharaonic Egyptians were practicing the ancient spirituality handed down from the Sumera- Mikoto of Japan. Although many of their practices mimicked the old beliefs, there is little if any symbology to support that they were part of the procession of ancient teachers who passed down the original form of ancient spirituality which inspired humbleness, humility, and a respect for all things. There is little of this in the pantheon of pharaohs and their search for grandeur. Quite the contrary: there was an obscene display of wealth and power.

The only connection with the ancients was not displayed by the Egyptians but by the Egyptian Jews and the Kushites. While in Egypt the Jewish slaves surreptitiously incorporated the ancient science of geoglyphology into the structures they built for themselves as living quarters. These geoglyphs tell a story of their journey from the near east to Egypt.

Geoglyphic Jewish Egyptian Slave Living Quarters

The Egyptian Kush

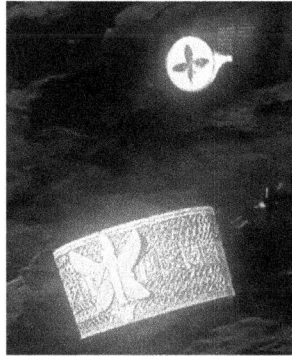

Elias Rovielo
Jewelry of a Kushite queen

The jewelry displays the four-sided cross of the ancients on the ring and a Sumerian god on the bracelet. This, and other evidence, indicate that it was the Kush, not the Pharonic Egyptians, who were following the ancient spiritual ways.

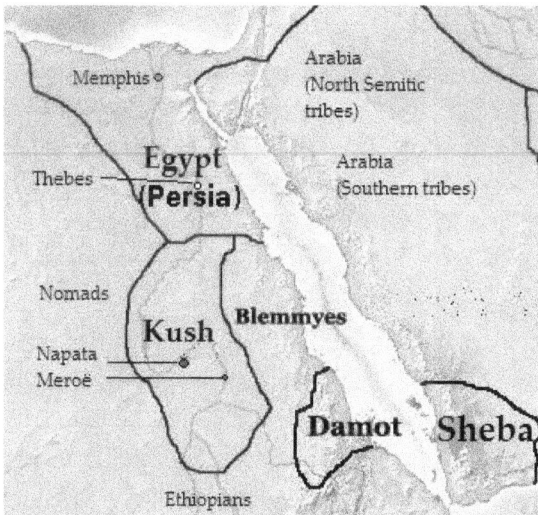

Pre-Pharaonic Kush, ca. 4000 BCE

Kush (/kʊʃ, kʌʃ/) was an ancient kingdom in Nubia, located at the Sudanese and southern Egyptian Nile Valley.

The Kushite era of rule in Nubia was established after the Late Bronze Age collapse and the disintegration of the New Kingdom of Egypt. Kush was centered at Napata (now modern Karima, Sudan) during its early phase. After the Kushites invaded Egypt in the eighth century BCE, the monarchs of Kush became the pharaohs of the Twenty-Fifth Dynasty of Egypt.

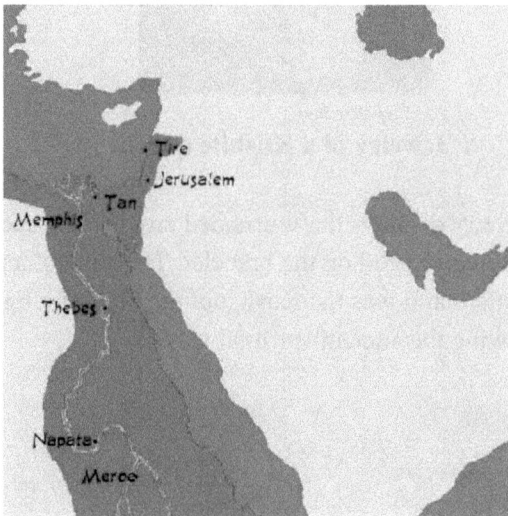

The kingdom of Kush at its height, ca. 800 BCE

The Kush were eventually defeated by the Neo-Assyrian Empire under the rule of Ashurbanipal and were finally expelled from Egypt by Psamtik I.

During classical antiquity, the Kushite imperial capital was located at Meroe. In early Greek geography, the Merotic kingdom was known as Aethiopia, now called Ethiopia. The kingdom of Kush, with its capital at Meroe, persisted until the fourth century CE, when it weakened and disintegrated due to internal rebellion. The seat was eventually captured and burned to the ground by the Nubian kingdom of Aksum. Afterward the Nubians established the three eventually Christianized kingdoms of Nobatia, Makuria, and Alodia.

Elias Rovielo

Kushite Pyramids

The Kushite pyramids were different from the Pharaonic pyramids in that they had much steeper sides and had entryways for easy entry to the side chamber. The Kushite pyramids, with their "H" shaped entryways, figure into the ancient conception and birthing sites covered in Chapter 7.

Mesopotamia—ca. 4000-1800 BCE

Sumerians

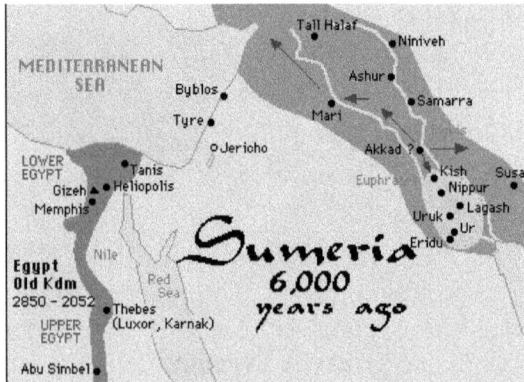

Google

     Any culture that lived in Mesopotamia except the Anunnaki has been called Sumerian. This is due to the fact that these cultures lived in and around the land of Sumer.

     According to Wikipedia, "Sumerian spiritual beliefs heavily influenced the religious beliefs of later Mesopotamian peoples. Elements of it are retained in the mythologies and beliefs of the Akkadians, Babylonians, Assyrians, and other Middle Eastern culture groups. Scholars of comparative mythology have noticed many parallels between the stories of the ancient Sumerians and those recorded later in the early parts of the Hebrew Bible." What I find interesting is that the Nile Valley and the Mesopotamian Valley were both considered as part of Sumeria at the same time that the Anunnaki came to earth. The culture of the Mesopotamian Anunnaki and the Egyptians seem very similar.

The Anunnaki (The Fallen Angels)

The Anunnaki are credited as the fallen angels that came to earth in Mesopotamia and changed society from an agrarian society, which was sustainable by the earth, to a technological society, which coveted wealth and materialism.

Encyclopedia Britannica explains that Anu was a "Mesopotamian sky god and a member of the triad of deities completed by Enlil and Ea (Enki). Like most sky gods, Anu, although theoretically the highest god, played only a small role in the mythology, hymns, and cults of Mesopotamia. He was the father of not only the gods but also of evil spirits and demons, most prominently the demoness Lamashtu, who preyed on infants. Anu was also the god of kings and the banner bearer of the Anunnaki. He was typically depicted in a headdress with horns, a sign of strength."

Again, from *Encyclopedia Britannica*: Lamashtu, "in Mesopotamian history, [was] the most terrible of all female demons, daughter of the sky god Anu (Sumerian: An). A wicked female who slew children and drank the blood of men and ate their flesh, she had seven names and was often described in incantations as the 'seven witches.' Lamashtu perpetrated a variety of evil deeds: she disturbed sleep and brought nightmares; she killed foliage and infested rivers and streams; she bound the muscles of men, caused pregnant women to miscarry, and brought disease and sickness. Lamashtu was often portrayed on amulets as a lion- or bird-headed female figure kneeling on an ass; she held a double-headed serpent in each hand and suckled a dog at her right breast and a pig at her left breast."

Eventually the Anunnaki were defeated in Mesopotamia, but rather than being erased from the earth, they scattered to spread their evil deeds among mankind. They are credited with bringing with them, from the heavens, the first written language, cuneiform. Cuneiform tablets have also been found in Peru.

Note: Sumerians - Basically any culture that lived in Mesopotamia, with the exception of the Anunnaki.

Semites, pre-4000 BCE

      The Jews have one of the longest histories in the near east. Their earliest recorded history is in the Mesopotamian valley ca. 2000 BCE. However, there is evidence that the Semites may have lived in the area of Palestine prior to that time.

      The Semites and Assyrians, two of the armies who helped to defeat the Anunnaki in Mesopotamia, returned to the east coast of the Mediterranean soon after the conflict. The Hebrew had practiced the ancient spirituality, as taught by the Sumera-Mikoto, for millennia. Ancient geoglyphs and symbols around the world point out the cultures that maintained these ancient ways.

UnitedwithIsrael.org

An Ancient Israeli synagogue mosaic with four and eight-sided symbols

Israeli synagogue zodiac mosaic with the four and eight-sided cross

Assyrians—ca. 1900 BCE

Ancient Assyrian symbol
Displaying both the four- and eight-sided symbols

Assyrian flag
Showing both the four- and eight-sided symbols

Tiglath-Pileser, Assyrian king, 745-727 BCE

This Sumerian king is wearing a crown displaying the ancient Japanese (Sumera-Mikoto) symbol of power, the chrysanthemum. Although pre-Sumerian in origin this symbol was copied by the Anunnaki from the gods and worn on their wrists as a symbol of power.

After the defeat of the Anunnaki, the Sumerians recaptured their pre-Anunnaki beliefs of love, respect for nature, and the energy forces that exist in all things. Nonetheless, the Anunnaki influence had altered the Sumerian, and world cultures forever.

Maya—ca. 1800-250 BCE, <u>Pre-classical period only</u>

Two of the ancient sacred symbols, the turtle and the cross, superimposed on one another in this "pre-classical" period of Mayan art.

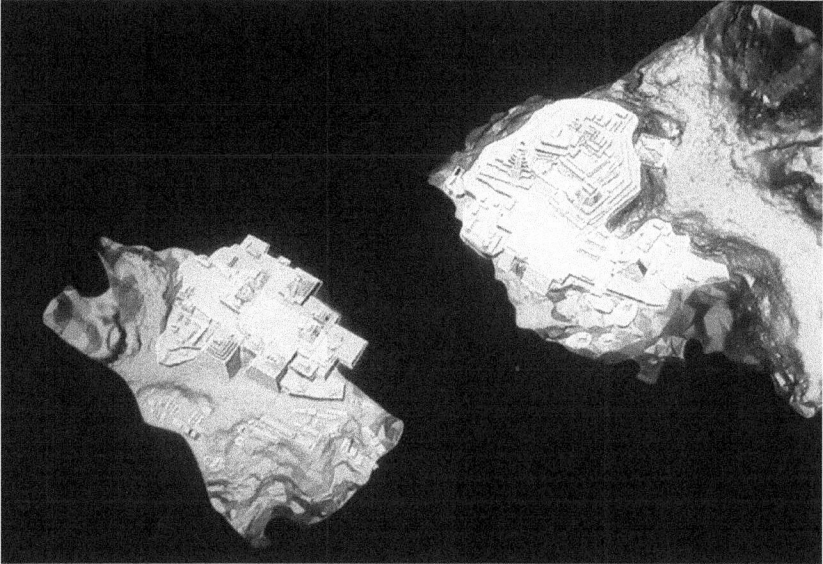

Google

Macabilero, Guatemala
Pre-classical Mayan structures with their geoglyphic properties

The Pre-classical Mayan people of Macabilero were known as the Turtle People. The turtle is one of the symbols of the ancient spirituality that dates back tens of thousands of years.

In the later "Classic Period" the Maya seemed to be different from the Pre-classical Maya. Not only did the Maya of the Classic Period not use geoglyphology in their structures, but they showed no tendencies toward using the ancient symbols. Research also shows that the Pre-classical Maya were peaceful farmers, while the later Maya were warlike. Sounds like a replay of the history of peaceful people around the world.

Ten miles north of Macabilero lay the city named Piedras Negras. The structures in Piedras Negras incorporate a more conventional style than those in Macabilero. History tells us that the soldiers from classical period Piedras Negras attacked and killed off the pre-classical inhabitants of Macabilero.

Few know the history of the Maya in Mesoamerica in the Pre-classical Period. The more well-known and studied Maya lived in the Classical Period ca. 250 BCE–900 CE. Research has shown that there were wars between the two. As can be seen in the image above, the Pre-classical Maya used the ancient practice of building geoglyphs into their structures to outline their territory. The Aztecs also followed this practice. Once again we see the age-old circumstance of the warrior cultures overpowering and eliminating the spiritual cultures. This has been a repeating pattern throughout history. Although little is known about the Olmec culture, they also lived during the Pre-classical Period.

Hittites—Anatolia (Turkey), ca. 1300 BCE

Quora.com
Hittite Tomb Ornament

The eight-sided cross, four-sided cross, and sun symbol, all in one ornament

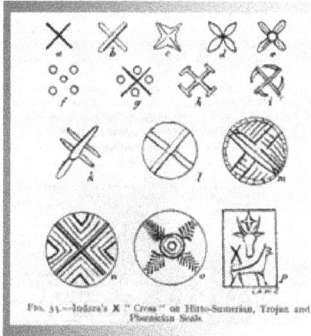
Hittite

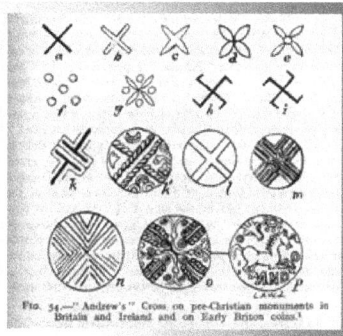
Celtic

Ancient symbols handed down through the Hittites of Anatolia and others, to the Celts

Hittite 1st Millennium BC

Hittitemonuments.com

Hittite stones bearing the Japanese mum and cross; Vedic, Hindu, ca. 1300 BCE.

Vedic India

The Hindu Sri Yantra

The Sri Yantra makes use of the ancient Japanese four- and eight-sided cross, the triangle, and the Japanese chrysanthemum.

Wikipedia explains, "Hinduism is the world's third-largest religion. It is an Indian dharma, or way of life, widely practiced in the Indian subcontinent and parts of Southeast Asia. Hinduism has been called the oldest religion in the world, and some practitioners and scholars refer to it as Sanātana Dharma, 'the eternal tradition,' or the 'eternal way,' beyond human history."

The words "religion" and "way of life" are sometimes used in the same paragraph to describe the Hindus, as well as other ancient cultures. One of the goals of this book is to show that religion is a modern word. When Hinduism is described as a way of life, the true nature of the ancient spirituality, as handed down for thousands of years, comes to light.

During our time true spirituality has been modified and infringed upon to the point of almost being lost in the whirlwind of what is now labeled as religion.

Egyptian Hebrew

It seems that Jews have been persecuted by civilizations and individuals from time immemorial. Could this be because they maintain secrets passed down from their ancestors whom others fear? Was the real reason the Jews were captured by the pharaohs to use their physical labor, or was it to use their secrets to build the pyramids?

Research shows that, while building their living quarters, the Jewish people surreptitiously built important geoglyphs into the orientation of the walls of their homes. These walls make up geoglyphs that point to internationally known monuments such as Gobekli Tepe, thereby indicating faraway monuments the Jews revered and were familiar with.

Geoglyphically oriented Jewish living quarters on the Upper Nile

Bearings generated by the structure walls

115

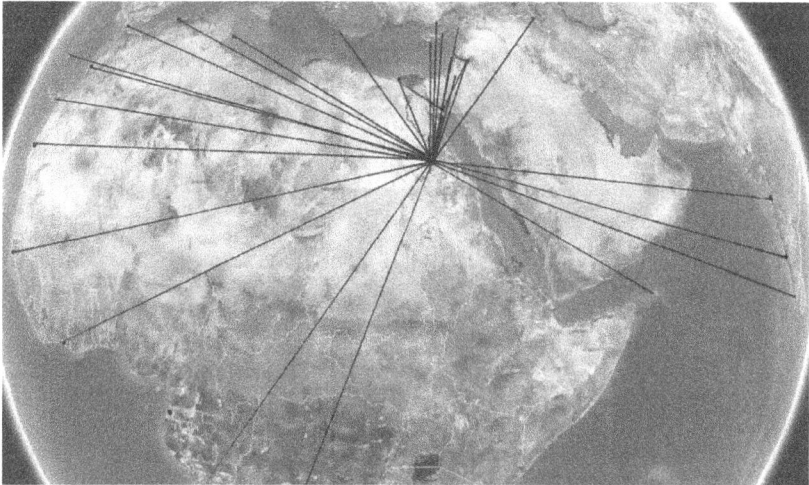

Points Described by Jewish Egyptian Structures

The angular lines running from Alexandria, to the Red sea, to the
Golan Heights might very well have been the original Jewish
territory.

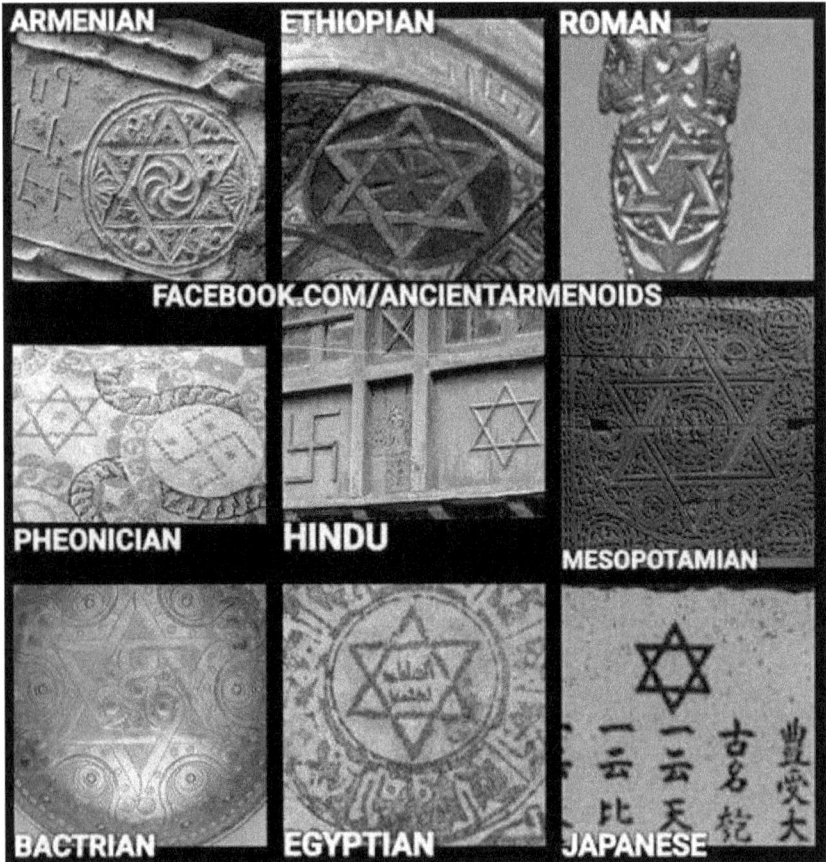

The Star of David, an ancient symbol

The star is not a Jewish symbol at all, but a sign that the bearer adhered to the teachings of the ancients. "Follow the symbols, not the names." The swastika is also an ancient symbol, just as is the snake symbol. Modern religious organizations tend to defile these and other ancient symbols in a self-serving attempt to get a person to shun anyone who uses them. This has the effect of negating the effects of the teachings of our forefathers and selling to the listener whatever might be the "religious" practice of the day.

The Phoenicians—ca. 1200 BCE

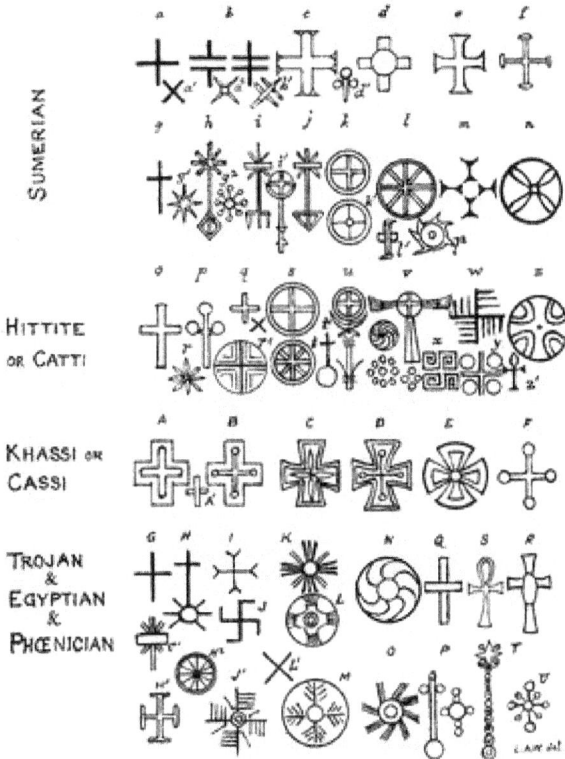

FIG. 46.—Sun Crosses, Hitto-Sumerian, Phœnician, Kassi and Trojan, plain, rayed, and decorated on seals, amulets, etc., 4000–1000 B.C.

Ancient Symbols and their users

Phoenicia was an ancient Semitic-speaking civilization that originated in the area of what we now call Lebanon. Scholars generally agree that it was centered on the coastal areas of Lebanon and included what is now northern Israel and southern Syria and reaching as far north as Arward. The Phoenician civilization spread across the Mediterranean between 1500 and 300 BCE.

The Phoenicians not only absorbed the information handed down from the ancients, but they were instrumental in passing the information down to their successors, the Celts and the Etruscans.

Many believe that the Phoenicians explored the Americas, even before the Celts. In ancient times the Phoenicians and the Jews were allies in what is now Israel. The Semitic influence covered most of the Middle East as far east as the northern Mesopotamian valley.

It is not certain what the Phoenicians called themselves in their own language; it appears to have been Kena'ani. In Hebrew, the word kena'ani has the secondary meaning of "a merchant," a term that well characterizes the Phoenicians and the Hebrews. Recent DNA studies on the origin of the Phoenicians show that they are the Canaanites from an ancient Mediterranean substratum.

Encyclopedia Phoenicia (Phoenicia.org) explains, "Many historians claim that Phoenicia ceased to exist in 64 BCE when it became part of the Roman Empire. But in 425 CE, official Roman records show the division of Phoenicia Prima into two provinces: Phoenicia Maritima and Phoenicia Libanensis. In the early Byzantine times, the count of Phoenicia governed. This means that Phoenicia was considered a separate entity."

Google

The Phoenicians were an ancient people who once ruled the Mediterranean. Despite little being known about them, as very few of their inscriptions have survived, their legacy has had an enormous impact on the world and is still felt today.

The Phoenicians were renowned as excellent mariners and used their expertise to trade all across the Mediterranean. One of the most notable signs of their trade activity is the establishment of

Carthage in present-day Tunisia. Carthage was founded as a colony in 814 BCE. The Phoenicians were also the originators of the modern alphabet.

The Carthaginians themselves became a dominant maritime power in the western Mediterranean. Apart from Carthage, the Phoenicians founded colonies on Cyprus and in Anatolia (Turkey) as well. The greater part of the territory they once occupied corresponds to modern-day Lebanon, but the Phoenicians also held parts of southern Syria and northern Israel.

Google

Phoenician trade routes

The direction taken by these influences can be followed from Egypt to Phoenicia, Syria, and Cyprus. The evidence comes thanks to a combination of excavated art forms that prove the direction of movement. During their westward movement, they carried Greek traditions with them. The latter lays great stress on what the early Greek philosophers learned from Egypt. The westward spread of this ancient philosophy did not stop in Eastern Europe. It continued on to the British Isles and later to pre-Columbian America.

Mesopotamian influence can be traced especially through the partial borrowing of Babylonian science, the divination by the Hittites, and later by the transmission of information through Phoenicia. The Egyptians and Mesopotamians wrote no theoretical treatises; information had to be transmitted piecemeal through personal contacts. The practice of transmitting information from memory left the Phoenicians' and their descendants' history at the mercy of their detractors. One of the cultures most affected by their lack of written history was the Celts, whose history was left to the Roman writers, a culture with whom they had been at war for over a thousand years. To this day the history of these cultures must be gleaned from stories written by other cultures and more importantly through the secret geoglyphological evidence they provided us.

The Phoenicians were instrumental in disseminating their form of writing, which became our modern alphabet. Both sciences and pseudo sciences spread from Egypt and Mesopotamia to Canaan, Phoenicia, and Anatolia. The Phoenicians in particular transmitted much of this ancient knowledge to the various lands of the Mediterranean, especially to the Greeks and Celts.

The Faram Research Foundation
The Juan de la Cosa map, ca. 1500 CE with geoglyphs numbered.

It is quite possible that the Phoenicians explored the Americas. It is little known that Celtic Galician Juan de la Cosa owned the ship *Santa María*, on which Columbus made his first voyage to the Americas. Not only did De la Cosa own the Santa Maria but accompanied Columbus as his navigator. The previous image shows a portion of the map he made shortly after his return from his first voyage with Columbus c1500 CE. The image shows a portion of the map depicting the southern coast of North America and the east coast of South America.

It was the practice in ancient times to claim all the land along a river by placing a geoglyph at the head of the river. You will notice the rivers of both southern North America and eastern South America are shown. At the head of each river is a dot indicating that a geoglyph exists at that location, claiming the river for the entity that placed the geoglyphic marker there.

It would have been impossible for anyone to explore and claim the rivers of North America and South America in the few years between when Columbus made his first voyage 1492 CE and when the map was made in 1500 CE. That would indicate that someone had explored and claimed the rivers shown on the map long before Columbus came to the Americas. A photo of each of the geoglyphs at the head of the rivers can be seen in the book *Ancient Signposts* (2011).

There were only three groups practicing geoglyphology at the time that also had the ships to travel to the Americas. These were the Phoenicians, the Etruscans (later to call themselves the Portuguese), and the Celts. Based on the time it would have taken to explore all this land, it would be reasonable to assume it was the Phoenicians who placed the markers in the Americas. This would also explain the Phoenicians' great prosperity.

The Etruscans—Italy, ca. 750 BCE

Etruscan amulet with all the appropriate symbols

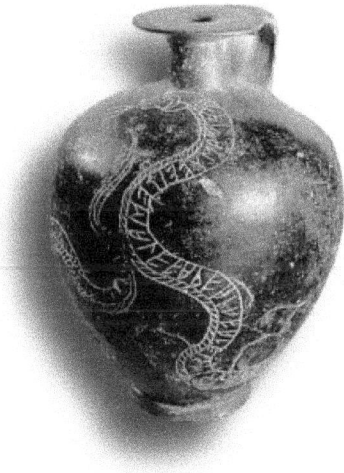

The sacred symbol of the snake and an Etruscan urn with double spiral

The Etruscans were the ancient people of Etruria, Italy, between the Tiber and Arno Rivers west and south of the Apennines. Their urban civilization reached its height in the sixth century BCE. Many features of Etruscan culture were adopted by the Romans after they displaced the Etruscans in Northern Italy.

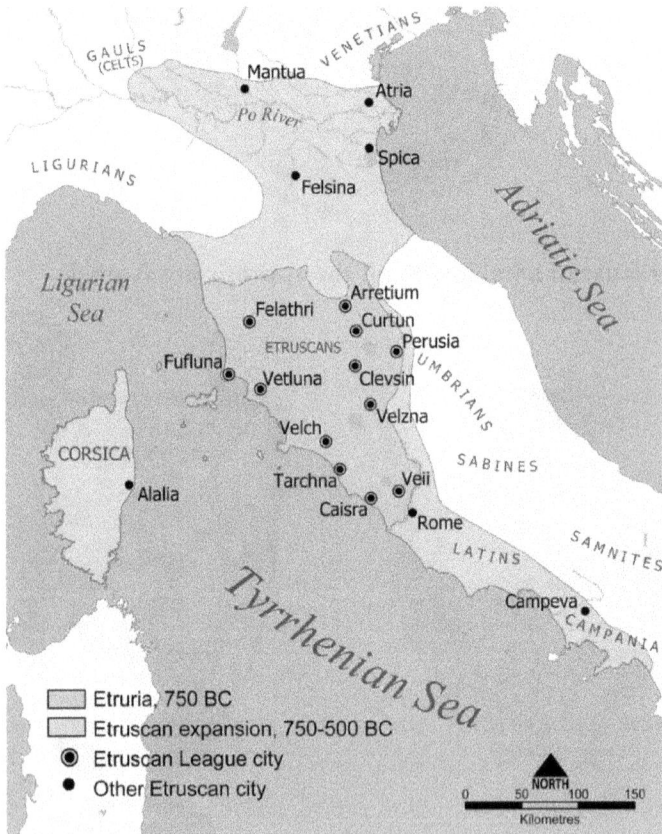

GAULS (CELTS)

VENETIANS

Mantua

Atria

Po River

Spica

LIGURIANS

Felsina

Ligurian Sea

Felathri

Arretium

Curtun

ETRUSCANS

Perusia

Fufluna

UMBRIANS

Vetluna

Clevsin

Velzna

Velch

CORSICA

SABINES

Tarchna

Veii

Alalia

Caisra

Rome

LATINS

SAMNITES

Campeva

CAMPANIA

Tyrrhenian Sea

Adriatic Sea

Etruria, 750 BC
Etruscan expansion, 750-500 BC
◉ Etruscan League city
● Other Etruscan city

NORTH
0   50   100   150
Kilometres

Google

"Academic" map of Etruria

The True Map of Etruria

Attached is a survey of the Etruscan Alatri Acropolis in Alatri, Italy. The acropolis has puzzled academics for centuries. Many say it was constructed in Roman times, while others say it is much older. What confuses people is the fact that the Catholic Church builds churches on top of mounds and pyramids of previous cultures. This is done all over the world to hide the fact that there was a spiritual culture there before they arrived. The Etruscans built the walled structure at Alatri ca. 900–100 BCE. However, the church was built by early Christians ca. 300–400 CE. Therefore the church bears the marks of both Etruscan and Roman influence.

The walled acropolis was built by the Etruscans, who still practiced using the ancient geoglyphic skills given to them eons ago. Later the church was built, presumably using Etruscan labor, and bears the symbols of the Etruscan ancients in the main window. There again are the eight- and four-pointed crosses used by the ancient cultures for eons. After the defeat of the Etruscans by the Romans, the Etruscan elite moved to the west coast of Iberia and reinvented themselves as the Portuguese.

The megalithic walls of Etruscans were built with access to the same technology as their predecessors, who built the monolithic walls in Peru and other places around the world. A geoglyphological survey of the Alatri Acropolis will bear this out.

Aerial photo of the Etruscan Acropolis of Alatri

The projected bearings of the linear walls

127

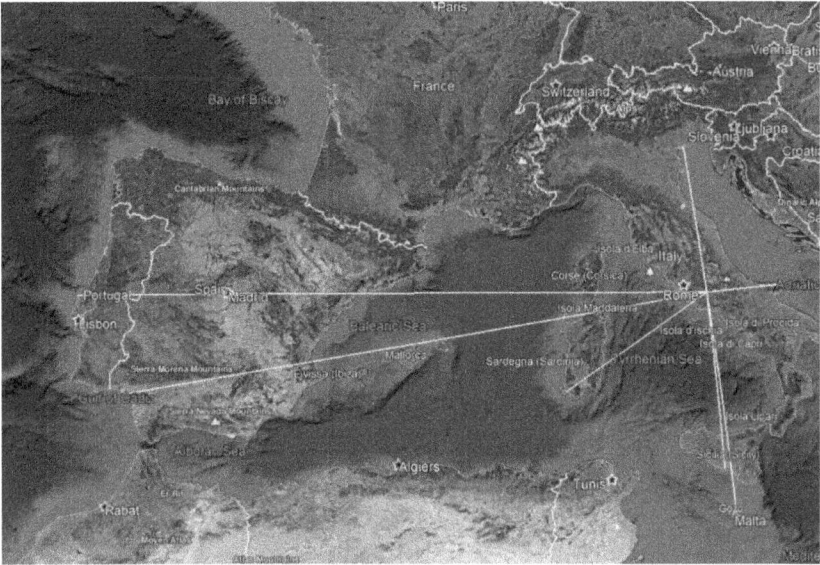

Extension of the bearings in the previous image

This displays the true territory of the Etruscans, not known until this survey.

A correction factor of –1 degree needs to be applied to each of the surveyed magnetic bearings emitted from the Etruscan structure walls at the Acropolis of Alatri. It was common practice to insert a correction code in order to prevent the unenlightened from decoding the geoglyph.

Window of church atop the Acropolis of Alatri

Notice the four- and eight-pointed symbols, which are found on churches that followed the ancient spirituality of Gnosticism, but not usually on a Catholic church. This is another telltale sign that there was a transition from the Gnosticism taught by Jesus to the Christianity taught by the Catholic Church. This most likely resulted from the structure being built by the Gnostic Etruscans during the transition period from Etruscan to Roman control.

Gavin Trilloch writes, "We know little about these pre-Roman engineering skills that seem to have been abandoned after the creation of these walled towns. The stones are enormous, up to at least 5 meters by 2 meters by 1.5 meters, a stone that weighs maybe twenty-five tons, not all that easy to move into its idealized position as the lintel above the minor gate on the western side of the acropolis of Alatri."

India and Tibet—500 BCE

Buddhism

As the British Library explains, "Gandhara was a vibrant crossroads of Indian, Iranian, and Central Asian cultures. At the peak of its influence, from about 100 BCE to 200 CE, it was perhaps the world's most important center of Buddhism and was almost certainly the gateway through which Buddhism was transmitted from India to China and elsewhere, to become one of the world's great (spiritualties) religions."

The Tibetan wheel of spirituality
Displaying both the four- and eight-sided crosses

Location of Tibet

Geoglyphology solves the dispute over stolen Tibetan land Sigiriya, Sri Lanka, ca. 480 CE

In October 1950 the Chinese army entered Tibet and occupied land the Tibetans had owned for hundreds of years. They claimed through some obscure reasoning that the land belonged to the Chinese. In actuality the move was made to crush the ancient spiritual practices practiced by the Tibetan monks. The Dalai Lama was supposed to have been captured, but he escaped.

On the following pages you will see two geoglyphological surveys done on two separate structures. One of the structures was constructed in Sri Lanka in 450 CE. The other structure was constructed by the Portuguese at Fort Daman, India, in 1559 CE. The following map of India shows the result of surveys conducted on the two structures.

Sigiriya, Sri Lanka

The following paragraphs pertain to these two forts:

The top of the Sigiriya mesa in Sri Lanka including geoglyphic bearings

Fort Daman, India - Portuguese ca. 1550 CE

Fort Daman, India, Geoglyphic Bearings

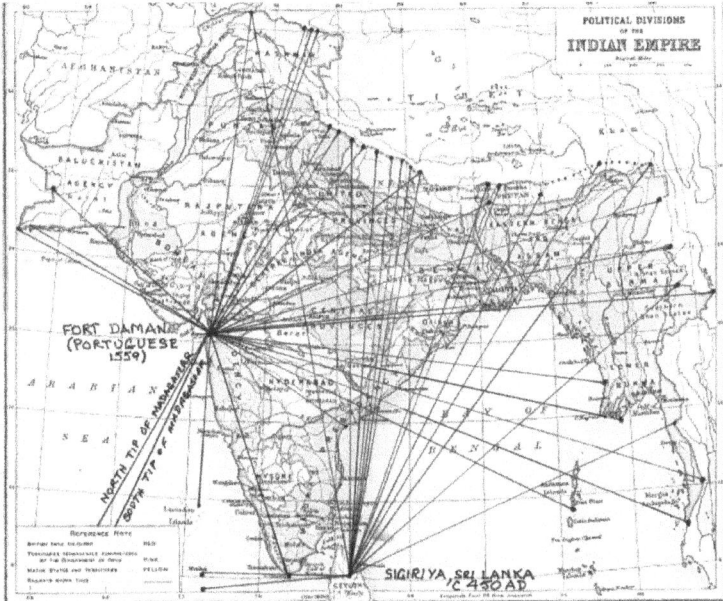

The Faram Research Foundation

Fort Daman, India, and the Sigiriya, Sri Lanka, radials

These two surveys show that the Indian and Tibetan territory used to be related. The smaller size today is the result of political and military intervention since the territory was first established. It also points out one of the beneficial uses of geoglyphology, that being the validation of the true boundaries of a country. You will notice there is a dotted line in the upper right-hand portion of the map. That line illustrates the land that the Chinese recently took from Tibet. Based on the Sri Lanka survey, the dotted line represents the original boundary of the ancient territory and shows that it belongs to the Tibetans. Also notice that, even though the western geoglyph was constructed much later in the form of a Portuguese fort, it coincides with the much earlier Sri Lanka geoglyph.

China—Daoism, ca. 221 BCE

Daoist symbol displaying the eight-sided cross

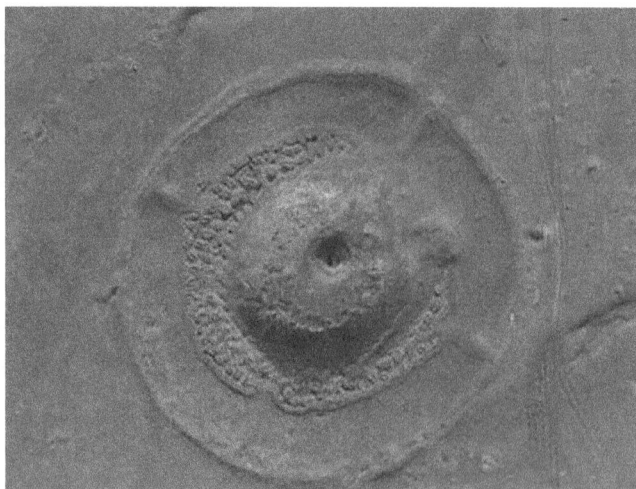

Celt-like hinge displaying the four-sided cross, Xinjiang, China, ca. 1000 BCE

Basic Concepts of Daoism

In 142 CE, in the mountains of the province of Sechwan, Zhang is said to have received a revelation from Taishang Laojun ("Lord Lao the Most High"). Laozi bestowed on Zhang his "orthodox and sole doctrine of the authority of the covenant" (*zhengyi mengweifa*). This was meant as a definitive replacement for the "religious" practices of the people, which are described as having lapsed into demonism and degeneracy. True spiritual practices require no organized religion. We are one with God and have been given the ability, and right, to communicate with our etheric God through prayer and meditation.

Certain concepts of ancient agrarian religion have dominated Chinese thought uninterruptedly from before the formation of the philosophic schools. This continued until the first radical break with tradition and the overthrow of dynastic rule at the beginning of the twentieth century. The most important of these concepts are (1) the continuity between nature and human beings, or the interaction between the world and human society; (2) the rhythm of constant flux and transformation in the universe and the return or reversion of all things to the Dao, from which they emerged; and (3) the worship of ancestors, the concept of heaven, and the divine nature of the sovereign. These have always been, and still are, the hallmarks of those practicing the ancient ways.

As can be seen here, the world is in constant state of flux, with good and bad often trading places in a constant struggle for control by the negative and a constant battle for spiritual autonomy by the good.

Portuguese—ca. 300 BCE

Portuguese national emblem

Religious Beliefs

Wikipedia describes the history of Portuguese political beliefs as follows:

>The bulk of the Portuguese population is nominally Catholic. However, during its history, Portugal has experienced waves of political anticlericalism. This is based on the Portuguese firmly entrenched ancient spiritual values attained prior to the forming of the Catholic Church in 300 CE. In the early half of the nineteenth century, religious orders were banned, and Catholic Church properties were confiscated.

>Then, under the First Portuguese Republic, 1910–1926, education was secularized and Coptic (the beliefs taught by Jesus and previous prophets) properties were confiscated, folk celebrations restricted, and the ancient spiritual beliefs abolished.

>This shakeup emphasized the rift between the Coptics and the Catholic Church, which had dominated Europe for over 1,800 years.

>In 1933, under the staunchly Catholic Salazar, Portugal experienced a Catholic religious revival, and the position of the local priest in the villages throughout the

country was greatly enhanced. Since 1974, the end of Salazar's "Estada Nova," the Catholic hierarchy has been challenged, and in recent years there has been a decline in the number of clergy. A form of "pious" anticlericalism exists among the people who view the priest as a spiritual leader on the one hand and a man like every other man on the other. Much of Portuguese religious life exists beyond the official structures of the Catholic Church.

It should be remembered that the Portuguese were the Etruscans before they moved to what is now called Portugal. The Etruscans practiced the ancient spirituality we now call Coptic well before Jesus taught it.

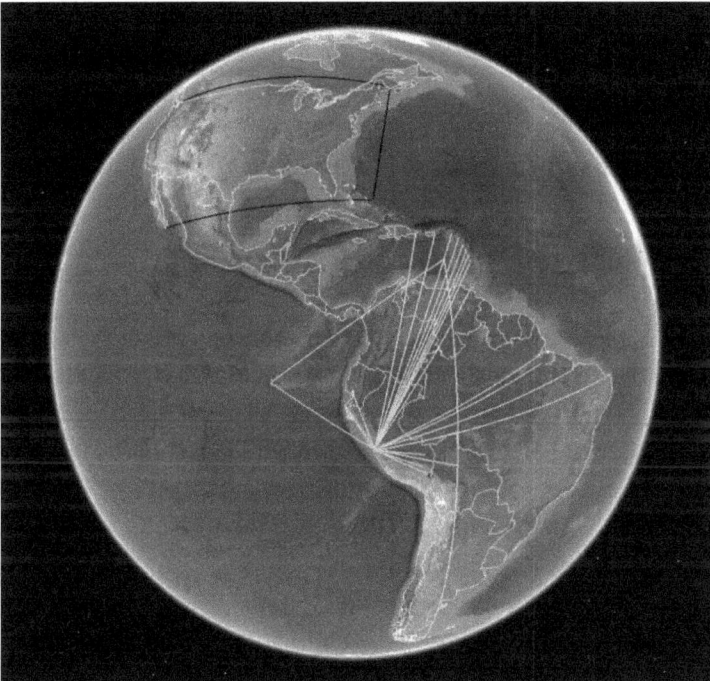

Google Earth – The Faram Research Foundation

The Post Columbus Portuguese Territory of South America
(As defined by the Caral Peru geoglyph ca.5000 BCE)

For millennia Portugal held claim to North and South America. These claims had been handed down to them through their predecessors, the Phoenicians. This territory was eventually further divided, as shown in the previous image, between the Portuguese (magenta lines) in South America, Spain (red lines) in Central America, and the Templars (black lines) in North America. This division of the Americas came about as the result of the war with the Moors on the Iberian Peninsula. The participants were the Templars, Portuguese, and Spanish against the Moors. The war lasted from ca. 700 to 1492 CE. Prior to this time, only the Portuguese and the Celts (Templars) knew about the Americas. During the Moorish war, the Spanish learned of their secret. Subsequently they had to have their piece of the pie. It was the job of the Columbian party to place geoglyphs around the Caribbean to cement Spain's claim to Mesoamerica. It was not long before Spain made incursions into the unprotected western coasts of both North and South America. The United States was not able to challenge this intrusion until they built up their military force.

The Coptics—ca. 5 BCE

In the following text, you will sometimes encounter the word Coptic in reference to ancient spirituality. That spirituality has been handed down through many thousands of years and was present in the loving teachings of Christ—"turn the other cheek". Coptic beliefs are not a religion but a way of life and are used by the individual as a way of communicating with the ethereal God through meditation or prayer. This spirituality was taught by prophets such as Jesus, Muhammad, Buddha, and other spiritual deities. This communication is achieved directly through meditation or prayer without the assistance of a worldly religion or intermediary. Both Jesus and Muhammad had their teachings distorted by earthly agendas after their death.

Due to misunderstandings regarding their theology and political allegiances, Coptic Christians have been persecuted for centuries, especially by the Romans. Coptic Orthodox churches split from the broader Christian community in 451 CE, just over a hundred years after the Roman Church was founded in 300 CE. The Coptic Church diverged from the Christian Church in part due to their departure from Christs teachings. After all, they had been practicing the Coptic teachings of Jesus for three hundred years prior to the establishment of the Catholic Church.

Coptic Christians trace their founding to the apostle St. Mark. Tradition holds that Mark brought the ancient beliefs, reiterated by Christ, to Egypt and founded the Coptic Church during the first century. The Coptic Church is the oldest church in the world that follows the teachings of Jesus. Several other apostles traveled to Portugal and other places to spread the Coptic teachings of Christ. A Coptic church in Egypt on the west bank of the Nile River was founded in 49 CE.

The Coptic teachings spread throughout Egypt within half a century of St. Mark's arrival in Alexandria. This is clear from the New Testament writings found in Bahnasa, Egypt. These writings date around the year 200 CE. A fragment of the gospel of John, written in the Coptic language, was found in Upper Egypt and can be dated to the first half of the second century.

Getty Images

Coptic theology and practice have much in common with Catholicism but diverge in several major areas. Like Catholics, Coptic Christians believe in the Ten Commandments, and they practice the sacraments of baptism and confirmation. But unlike Roman Catholics, they don't believe in the infallibility of the Pope or in purgatory. Unlike other Christians, Coptics believe in reincarnation. Belief in reincarnation was deleted from practice by Catholics during the first Catholic ecumenical council in 300 CE. Also, Coptic priests are allowed to marry.

Just like their Templar brothers a thousand years later, in order to survive in a Catholic-dominated world, orthodox Coptic Christians eventually adopted many Catholic rituals and practices, albeit not their beliefs.

The Coptic Christians were originally well founded in theology in churches and cities throughout the Roman Empire. Others looked up to them with great admiration and respect, willingly following their lead in doctrinal like-mindedness and unity.

141

It is documented that the first ecumenical council used Egyptian Coptic texts as the basis for the new Catholic Bible.

It is interesting to note that while the Coptics were under the rule of the Roman Empire, they suffered severe persecution and death for their steadfast faith and beliefs in Christ while refusing to worship self-appointed clerics. As the belief in the original teachings of Jesus spread, especially in the ranks of the Roman soldiers, Rome realized that something had to be done. The resulting solution was that the Catholic Church was founded in 300 CE. The Catholic Church and Islam became the religious standards of the time. After the death of the two beloved prophets, Jesus and Muhammad, disruptive forces developed systems by which the believer was controlled by teachings of damnation, fear, and religious condemnation. Confession was included to keep the Romans abreast of any disruptive influences in their empire.

Wikipedia notes, "According to tradition, several of Muhammad's companions served as scribes and recorded his revelations. Shortly after Muhammad's death, the Quran was compiled by the companions, who had written down or memorized parts of it. The codices showed differences that motivated Caliph Uthman to establish a standard version, now known as Uthman's codex, which is generally considered the archetype of the Quran known today."

So it seems that, after their death, the significant influence of both of the modern prophets was used by the politicians of the day to further their own agendas, resulting in the writing of the amended versions of the Bible and the Quran.

In 641 CE, yet another tribulation began when the Arab conquest took place, overthrowing the Romans' rule in Egypt and at first relieving the Coptic Church from persecution by the Catholics. But what appeared to be their freedom became, yet again, bondage. The Arabs' societal strength and control caused the Coptics to endure a major language and culture change, as well as a confrontation with the Islamic faith. Unfortunately, over the centuries, most Coptics converted to Islam.

Orthodox Churches, ca. 100 CE

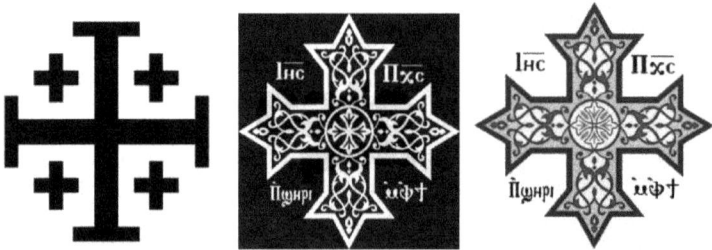

Greek Orthodox   Egyptian Orthodox   Russian Orthodox
Notice the four- and eight-sided aspects of the crosses.

Orthodox churches are basically Coptic churches that refused to change the Coptic teachings of Jesus while under the Roman domination. To this day they maintain their basic Coptic beliefs.

Greek Orthodox

Greek Orthodox churches are united in communion with each other, as well as with the other Eastern Orthodox churches. Orthodox Christians hold a common doctrine and a common form of worship, and they see themselves not as separate churches but as administrative units of one single church. They are notable for their extensive tradition of iconography (see also: Byzantine art), for their veneration of the mother of God and the saints, and for their use of the Divine Liturgy on Sundays.

The current territory of the Greek Orthodox churches more or less covers the areas in the Balkans, Anatolia, and the eastern Mediterranean, which used to be a part of the Byzantine Empire. The majority of Greek Orthodox Christians live within Greece. However, there is a strong influence in the southern Balkans (especially in

Albania), as well as in Jordan, the occupied Palestinian territories, Iraq, Syria, Lebanon, Cyprus, Anatolia, European Turkey, and the South Caucasus. In addition, due to the large Greek diaspora, there are many Greek Orthodox followers who live in North America and Australia. Orthodox Christians in Finland, who compose about 1 percent of the population, are also under the jurisdiction of a Greek Orthodox church (the Ecumenical Patriarchate). There are many Greek Orthodox churches with origins dating back to the Byzantine Empire ca. 364 CE.

Ethnic Greeks in Russia, as well as Pontic and Caucasus Greeks from the former Russian Transcaucasia, often consider themselves both Greek Orthodox and Russian Orthodox, which is consistent with the Orthodox faith. (Orthodoxy is the same across ethnic boundaries.) Thus, they may attend services held in old Russian and old Slavonic languages, without this in any way undermining their Orthodox faith or distinct Greek ethnic identity. Over the centuries, these Pontic Greek–speaking communities have mixed through intermarriage in varying degrees with ethnic Russians and other Orthodox Christians between the Middle Ages and early nineteenth century.

Byzantines—ca. 364 CE

Byzantine coat of arms with the four orders

The Byzantine Empire is a continuation of the Orthodoxy that existed in the face of the Roman Empire. The Orthodox territory was known as the Eastern Roman Empire. Notice that the symbol for all four of the Byzantine orders is the four-sided cross. It is interesting to note that the four types of crosses all have four main extensions. If you look closely, you will notice that the ends of the arms of the four-pointed star are splayed. By doing this they have incorporated both the four- and eight-sided crosses into one. If you count only the legs of the cross, you will have a four-sided cross; however, if you count the points on the cross, the total will be eight.

Google Images

The Byzantines Used the Ancient Symbols

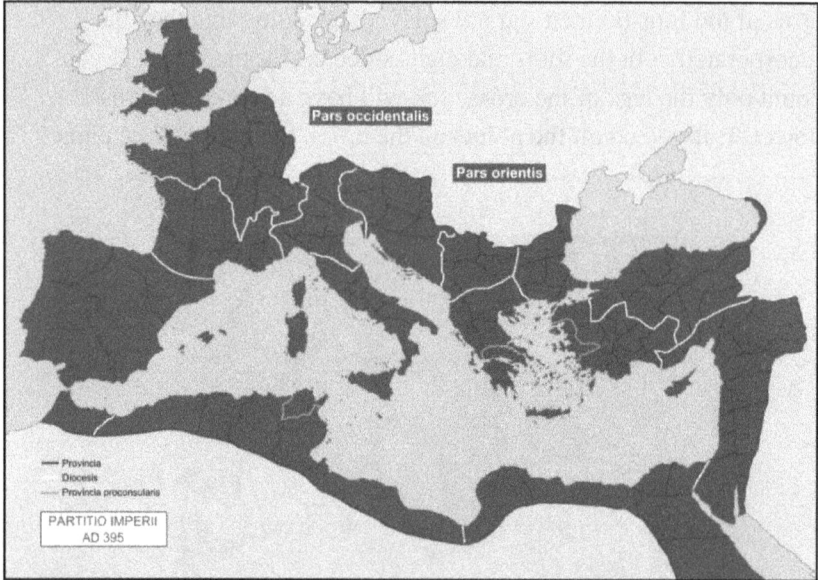

The Roman Empire, showing the Eastern and Western Empires

The eastern portion of the Roman Empire refused to convert from the Coptic teachings of Jesus to the Christian teachings of the newly established Catholic Church. As a result they adopted all the trappings of the Catholic Church, but their beliefs remained Coptic. After the collapse of the Roman Empire ca. 400 CE, the Western Roman Empire took on the name of the Byzantine Empire and occupied what was previously called the Eastern Roman Empire.

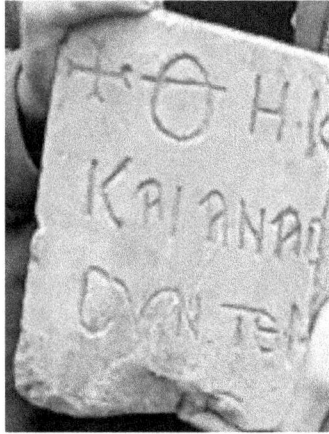

Byzantine Tombstone with the Splayed Four-Sided Cross

Native Americans – Unknown to present

Native American Sun Cross – Sun Cross with Heavenly Spiral

Most eastern and some western North American native tribes express beliefs similar to the teachings of the ancients. However, the tribe that has managed to adhere more closely to the ancient teachings is the Hopi tribe.

A great number of the Native American tribes display many of the same ancient symbols as the Celts of Europe. Although research has proven that the Celts existed in the New World along with the natives, it is currently unclear if the natives obtained the symbols from the Celts, or if both the Celts and the Native Americans had the symbols handed down to them from the ancients independently of one another.

Wikipedia Commons
Spiro Mounds, Oklahoma, United States, ca. 1000 CE

Wikipedia Commons

Spiro Mounds, Oklahoma, United States, ca. 1000 CE

The Hopi flag with the four-plus-four star configuration

The Hopi people are Native Americans who have lived in the high mesas of Arizona for several thousand years. Today there are several hundred villages, all autonomous, each with their own form of self-government. The clans are matriarchal and matrilineal. Religious observance is led by the men who own the livestock and fruit trees, but women own the land. The culture is a matriarchal society. Matriarchy was the practice throughout much of the history of those who practiced the ancient spirituality. One of the issues that caused the demise of the Templars was that they venerated the Virgin Mary. Matriarchy is demonstrated in the Russian religious icons of the

Virgin Mary with child, which are so sought after today. These images were generated by Russian Orthodox followers. The true followers of the ancient teachings were matriarchal in nature. The ancient practice of the veneration of the sacred feminine was the impetus behind the ancient veneration of the female Isis.

Isis and Horus   **Isis and Pharaoh**   **Mary and Jesus**

The Book of the Dead describes Isis as "she who gives birth to heaven and earth, knows the orphan, knows the widow, seeks justice for the poor, and shelter for the weak." Due to her association with Horus, Isis also became the eye of Ra when the two gods merged as Ra-Horakhty. The worship of Isis spread throughout the Roman Empire between the time of Jesus and the birth of Christianity through the Catholic Church. This was evident in wall paintings and objects found at Pompeii, among other places. The loss of control of the Roman Troops to the Coptic beliefs taught by Jesus was the impetus behind the start of the Holy Roman Catholic Church ca. 300 CE

It is no wonder that the Catholic Church would imitate Isis in order to win over the spiritualists. As were many of the ancient religious icons, Isis has been given a negative connotation in order to discourage worshipers from learning the truth. Isis was one of the most revered and widespread spiritual icons until recent times, gaining her the name "The Woman of Ten-Thousand Names."

Spiritual Beliefs

The Hopi culture, as are other spirituality based cultures, based on their spiritual concept of harmony with nature and cycles of rebirth. From birth to death, every event is marked by ritual, and throughout the year ceremonial lessons are given. The most important rituals concern rain and corn, the two essential elements of Hopi life.

The Hopi worldview accepts that time and distance are linked concepts and that that symbolism equates to reality, similar to the modern line of thought called "the power of positive thinking". They believe a form of reciprocity between men and spirits, so that if men observe the rituals that give spirits form, the spirits are obligated to hear their petitions, send rain, and protect the harvest.

Harold Courlander (1971) shares this Palatkwapi story: "When a stranger comes to the village, feed him. Do not injure one another, because all beings deserve to live together without injury being done to them. When people are old and cannot work anymore, do not turn them out to shift for themselves, but take care of them. Defend yourselves when an enemy comes to your village, but do not go out seeking war. The Hopi shall take this counseling and make it the Hopi way."

The Hopi universe consists of earth, metaphorically spoken of as "our mother," the upper world, and the underworld from which the Hopi came and to which their spirits go after death. The universe is balanced between a feminine principle, the earth, and a masculine one, manifested in the fructifying but dangerous powers of sun, rain, and lightning.

There are three major classes of supernatural. The most individualized are the gods and goddesses, each having his or her special area of concern. Figures or impersonations of these deities are used in ceremonial activity. The next category is the Kachinas. A few of the Kachinas are individuals, but most of them are classes of beings each with its different character and appearance. In kachina dances the dancers wear the costume appropriate to the kachina type they portray. Some types are more popular than others; new ones are invented, and old ones drop out of use. Finally, there are the generalized spirits of natural objects and life-forms, who will be offended if one of their earthly representatives is treated improperly. Thus, when a game animal is killed, its spirit, and the generalized spirits of that animal type, must be placated. This harmony with nature is a key part of the ancient spirituality.

The Native Americans suffered the same fate as the Celts and the Jews. Groups wishing to further their own agendas labeled them as barbarians or savages to give their warriors a clear conscience while committing genocide. What is incredible is that the three cultures just mentioned were peaceful cultures that followed the ancient spiritual teachings of living in peace and harmony with their environment. It makes you wonder if the term savages and barbarians was misplaced.

Before the wave of Europeans came to the Americas ca. 1500 CE, the Freemasons and Celts had been living in peace and harmony with their neighbors, the Native Americans. There were numerous treaties that were ratified and were being honored by the colonists before the wave of early European immigrants arrived. (See the book *La Merica*, 2013.)

The Knights Templar—ca. 1118 – 1450 CE

(1450 CE is the date that the Freemasons officially replaced the Templars in Edinburgh, Scotland.)

ST-SÉPULCRE   MALTE   TEMPLE   ST-JACQUES DE L'ÉPÉE   TEUTONIQUE

Pinterest.at

Orders of the Knights Templar displaying the four-sided cross

The Poor Fellow-Soldiers of Christ of the Temple of Solomon, commonly known as the Knights Templar or the Order of the Temple, were among the most famous of the Western Christian military orders. The organization existed for approximately two centuries in the Middle Ages. The order was created earlier but not officially endorsed by the Roman Catholic Church until 1129 CE.

According to author Robert Lomas, the Sinclairs of Scotland and their French relatives, the St. Clairs, were instrumental in creating the Knights Templar. He claims that the founder of Templars, Hugh de Payns, was married to a relative of the Duke of Champagne (Henri de St. Clair), who was a powerful broker of the first Crusade and who had the political power to nominate the pope. The duke suggested the idea and empowered it to the pope.

Although the order was endorsed by the Catholic Church, their true origins lie in the Celtic hierarchy who knew that the only way to exist in the Catholic monopoly was to create an order that would be accepted by the pope. This order grew so important in Europe that in 1312 CE a French king who owed the Templars vast sums of money convinced the pope of Templar wrongdoings in order to abolish the order.

The Templars' existence was tied closely to the Crusades; when the Holy Land was lost, support for the order faded. Rumors about the Templars' secret initiation ceremony created mistrust, and King Philip IV of France, deeply in debt to the order, took advantage of the situation. Philip coordinated with the pope to eliminate the growing power of the Templar organization. In 1307, many of the order's members in France were arrested, tortured into giving false confessions, and then burned at the stake. Under pressure from King Philip, Pope Clement V disbanded the order in 1312 CE.

King Phillip had borrowed tremendous amounts of money from the Templars. By creating a scandal and eliminating the Templars, he would also eliminate his debt. The abrupt disappearance of a major part of the European infrastructure gave rise to speculation and legends, which have kept the Templar name alive into modern times.

With the Templar order in disarray, the remaining members allegedly collected the immense wealth that the Templars had amassed and boarded ships in France for trips to Scotland, Portugal, and North America. (See the book: *La Merica* – 2013)

A Templar ship. Notice the square sail, similar to the Viking ships.

In Scotland the Scottish independence movement provided an excellent cover for disenfranchised warriors. The Templars would assist their Scottish hosts by defeating the English at the Battle of Bannockburn in 1314. During the late thirteenth and early fourteenth century, England, under King Edward I, was at war with Scotland. In 1314 his son, Edward II, engaged the Scots at the Battle of Bannockburn. The Scots won the battle largely due to the intervention of the Knights Templar on the side of their king, Robert the Bruce. There are no records of the Knights Templar engaging in the battle of Bannockburn. The excommunicated King Robert had very good reason to hide the Templars' part in the battle. He was desperate to keep on the right side of the pope and of the king of France. It is also worth noting that two members of the Knights

Templar had fought for Edward I at the battle of Falkirk in 1297. The Templars became the Freemasons ca. 1450 CE. In the Freemasons there are two rites of ascendance, the York Rite and the Scottish Rite. The Order of the Knights Templar is the highest rank in the York Rite.

Templar Beliefs

The order of the Temple of Soloman tells us;

"Perhaps the most attractive and inspirational aspect of the Order of the Temple of Solomon is its traditional focus on a unique heritage of spirituality, which has prominently colored its distinct character as an Order of Chivalry. In the modern era, this has given rise to great popular interest, seeking to discover the true nature of the legendary "Templar Spirituality", and its connection with the most ancient Priesthood of Melchizedek from the Biblical Magi. (Authors Note: Notice that the article refers to spirituality rather than religion.)

Under the Temple Rule of 1129 AD, the Order strictly operates "according to Canon law" as a "canonical institution". However, the same Temple Rule of Saint Bernard, which converted the Order to Christianity, also specifically highlights its unique path of spirituality with its own Templar Priesthood...

The Knights Templar were founded in the Biblical Temple of Solomon, which they excavated for a nine year period. This Solomonic Temple embodied the most ancient Magi Priesthood of Melchizedek (Genesis 14:18-20; I Kings 1:39) of the Biblical Magi (II Samuel 15:25-27; Ezekiel 44:15, 48:11; Matthew 2:1-2), of which Jesus was High Priest (Hebrews 5:5, 5:6, 5:10, 6:20, 7:17, 7:20).

The legendary Templar Priesthood thus consists of the earliest origins of classical Spirituality, since the beginning of recorded history, tracing back to ca. 10,068 BC. Prior to the development of the Templars the Romans had instituted the Catholic Church. It is precisely for this reason that under the Temple Rule, the Order continues to serve as Defenders of the Church, primarily as Guardians of the origins of Christianity, which are the foundational pillars essential to restore and preserve the Orthodox Church.

For that same reason, because the Ancient Priesthood of the Templars predates and thus is the foundation of all religions, the Temple Rule also established that the Order is authentically interfaith and non-denominational for individual membership, while still upholding its traditions of the ancient spirituality.

While the Order actively defends the Church, it is not itself a Church, but rather an Order of Chivalry, which always included "Secular Knights". Therefore, authentic Templarism does not impose any particular beliefs upon its members, and does not require any specific religious practices. The original Templar traditions thus fully accommodate and support religious diversity and spiritual individuality.

Notice: Templar interfaith cooperation rejects and prohibits the modern "ecumenical" trend of "mixing" and "blending" of religions, and requires strictly preserving the distinct and authentic heritage of each historical tradition separately.

Before we can explore the depths of Templar accomplishments, it is important to understand a few of their beliefs and appreciate the knowledge they possessed.

In order to protect themselves and their valuable knowledge, they resorted to secret societies that have existed down through time to this very day. The Templars and Freemasons are two of those societies. The reason their secrets have remained private is that they take a seldom oath to protect them.

The Celts, Etruscans, and their predecessors, from which the Templars evolved, were experts at geometry and astronomy. They enjoyed and excelled at putting together numeric and geological puzzles that we are just today deciphering. The Celts were also very spiritual; however, when the Roman emperor Constantine instituted the Roman version of Christianity, three hundred years after the death of Jesus, the Celts now had two reasons to keep their religion hidden. The Celts, who believed that Mary was also a deity, had to go underground or be persecuted by Rome for their beliefs. The gnostics, as the followers of the teachings of Jesus, existed before the Catholic Church was established. The gnostics believed that Jesus was the son of God and that Mary, having had an immaculate conception, was the earthly embodiment of the feminine side of God (the sacred feminine), just as Jesus was the earthly embodiment of the Son of God. This would explain the Trinity as the Father, the Son, and the Holy Spirit (Mary). By giving the feminine side of the Trinity the name "Holy Spirit," the Catholic Church eliminated any reference to Isis, the pre-Christian female deity, and erased any part a female might play in the Catholic rituals. Before, during, and after this period, many Celts became priests in the Catholic Church but retained their Coptic beliefs. This was necessary to coexist in a predominantly Catholic society. This is demonstrated by the participation of Bernard de Clarvaux in establishing the Order of Templars while practicing as a Catholic abbot.

Up to the time of the Virgin Mary, Isis had been the universal personification of motherhood and fertility. Isis's reputation as the mother of the world earned her the name of "The Woman of Ten Thousand Names." The Roman numeral for ten thousand is an X with a line over it. However, displaying such a symbol in the Middle Ages would have been very dangerous. It is this writer's opinion that the X with a line over it was abbreviated as an X with a short line on the top right-hand leg so that believers in the ancient spirituality could set themselves apart from Catholics without detection. Not surprisingly, any runic writings by the Cistercians (Coptic) monks also contain an X with a short line attached to the upper right leg.

"Hooked X"

Shield of the Cistercian Order

Notice the French fleur-de-lis design (Sinclair, Templars and Cistercians) in the shield image above. Also notice the four-sided cross symbol of the ancients. It should be noted that the Jesuit order of the Catholic Church replaced the Templars as the Coptic insiders of the Catholic Church. Their origin was the Basque culture which resided on the border of Celtic Galicia and Spain.

Historically, one of the accusations that caused the downfall of the Templars was that they were worshiping a woman. During its formation, the Catholic Church adopted many ancient symbols in order to entice Coptics to convert to Catholicism. Giving a woman any status above motherhood was not one of them.

What follows are excerpts from an overview of the book *Templars in America* (2004), by Tim Wallace-Murphy and Marilyn Hopkins, published by Beliefnet.com.

The book *Templars in America* tells the story of a European noble family that explored America nearly one hundred years before Columbus. In their study, authors Tim Wallace-Murphy and Marilyn Hopkins write that the medieval warrior monks of the Knights Templar had trading links with Native Americans in Nova Scotia and New England, and that the European families—who were members of the Templars and claimed to be descended from Jesus—passed their beliefs through Masonic teaching into the US Constitution and the Declaration of Independence.

The main point of their new book, however, is to report evidence they believe ties those European families more directly to America. They say that a member of one of the European families, Earl Henry Sinclair, voyaged to New England in the 1300s and ultimately assimilated with the Native American people and died there. These assertions were further validated in the 2013 book *La Merica*, by Arthur Faram.

Who Were the Knights Templar?

On the surface the Knights Templar were a medieval monastic order who gave the appearance of being part of the church and being devout Christians. In actual fact, they were anything but that. Yes, they were a monastic order that had been approved by the Pope. However, they were virtually independent of all civil and other church authorities, being responsible through their grandmaster to the pope and the pope alone.

In actuality they had been founded by a group of families who had a very different view about spirituality and recognized the true ancient spirituality which had been passed down from our creator. The Celts had kept the true ancient spiritual teachings, which Jesus also taught, alive for nearly 1,100 years after having them passed down from their predecessors.

Freemasonry is an extension the Knights Templar and their beliefs. It was most certainly created and formed by enlightened families. Freemasonry played a pivotal and formative role in the creation of the American Constitution and the american way of life. If you study the history of the people who led the American Revolution, you find that the leading figures, militarily, politically, and philosophically, were members of the Freemasons, including George Washington. A percentage of people who composed and created the American constitution came from the same background. Masonic principles are bound in the Constitution.

Templar accomplishments after they were disbanded in 1312 CE include:

1. They fought for Robert the Bruce, king of Scotland, and secured Scottish independence from England at the Battle of Bannockburn in 1314.

2. In 1450, in Edinburgh, Scotland, the Templars became the Freemasons through the Wall Builders Lodge. Although their inner structure may have changed, their spiritual beliefs remained.

3. They fought for Portugal and Spain to rid the Iberian Peninsula of Muslims ca. 1362–1492.

4. Under the command of Sir Henry Sinclair, they assisted in subduing the Norse, who were colonizing Celtic territory in North America ca. 1314–1450. (See the book La Merica – 2013.)

Many are not familiar with the Templars' participation in the Iberian war against the Muslims. Most people believe that the

Templar order ceased to exist upon the death of its last acknowledged master in 1313 CE. The Templars assistance provided to Portugal and Spain by the remaining Templars, during their battles to rid Iberia of Muslims, is the basis for the Portuguese land grant to the Templars that would later become the United States of America. This fourteenth-century Portuguese grant is laid out by the combined geometry of the Kensington Runestone in Alexandria and Inspiration Peak, both in Minnesota, and the Newport Tower in Newport, Rhode Island. This land grant was validated by the Pyramids of Guimar, built by the Portuguese ca. 1822 CE, on the island of Tenerife in the Canary Islands. (See Narratives N and O.)

The main window of the Templars' Rosslyn Chapel, Edinburgh, Scotland

Notice the Celtic cross, with a square, at the top of the window. This same pattern appears in only one other place, on the shore of Farum Sound in Farum, Denmark. (See the book *La Merica*.) On the bottom of the window appears the French fleur-de-lis commemorating the French origins of the Sinclair family and the Templars.

The Freemasons, ca. 1450 CE – Present

The Faram Research Foundation
Masonic temple windows, Fort Worth, Texas
Eight-pointed crosses, above and below

The eight-pointed crosses on the lower windows of the Charlotte–Mecklenburg, North Carolina, police station

Informed architects around the world incorporate ancient symbols into their buildings in hope that the proceedings within the building will be blessed with the truth.

The eight-pointed cross on courthouse windows

The eight-pointed star frequently appears on Freemason buildings or buildings built by Freemasons. Since the eight-pointed cross is the ancient symbol for God or a supreme being, the symbol is placed on buildings where the Freemasons hope decisions will be just and that God will watch over the proceedings.

Masonartstore.com

The eye of God is a symbol that is representative of a divine supreme being watching over the entire universe. It is shown as a single human eye enclosed in a triangle and often surrounded by clouds or burst of light. Also known as the all-seeing eye and the Eye of Providence, the symbol has been used since the ancient times to signify the omniscience and omnipresence of God and his power, preserving and guarding character.

Throughout history, eye iconography has been used in different cultures. Hebrew literature talks of the watchful eyes of the Lord looking over all creation. The Egyptians have the Eye of Horus that symbolizes protection, good health, and royal power. In Hinduism, there are references to Lord Shiva's third eye, and in Buddhism, the Buddha is known as the eye of the world.

The eye of God symbol has a significant Masonic connection also. It appeared as a part of Freemasonry iconography in 1797. The Freemasons view God as the great architect of the universe, and the symbol of his vigilant eye serves as a reminder to all Masons that he is always watching their thoughts and actions.

You will see the eight-pointed star incorporated into most courthouses.

From Templars to Freemasons

The trial of the Templars supposedly terminated the order. Although the order officially ceased to exist, it did not actually disappear. During their sudden arrest in 1307, most Templars escaped. According to a thesis based on various historical documents, a significant number of them took refuge in the only kingdom in Europe that did not recognize the authority of the Catholic Church in fourteenth century, Scotland. There they reorganized under the protection of the Scottish king, Robert the Bruce. Sometime later, they found a convenient method of disguise by which to continue their clandestine existence. They infiltrated the most important guild in the medieval British Isles, the Wall Builders' lodge, and eventually took control of those lodges. Later the Wall Builders' lodge changed its name, calling itself the Masonic lodge. This name satisfied both the wall builders and the Freemasons.

The Scottish Rite lodge is the oldest branch of Freemasonry and also dates back to the fifteenth century. The names given today to the highest degrees in the Scottish Rites are titles attributed centuries earlier to the Order of the Knights Templar. These are still employed to this day. In short, the Templars did not disappear, but their philosophy, beliefs, and rituals still persist in the form of Freemasonry. These facts are supported by much historical evidence and are accepted today by a large number of Western historians. See "The New Masonic Order", by Harun Yahya). the Temple Rule also established that the Order is authentically interfaith and non-denominational for individual membership, while still upholding its traditions of the ancient spirituality.

While the Order actively defends the Church, it is not itself a Church, but rather an Order of Chivalry, which always included "Secular Knights". Therefore, the brotherhood does not impose any particular beliefs upon its members, and does not require any specific religious practices. These original Templar traditions thus fully accommodate and support religious diversity and spiritual individuality. The thesis that traces the roots of Masonry to the Templars is often referred to in magazines published by Masons for their own members. Freemasons are very accepting of the idea. One such magazine is called *Mimar Sinan* (a publication by Turkish Freemasons). In one issue, in the article "Global Freemasonry," Harun Yahya describes the relationship between the Order of the Templars and Freemasonry:

In 1312, when the French king, under pressure from the Church, closed the Order of Templars and gave their possessions to the Knights of St. John in Jerusalem, the activities of the Templars did not cease. The great majority of the Templars took refuge in lodges that were operating in Europe at that time. The leader of the Templars, Mabeignac, with a few other members, found refuge in Scotland under the guise of a wall builder using the name of Mac Benach. The Scottish king, Robert the Bruce, welcomed them and allowed them to exercise great influence over the Wall Builders' lodges in Scotland. As a result, Scottish lodges gained great importance from the point of view of their craft and their ideas.

Today, Freemasons use the name Mac Benach with respect. Scottish Masons, who inherited the Templars' rituals, returned to France many years later and established there the basis of the rite known as the "Scottish Rite." It is clear that the roots of Freemasonry stretch back to the Order of Templars and before. Freemasons themselves do not deny this. Even though the Templars were formally disbanded in 1312 they lived on in both Europe and North America until retired through the building of Roslyn Chapel, in their honor, in 1450 CE.

St John's Church, Chester, England. The stained-glass window ca. 1900 CE shows Hiram Abiff, the architect of the Temple in Jerusalem.

In Ancientpages.com (2019), A. Sutherland writes, "Hiram Abiff is, according to the Freemasons' legend, the master and chief architect at the building of King Solomon's Temple in Jerusalem. No doubt, Hiram is an extraordinary figure in modern Freemasonry and known to all members of the fraternity. Those who were involved in the construction of the temple organized the first skilled Masons, and, as the order maintains, Hiram Abiff was the only one who was consecrated in the secret knowledge required to build this unique structure." There were some very curious fellow craftsmen who tried (in vain) to obtain the hidden knowledge that Hiram possessed. When Hiram refused, they murdered him. (This knowledge is most likely the same knowledge which allowed the building of the ancient monolithic structures, and territorial geoglyphs, which exist around the world.

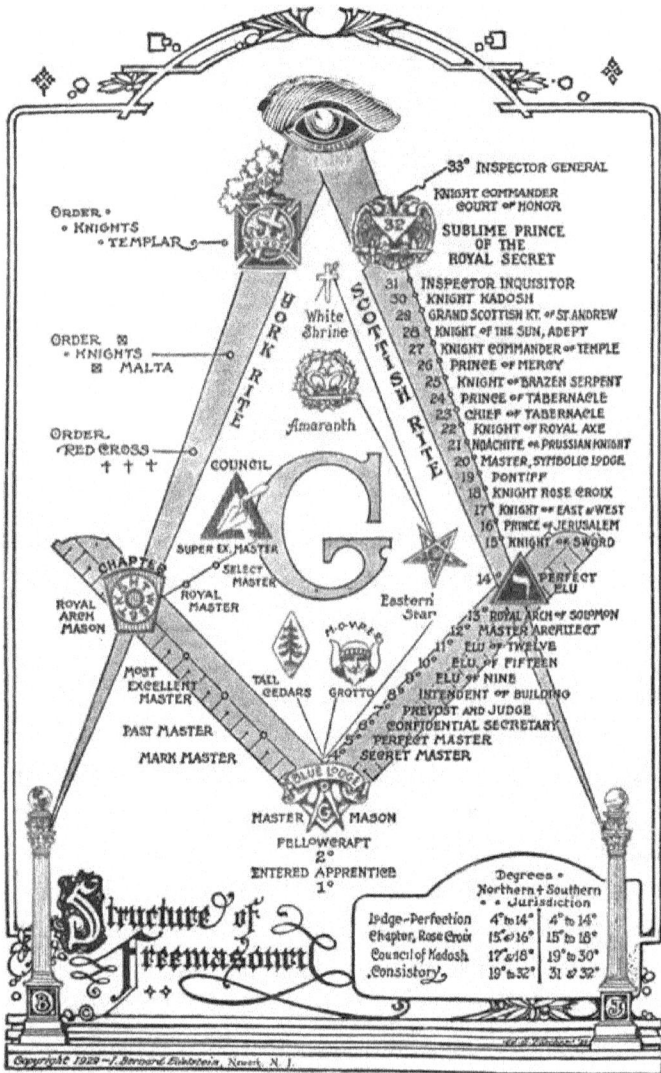

The York and Scottish Rites

The image shows the Knights Templar as the highest order in the
York rites.

Until recently the Freemasons played a large part in American politics

172

The Freemason Placement of Washington, DC

Image Credit: Wayne Herschel and Mark Scott

Nothing could better tie the Celts, Templars, and Freemasons to the pre-Columbian colonization of North America than the Ohio Serpent Mound, constructed during the Adena period ca. 1000–200 BCE.

Throughout Eastern North America, there once existed a culture known as the Adena. The culture was replete with the symbols and structures of the early Celtic culture. Although the Adenas appear to be the first to display Celtic influence on North America, they were far from the last. The culture eventually spread to include most of the territory east of the Mississippi River. This later homogenous culture was eventually known as the Hopewell culture or the Mississippi Mound culture.

According to Wikipedia,

The Adena culture was a pre-Columbian, North American culture that existed from 1000 to 200 BCE, in a time known as the Early Woodland period. The Adena culture refers to a number of related Native American societies sharing a common cultural and ceremonial system. The Adena lived in an area including parts of present-day Ohio, Indiana, Wisconsin, West Virginia, Kentucky, and New York.

The importance of the Adena complex comes from its considerable influence on other contemporary and succeeding cultures. The Adena culture is seen as the precursor to the traditions of the Hopewell culture, which are sometimes thought as an elaboration, or zenith, of Adena traditions. The Adena were notable for their agricultural practices, pottery, artistic works, and extensive trading network, which supplied them with a variety of raw materials, ranging from copper from the Great Lakes to shells from the Gulf Coast. It was here, where the Adena culture would eventually flourish and where the Bell Beaker Celts begin their first serious colonization of North America.

The Celts and their allies, the Etruscans, had known about the Americas for millennia prior to this. However, ca. 800 BCE the Celts and the Etruscans begin losing their longtime hold on Northern Italy. The two allies had been fighting the Roman Republic (Later called the Roman Empire) for centuries. It was about this time that the Romans became strong enough to start pushing the two allies out of the northern Mediterranean. This displacement precipitated a move by the two allies to the west coast of Iberia. The Etruscans became known as the Portuguese, and the Celts colonized Galicia (the northwest corner of Iberia). See the book *La Merica* (2013).

The reason for including the Ohio Serpent Mound here is to tie the three cultures together, further validating that the Celts, Etruscans, and their predecessors, the Phoenicians, were in the Americas long before Columbus, and to explain why Washington, DC, was moved to its current location.

What follows is a geoglyphological survey of the Ohio Serpent Mound, along with some very Celtic-looking Mound culture artifacts. As you will notice in the survey, the ninety-degree radial points directly to Washington, DC. In any geoglyph the ninety-degree radial is the most important and sacred radial. In a legitimate geoglyph, which contains a ninety-degree radial, there will most likely be something important at the end point of the 90 degree bearing.

If you remember your history lessons, you will recall the country's capital used to be in Philadelphia. Why would the Freemasons, who were in control of the political system at the time, move the capital from a place centrally located to the population to a place not centrally located geographically or population wise? Well, the answer is simple. The Freemasons were aware that the site where Washington, DC, now stands was a sacred site hundreds if not thousands of years old.

Serpent Mound Historical Site

Google Earth – The Faram Research Foundation

Ohio Serpent Mound bearings. The bearings are aligned with the coils of the serpent.

Each of the bearings on the Serpent Mound has a one-degree offset. This is done on many of the older geoglyphs to prevent their being decoding by the uninitiated. One degree must be added to each of the bearings to make the geoglyph accurate.

Something that must be remembered about geoglyphic sites is that they were mapped out millennia ago and were used repeatedly as time passed.

Google Earth – The Faram Research Foundation
Ohio Serpent Mound—Radials

Radial End Points:
037+1 – Niagara Falls
068+1 – The tip of Cape Cod
074+1 – Entrance to the Hudson River and the southern tip of Long Island
089+1 – Washington, DC
127+1 – The south end of Pimlico Sound, NC
282+1 – Southern tip of White Island (Adena Culture Boundary) in the Mississippi River

Notice that the previously mentioned geoglyphological map of the Ohio Snake Mound outlines the Eastern Woodlands Culture territory map just as it was described in the preceding Wikipedia segment and the following map.

Google

Notice that the boundaries of the Adena East Woodlands culture conform to the Ohio Snake Mound geoglyphic boundaries previously shown.

The Freemasons and the Mexican–American War

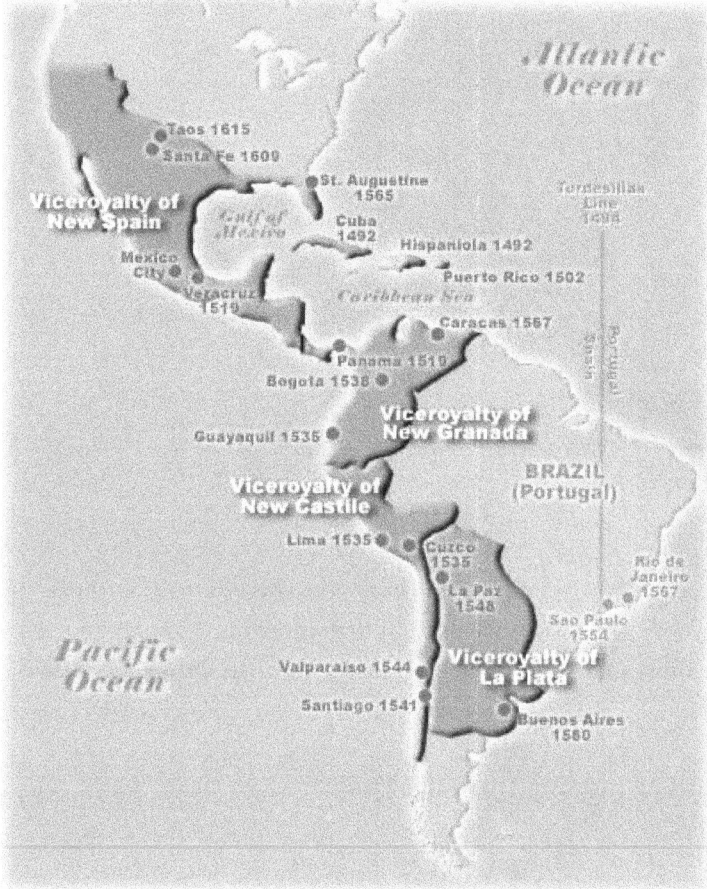

Google

Illustration of the Spanish intrusion into territories claimed by what was now the United States (North America) and Portuguese Territory (South America).

Spain's blatant disregard for territorial boundaries of the U.S. to the north and the Portuguese to the south was the catalyst for the Mexican–American War.

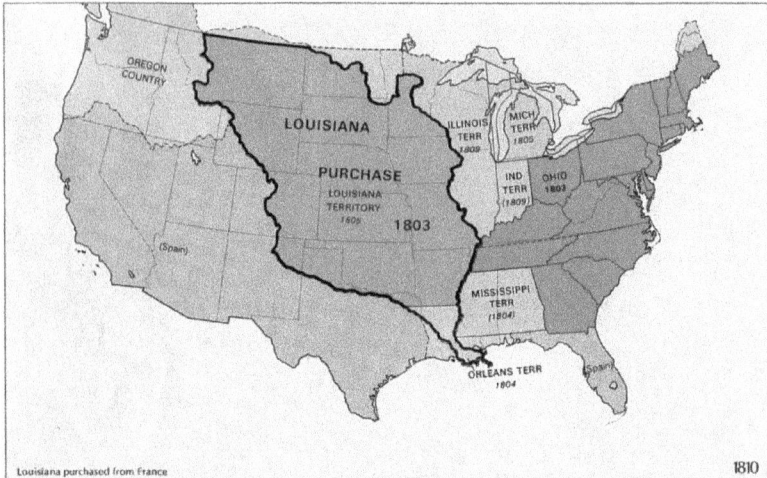

Google

The US territory in 1810.

Unofficially, the colonial territory consisted of the Louisiana Territory and everything east of that, including everything north of a line drawn from the southern tip of Florida to the southern tip of Baja.

Timeline Leading Up to the Mexican–American War

1802—France's acquisition of the Louisiana Territory from Spain. Napoleon Bonaparte, a Freemason himself, purchased the Louisiana Territory for the United States from Spain. He agreed not to sell the territory. Within weeks he sold the territory to the United States.

1803—Louisiana Territory sold to the United States by Napoleon Bonaparte of France. Upon completion of the agreement, Napoleon stated, "The accession of this territory affirms forever the power of the United States, and I have given England a maritime rival who sooner or later will humble her pride."

179

1821—Mexico's independence from Spain.

1822—Approximate date of the construction of the Tenerife Guimar Pyramids. The pyramid's geoglyphic radials coincide precisely with the US territory described by the Kensington Runestone, Inspiration Peak, and Newport Tower alignments. (See Narrative N.)

1836—Texas's independence from Mexico.

1845—Texas admitted to the Union.

1846—Beginning of the Mexican–American War (led by General Zachary Taylor, later the twelfth president of the United States).

1848—End of Mexican–American War and establishment of the current southern boundary of the United States.

The date 1821 in the preceding chronology is important. As mentioned previously, the Guimar pyramids in the Canary Islands were built by the Portuguese ca. 1822 CE to validate the fact that they had given certain countries their freedom and were validating the United States territory. This was no doubt a response to the intrusion of Spain into Templar/Freemason territory.

The Mexican American War

The Treaty of Guadalupe Hidalgo
The Treaty of Guadalupe Hidalgo was negotiated after the Mexican–American War (1846–1848). It was signed by Nicholas Trist on behalf of the United States and Luis G. Cuevas, Bernardo Couto, and Miguel Atristain as representatives of Mexico. The signing occurred on February 2, 1848, at the main altar of the old Basilica of

Guadalupe at Villa Hidalgo as US troops under the command of Gen. Winfield Scott who occupied Mexico City.

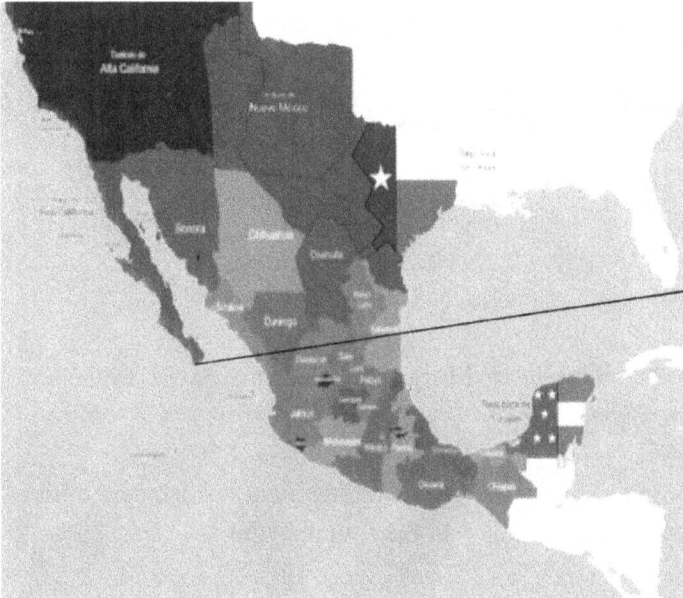

The Southern boundary of the Templar/Freemason territory until the Treaty of Guadalupe Hidalgo (See Narrative N)

The black line indicates the southern boundary of the territory given to the Templars by the Portuguese and later validated by the Tenerife pyramid geoglyphs. (See narrative M.) The Tenerife pyramids were constructed by the Portuguese ca. 1822 to validate the Templars' (by then the Freemasons) claim to North America.

The boundary depicted by the green area (Mexico) is the treaty boundary between the United States and Mexico after the Mexican–American War. The line running through Mexico to the tip of Baja California is the old Templar/Freemason boundary outlined by the information obtained from the Kensington Runestone, the Newport Tower, and Inspiration Peak. (See narrative N.) The preceding image is important in understanding the following story.

After the war and prior to the Treaty of Guadalupe Hidalgo being ratified, Jefferson Davis and a number of other Freemason senators proposed an amendment to the treaty. (Senator Davis served as the US secretary of war under Democratic president Franklin Pierce as well as the Democratic senator representing Mississippi. Later, during the American civil war, he served as president of the Confederate States.) The amendment by Jefferson Davis would have retained for the United States most of the territory given to the Templars and lost by the Treaty of Guadalupe Hidalgo. This territory consisted of the area between the black line on the preceding image and the current boundary of the United States. In other words, these senators were aware that the land, which was secretly part of the United States, was being given to Mexico.

The treaty was so egregious to the Freemasons in the Senate that they proposed an amendment to the treaty before it was ratified. The land in question consisted of the Mexican parcels named Tamaulipas, Nuevo Leon, all of Coahuila, and a large part of Chihuahua. This amendment was supported by both senators from Texas (Sam Houston and Thomas Jefferson Rusk), Daniel S. Dickinson of New York, Stephen A. Douglas of Illinois, Edward A. Hannegan of Indiana, and senators from Alabama, Florida, Mississippi, Ohio, Missouri, and Tennessee. Most of the leaders of the Democratic Party were opposed, and the amendment was defeated forty-four to eleven.

Unlike most treaties, the Treaty of Guadalupe Hidalgo was labeled secret in the US Senate. But one of the senators that were opposed to the land transfer intentionally leaked the terms of the treaty to the press. In March 1848, three days after the treaty reached Washington for ratification, the *New York Herald* published the treaty ending the war with Mexico. John Nugent was the reporter who prepared the story revealing the contents of the secret treaty.

Under questioning, John Nugent refused to disclose his source to Senate investigators. Nugent was jailed for a period of six months until the Senate, in desperation, released him. It was later discovered that James Buchanan, the fifteenth president of the United States, was the senator that leaked the information to Nugent. This was most likely to obtain enough support to amend the treaty to prevent part of the US territory from being given to Mexico.

The treaty was subsequently ratified by the Senate by a vote of thirty-eight to fourteen on March 10, 1848. The treaty was also adopted by Mexico through a legislative vote of fifty-one to thirty-four and a Senate vote of thirty-three to four, on May 19, 1848.

The US Senate, perhaps unknowingly to non-Masons, had just given away part of the territory given to the Templars for assisting Portugal in liberating Iberia.

The Forgotten Land

The following images show the districts that were in the Templar (Freemason) territory prior to the Treaty of Guadalupe Hidalgo. The western Mexican states of Sonora and Baja were accidentally left out the treaty.

Tamaulipas, Mexico

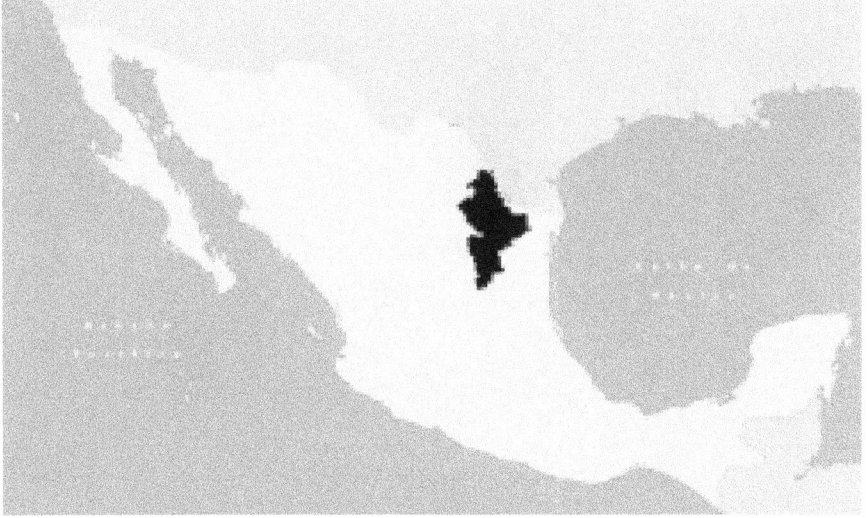

Nuevo Leon, Mexico

Coahuila, Mexico

Chihuahua, Mexico

As you can see from the previous four images, the Treaty of Guadalupe Hidalgo did not conform to the boundaries previously established and agreed upon between Spain, Portugal, and the United States. The transfer of Templar/Freemason land to Mexico infuriated the Freemasons, who watched as land whose boundaries were known only to them was given to Mexico.

But this was not the end of the story. As you can see, somehow the land known as Sonora and Baja California did not appear in the treaty. The Freemasons knew that these two districts (Shown below.) lay within the ancient territorial boundaries established by the Portuguese land grant years ago.

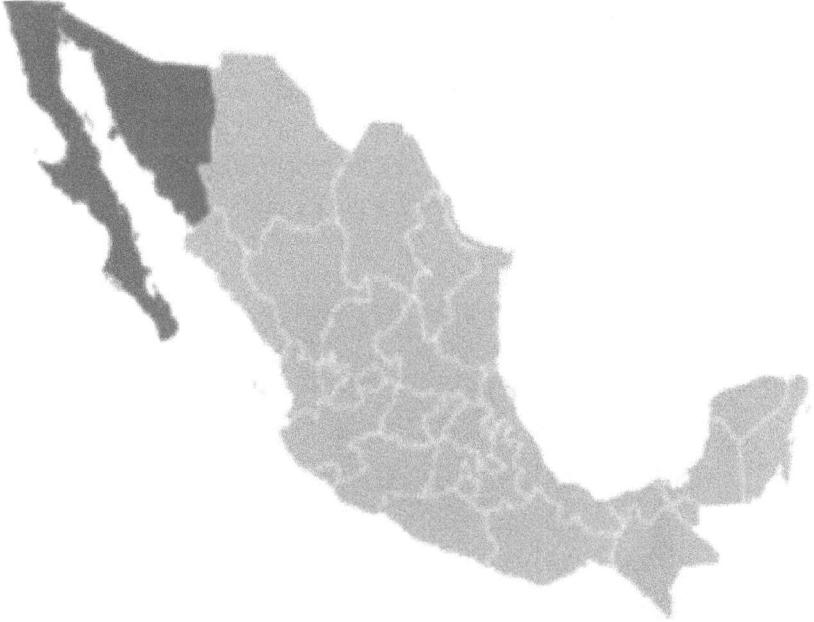

The Republic of Lower California, 1854

The dark area represents Sonora and Baja California, which were not included in the Treaty of Guadalupe Hidalgo. Their status therefore remained in limbo for many years. This oversight did not go unnoticed by Senator Walker, who had inside knowledge on the subject. Senator Walker notified his son, a merchant in San Francisco, that the Baja territory was not owned by either Mexico or the United States. William Walker immediately began making plans to claim Baja and Sonora for themselves. The new Republic of Baja California was proclaimed in 1853 by soldier of fortune William Walker.

On October 15, 1853, Walker set out with fifty men to conquer the Mexican territories of Baja California and Sonora. He succeeded in capturing La Paz, the capital of sparsely populated Baja California, which he declared the capital of the new Republic of Lower California, with himself as president and his partner, Watkins, as vice president. He then patterned the constitution after the laws of the American state of Louisiana, in which slavery was legal. The declaration of independence from Mexico was written on January 10, 1854. He moved his headquarters to Ensenada to maintain a more secure position of operations. Although he never gained control of Sonora, less than three months later, he pronounced Baja California and the larger Republic of Sonora as the Republic of Lower California.

Flag of the Republic of Lower California, 1853

A serious lack of supplies, discontent within his party, and an unexpectedly strong resistance by the Mexican government forced Walker to retreat. Back in California, Walker was put on trial for conducting an illegal war. The jury took eight minutes to acquit him.

Although William Walker did not succeed in his misadventure, his actions were enough to put Baja California in limbo until 1953. In 1953 the United States and Mexico agreed that Baja California belonged to Mexico.

Without the information held by the Templars and passed to the Freemasons, no one would have ever known about the secret that placed the six Mexican republics within the true territory of the United States.

Transcendentalists—ca. 1830 CE

American transcendentalism is similar to Buddhism, Hinduism, Gnosticism, and other practices that adhere to the ancient spirituality.

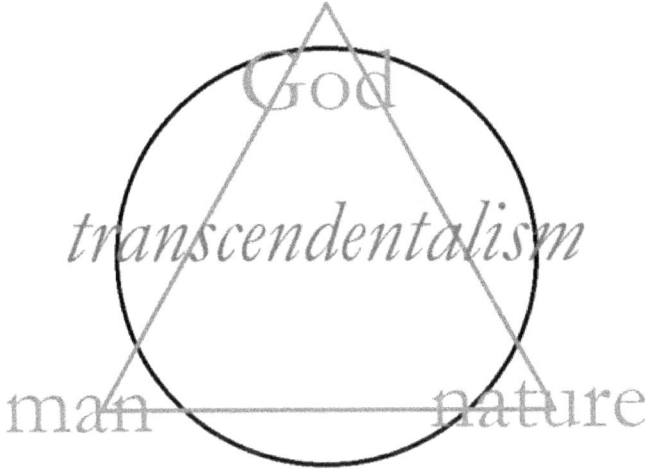

God

transcendentalism

man   nature

Transcendentalism is an Eastern philosophical practice that once enveloped the entire earth in its grace. In the late 1820s and 1830s, in the face of the rapid Christianizing of the eastern United States, transcendentalism arose as a reaction against the general state of intellectualism affecting the ancient spirituality being practiced at the time by Freemasons and others. The doctrine of the Unitarian Church, as taught at **Harvard Divinity School,** was of particular interest, as it sought to dilute the ancient teachings being practiced by the Freemasons and other colonists.

A core belief of transcendentalism is in the inherent goodness of people and nature. Adherents believe that society and its institutions have corrupted the self-reliance of the individual, and they have faith that people are at their best when truly self-reliant and independent.

Transcendentalism emphasizes using meditative intuition to aid in the success of the physical individual. Adherents believe that individuals are capable of generating wisdom and original insights through meditation.

Transcendentalism is the American version of the ancient spirituality which has been handed down through the ages. The practice is a nineteenth-century school of philosophical thought that combined respect for nature, moderation, self-sufficiency, self - reflection and meditation.

This ancient philosophy was handed down through time to the Freemasons. Writer Ralph Waldo Emerson was the primary practitioner of the transcendentalist movement, which existed loosely in Massachusetts in the early 1800s before becoming an organized group in the 1830s.

Transcendentalists espoused four main philosophical points. Simply stated, these are self-reliance and responsibility for one's own actions; individual conscientiousness and meditation to aid conscious reasoning. Transcendentalists believe in the unity of all things in nature. In other words, individual men and women can make their decisions based on knowledge obtained through the use of their experience, intuition, conscience and the knowledge that every action will have an affect the universal environment.

The transcendentalist movement was centered in New England and included a number of prominent individuals, including Ralph Waldo Emerson, George Ripley, Henry David Thoreau, Bronson Alcott, and Margaret Fuller.

Because of the beliefs in self-reliance and individualism, transcendentalists became huge proponents of progressive reforms. They wished to help individuals find their own voices and achieve to their fullest potential. Margaret Fuller, one of the leading transcendentalists, wished to see women treated fairly and argued for women's rights. She argued that both sexes should be treated equally. In addition, transcendentalists argued for the abolition of slavery. In fact, there was a crossover between women's rights and the abolitionist movement. Other progressive movements that they espoused included the rights of those in prison and help for the poor.

Importance of Nature

Public Domain

Transcendentalists have a deep gratitude and appreciation for nature, not only for aesthetic purposes but also as a tool to observe and understand the structured inner workings of the natural world. Emerson emphasizes the transcendental beliefs in the holistic power of the natural landscape in nature. The conservation of an undisturbed natural world is extremely important to the transcendentalists.

Transcendentalism and God

Martin Kelly (2017) writes,

> As a philosophy, transcendentalism is deeply rooted in faith and spirituality. Transcendentalists believe in personal communication with God leading to an ultimate understanding of reality. Leaders of the movement were influenced by the elements of profound truths found in

Hindu and Buddhist religions, the pre-Catholic teachings of Jesus, as well as the American Puritan and Quaker faiths. The transcendentalists equated their belief in a universal reality to the Quakers' belief in a divine inner light as a gift of God's grace.

During the early 1800s, transcendentalism was suppressed by the doctrine of the Unitarian Church, as taught at Harvard Divinity School. While Unitarians stressed a rather calm and rational relationship with God, transcendentalists sought a more personal spiritual experience. As expressed by Thoreau, transcendentalists found and communed with God in gentle breezes, dense forests, and other creations of nature. Since transcendentalism teaches self-reliance and the direct communion with God, transcendentalism never evolved into its own organized religion but remains more of a close, personal relationship with God.

Thinkers in the movement embraced ideas brought forth by philosophers Immanuel Kant, George Wilhelm, and Friedrich Hegel, poets Samuel Taylor and Kent Coleridge, and religious founder Emanuel Swedenborg. Ancient East Indian scriptures known as the Vedas were also important.

Transcendentalists advocate the idea of a personal relationship with God, believing that no intermediary is needed for spiritual insight. They embraced idealism, focusing on nature and opposing materialism.

By the 1830s, literature began to appear that bound the transcendentalist ideas together in a cohesive way and marked the beginnings of a more organized movement.

The Transcendental Club

On September 12, 1836, four Harvard University alumni—writer and Bangor, Maine, minister Frederic Henry Hodge, Ralph Waldo Emerson, and Unitarian ministers George Ripley and George Putnam—left a celebration of the bicentennial of Harvard to meet at Willard's Hotel in Cambridge. The purpose was to follow up on correspondence between Hodge and Emerson and to talk about the state of Unitarians departure from the transcendentalist practices of the current culture and what they should do about it.

One week later, the four met again at Ripley's house in Boston. This was a meeting of a much larger group that included many Unitarian ministers, intellectuals, writers, and reformers. There would be thirty more meetings of what was called the Transcendental Club (notice they did not call themselves a church) over the next four years, featuring a shifting membership that always included Emerson, Ripley, and Hodge.

The only rule the meetings followed was that no one would be allowed to attend if their presence prevented the group from discussing a topic. Emerson's essay "Nature," published in 1836, presented transcendentalist philosophy as it had formed in the club meetings.

This group ceased to meet in 1840 but was involved in *The Dial*, a publication first headed by member and pioneering feminist Margaret Fuller and later by Emerson, with the mission of addressing transcendentalist thought and concerns.

Transcendentalism Fades Out

History.com (2017) explains, "As the 1850s arrived, transcendentalism was considered to have lost some of its influence, particularly following the untimely death of Margaret Fuller in an 1850 shipwreck" and the overwhelming surge of Christians from Europe.

William Channing

William Channing is credited with almost single-handedly turning New England and eventually the entire country away from the founding fathers' institution of transcendentalist practices. Although not called transcendentalism at the time, the country was spiritually redirected from conservatism and spirituality to the new practice of institutionalized communication with God and materialism.

In 1792 Channing was sent to study with his uncle, Henry Channing, a liberal minister in New London, Connecticut. At age fifteen he entered Harvard College. His college reading of Francis Hutcheson, a Scottish common-sense philosopher, was transforming. The Christian Calvinist doctrine of original sin divided humanity into the "unredeemed," who required institutionalized redemption, and the "redeemed," who required constant institutional monitoring of their loyalty to the church.

William Ellery Channing (April 7, 1780–October 2, 1842), minister of the Federal Street Church in Boston, Massachusetts (1803–42), was a spokesman during the Unitarian transformation for the more liberal—or Unitarian—churches within the Massachusetts Standing Order of Churches. His published sermons, his path between orthodoxy and infidelity, were widely influential abroad as well as throughout the United States. His Christian humanism borrowed both religious and literary features of the transcendental movement. An exemplar of Christian piety and a champion of human rights and dignity, he effectively fostered social reform in areas of free speech, education, peace, relief for the poor, and slavery. His pulpit orations made him, according to Emerson, "a kind of public conscience."

William Channing, possibly introduced to transcendentalism while at Harvard, was largely responsible for the transition of a country founded on the principles of transcendentalist spirituality through the Freemasons into the Christian-labeled Unitarian Church.

Although Channing subscribed to many of the transcendentalists' fundamental beliefs, he could not accept them all. However, many of his transcendentalist beliefs were carried over to the institutionalized Unitarian Church.

After years of sparring with the existing clergy over changes that Channing perceived were needed to practice Christianity, it became clear that Unitarians would separate from the churches of the Standing Order, which had existed since colonial times and was rent asunder by the refusal of "orthodox" ministers to exchange pulpits with Unitarian Christian ministers. In 1819, to make clear the liberals' theology in a time of conflicting reports, Channing delivered a landmark sermon, "Unitarian Christianity," at the ordination of Jared Sparks by the new First Independent Church in Baltimore. Tens of thousands of copies were sold.

Channing was responsible, through the development of the Unitarian movement of the time, for moving the country away from the spiritual practices of his predecessors, the Freemasons. As a result, the country slowly began to convert to Protestant versions of the Catholic Church and the Church of England, founded on the Roman and English ideology of their time.

Without this liberal transformation away from conservative spiritualism, the fast-growing army of European entrepreneurs would not have been able to institute the practice of capitalism. As a tribute to his life, Channing's statue stands in the prestigious Touro Park in Newport, Rhode Island. In a bit of irony, the statue stands next to the Newport Tower,
which purportedly was commissioned by the Freemasons. (See narrative N.)

End Chapter 5

Chapter 6
Easter Island

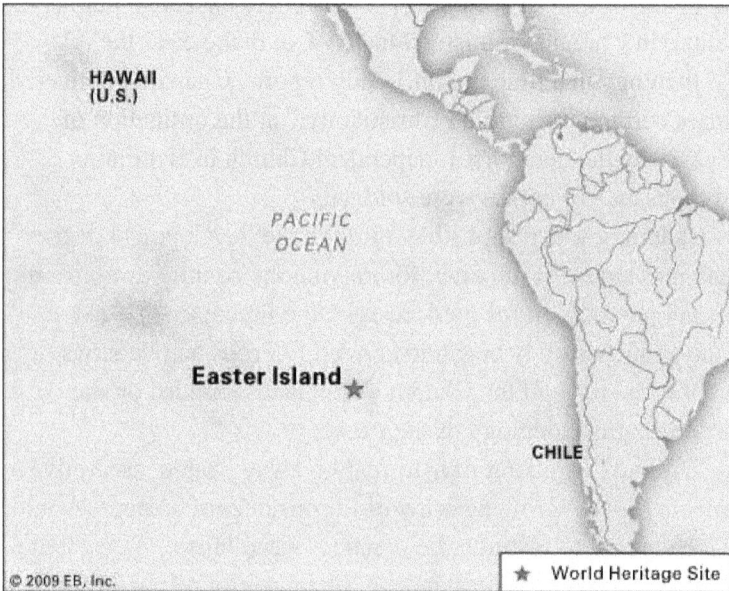

HAWAII
(U.S.)

PACIFIC
OCEAN

Easter Island

CHILE

© 2009 EB, Inc.

★ World Heritage Site

Among the numerous questions regarding Easter Island (many of them still unanswered) are the origin and the date of the first immigrants. The great Sebastian Englert, a priest and scientist who loved the islanders like his predecessor, his brother Eyraud, came to the conclusion that the island's culture had been defined after three consecutive invasions, probably distant in time. As you will see in the following paragraphs, modern technology is opening our eyes to many unexplained phenomena that have been eluding man for centuries.

Easter Island covers roughly sixty-four square miles in the South Pacific Ocean, some 2,300 miles from Chile's west coast and 2,500 miles east of Tahiti. Known as Rapa Nui to its earliest inhabitants, the island was christened Paasch-Eyland, or Easter Island, by Dutch explorers in honor of the day of their arrival in 1722. It was annexed by Chile in the late nineteenth century and now maintains an economy based largely on tourism. Easter Island's most dramatic claim to fame is an array of almost nine hundred giant stone figures named Moai that date back many centuries. The statues reveal their creators to be master craftsmen and engineers and are distinctive among other stone sculptures found in Polynesian cultures. There has been much speculation about the exact purpose of the statues, the role they played in the ancient civilization of Easter Island, and the way they may have been constructed and transported.

Easter Island's inhabitants are of Polynesian descent, but for decades anthropologists have argued the true origins of these people, some claiming that ancient South American mariners settled the island first. What many early explorers who visited Easter Island found was a scattered population with almost no culture they could remember and without any links to the outside world.

The Easter Islanders were easy prey for nineteenth-century slave traders, which depreciated even more their precarious culture, knowledge of the past, and skills of their ancestors.

Livescience.com

There are over eight hundred Moai on Easter Island.

The Ahute Pito Kura, Easter Island

The above image shows a pit with a stylized four-sided cross, the symbol of the ancients. Two possible phallic symbols can also be seen. (More on this in the next chapter.)

The Walls on Easter Island

The Easter Island walls.

These walls are similar to the ones in South America.

Easter Island Tours

Koyeka, an ancient birthing symbol, at Rapa Nui (Easter Island)

At this point Easter Island is beginning to look less like an isolated island and more like part of the worldwide network we have been discussing throughout this book. Oh, but we have just started.

The Geoglyph on Easter Island

As you can see there is a never-before-mentioned geoglyph on Easter Island. Easter Island has always been a place of enigmatic theories but has never had any physical evidence to substantiate the theories about it. This geoglyph may provide the answer.

As is the case in other geoglyphs, this one has a specific purpose. The purpose of most geoglyphs can be determined by the similarities of the sites to which it points. In the case of the Easter Island geoglyph, the similarities seem to be many of the birthing sites, which are the subject of the following chapter.

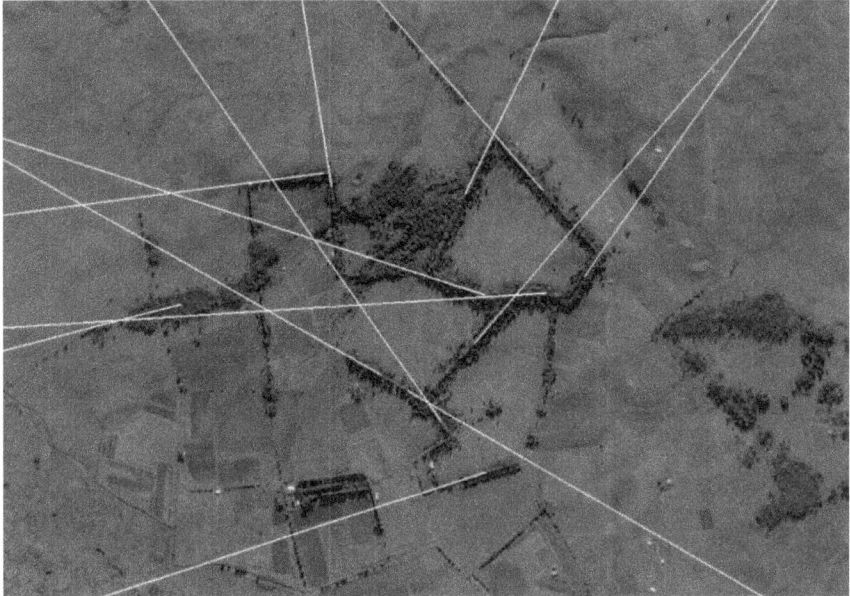

Google Earth – The Faram Research Foundation
Easter Island geoglyph bearings

      The bearings are obtained by simply extending the straight lines in the geoglyph and then reading the magnetic bearings. Magnetic measuring of a bearing at the site is possible because there is no magnetic deviation while standing in one spot. However, once you leave the site of origination, a true line must be followed to eliminate magnetic deviation. Magnetic deviation has been already figured into all Google Earth radials, so the bearing remains true all the way to the end point.

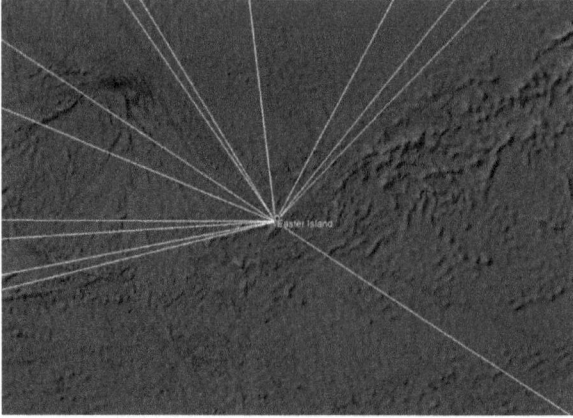

Easter Island geoglyphs extended radials

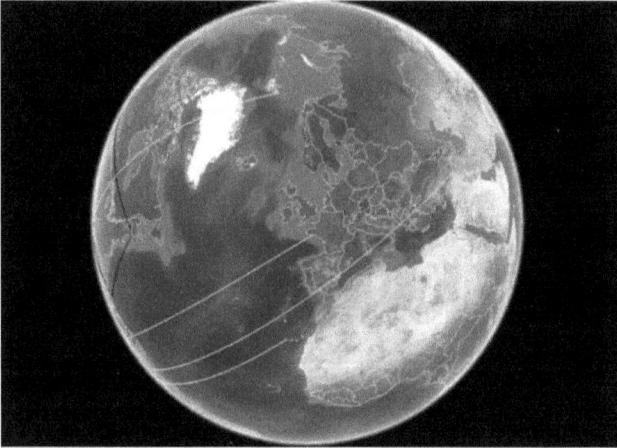

The end points of the eastern radials

Although the end points of a geoglyph may seem random, they are validated by their repetitive use in places around the world. This alone proves that there was a worldwide network in place thousands of years ago. What follows is a description of each of the eastern Easter Island end points, from the northernmost radial and working south.

1. Southern tip of Svalbard Island
The northern limit of the Norwegian territory.

Aqua-firma.com

The same round stones as found in Bosnia, Costa Rica, and other ancient places around the world

2. Carnac

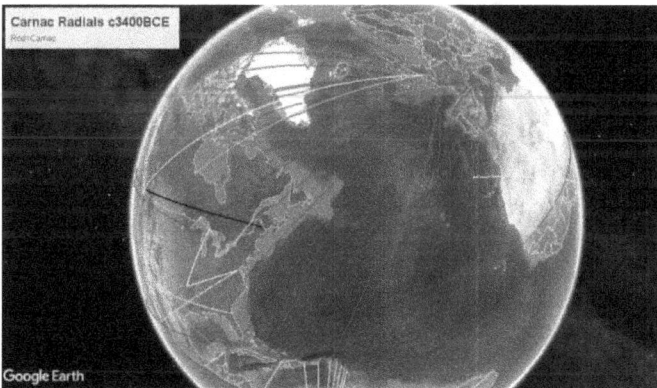

Google Earth – The Faram Research Foundation

Location of the geoglyphic stones at Carnac, France.

(See Narrative H)

3. Gobekli Tepe, Turkey

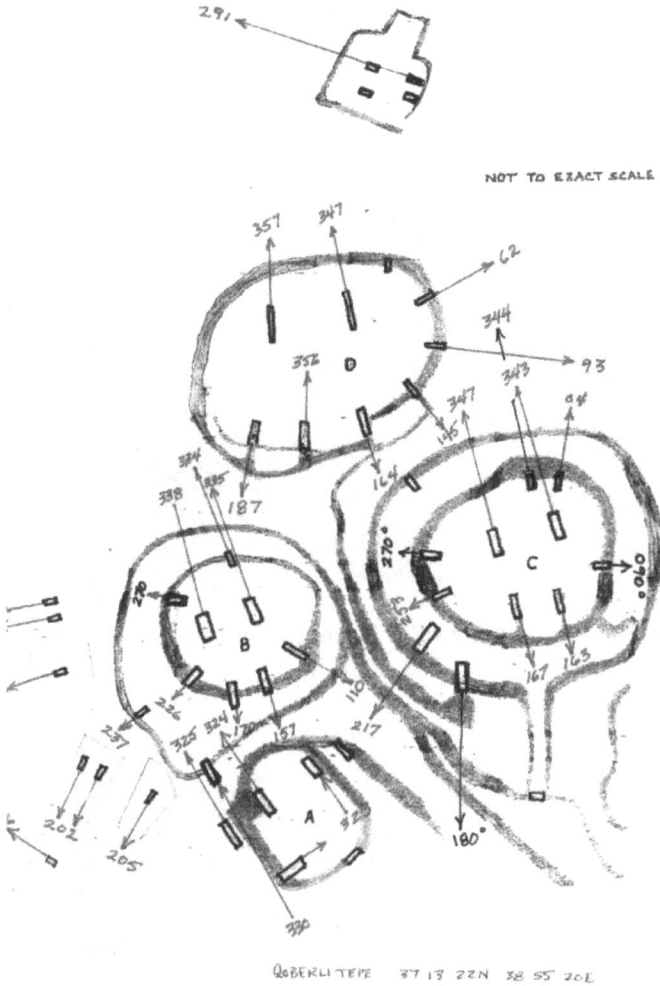

Gobekli Tepe, Turkey, one of the birthing sites, ca. 10,000 BCE
(See Chapter 7 for the story on birthing sites)
For the story on Gobekli Tepe, see Narrative D.

The Faram Research Foundation

4. Canary Islands

The Canary Islands are shown as the southern tip of the Celtic empire on numerous Celtic geoglyphs down through time.

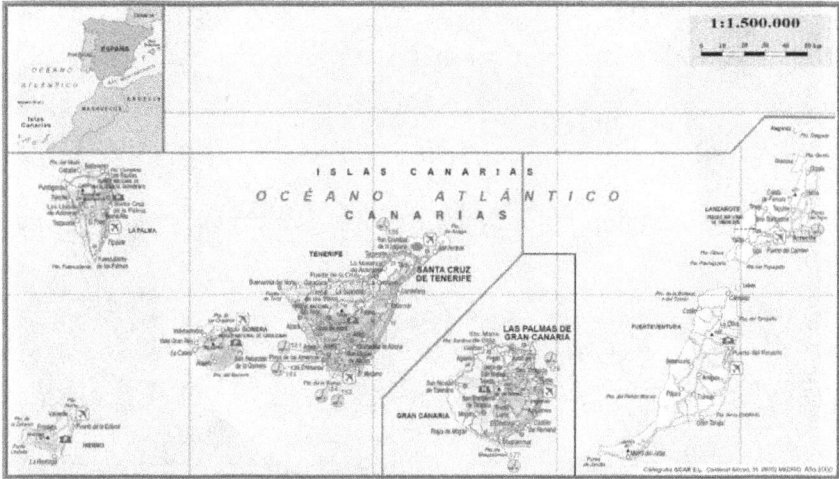

Google

Gran Canaria Island is where Columbus stopped to pick up supplies prior to his first voyage to the Americas. The majority of the island's male citizens are Freemasons.

The Western Radials of the Easter Island Geoglyph

Google Earth - The Faram Research Foundation
Easter Island Western Radials

End Points of Easter Island's Western Radials, Working from North to South:

1. South tip of Alaska
An ancient reference point and the southern tip of Alaska. This point has been the end point on many ancient geoglyphs in the past, such as the Oak Island Triangle. It was also a point of contention in Britain's negotiations with the United States for where to place the US–Canadian border during the negotiation of the Treaty of Oregon.

2. Boundary between Alaska and Canada

This is another boundary point used by the ancients long before Russia or the United States. Japan owned the Alaskan Territory before Russia, and evidently one of the Aleutian Islands, named Attu, had a special meaning to them. See number 3.

3. Southern tip of Alaska's Aleutian Islands, Attu Island

Attu is a single island at the tip of the Aleutian chain. This island was so important to the Japanese that they were willing to fight for it in WWII, even though it was of no use and was indefensible. Attu Island was also pointed out by the Yonaguni pyramid Nan Madol geoglyphs.
(See Narrative E.)

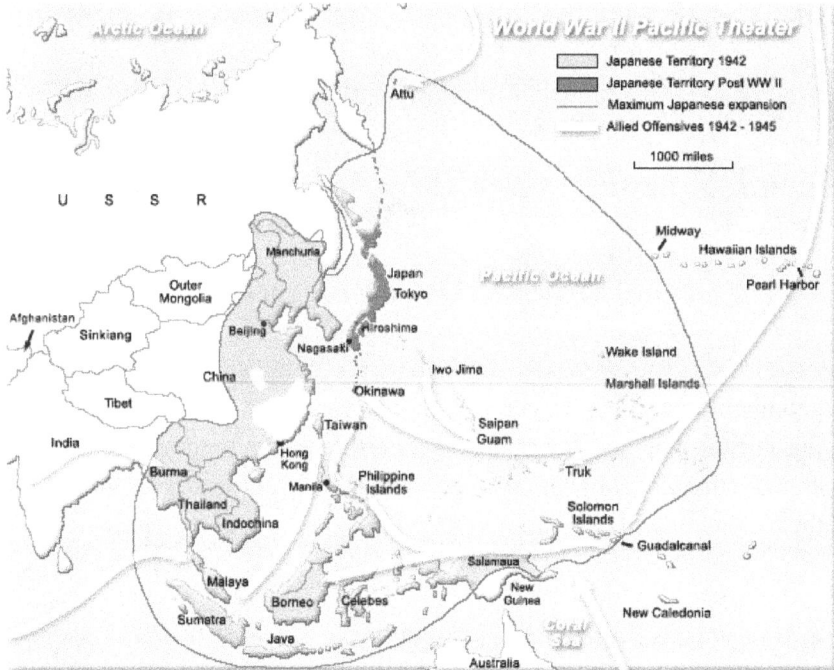

World War II Pacific Theater

Japanese Territory 1942
Japanese Territory Post WW II
Maximum Japanese expansion
Allied Offensives 1942 - 1945

1000 miles

Google

Attu Island appears at the north end of the area in which Japan fought during WWII and is pointed out by the Yonaguni, Easter Island, and the Nan Madol geoglyphs.

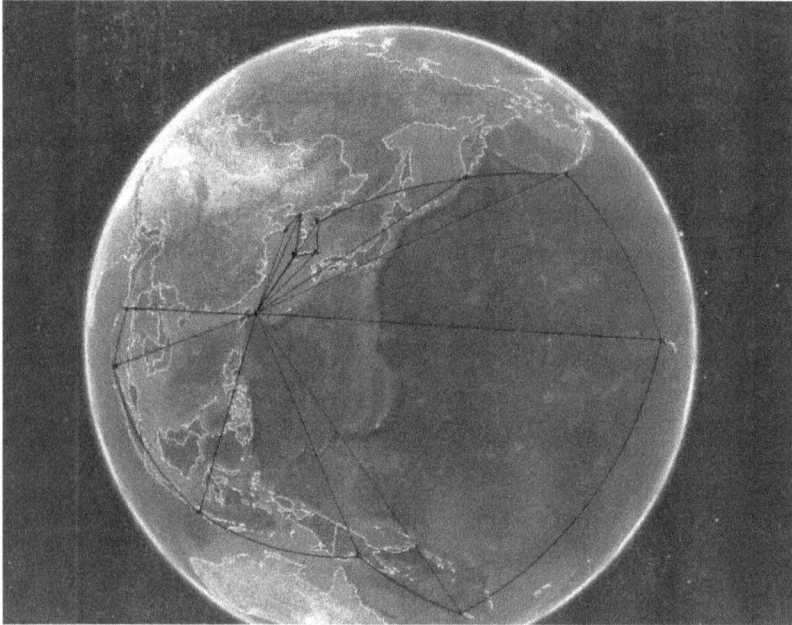

Google Earth – The Faram Research Foundation
The Yonaguni Pyramid territory

This is the territory outlined by the Yonaguni Pyramid geoglyphical survey. As you can see, Attu Island is also at the top of this territory, which shows an area almost identical to the Japanese area of conquest shown in the previous image. (For information on the Yonaguni territory, see narrative E.)

4. Hawaiian Islands
Hawaii is on the boundary between the territory claimed by ancient Japan and the ancient Pacific territorial boundary of the Americas. As you will see in the next chapter, the round object between the

woman's legs is a baby being born. This signifies that this was also a birthing site.

(See next chapter)

Hawaii - Two females giving birth, and a male

5. Southern tip of Japan
It is documented that Japan was the birthplace and center of ancient civilization long before Mesopotamia, and so it would logically be pointed out.

6. Amami Island, Japan
Amami means "goddess of creation" and therefore could be one of the birthing sites. It is currently barren, as is Attu Island, Alaska.

7. Yonaguni Island, Japan
One of the birthing sites mentioned and the geoglyph that outlines Japan's ancient, post-apocalyptic birthing territory.

8. Mojenjo Doro, Indus Valley, Pakistan

One of the birthing sites and the site of one of the possible atomic blasts in ancient times.

(See Narrative C.)

Easter Island's Iconic Relationship to Other Sites

AncientOrigins.net

Easter Island, feathered headdress

Yonaguni, Japan, feathered headdress, ca. 8000 BCE

Tiwanaku headdress, Peru

Feathered headdress petroglyph

Aztec chieftain, feathered headdress

211

Caribbean native, feathered headdress

Mayan, feathered headdress

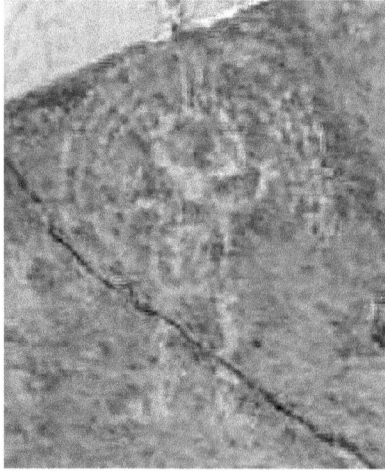

Nazca Headdress Petroglyph

Native American, feathered headdress

End Chapter 6

The Faram Research Foundation writes,

After many years of research, there appeared to be a worldwide theme developing which leaned toward certain of the many ancient sites having been dedicated to replenishing the human population after the preceding apocalypse. The type of artifacts found, or more importantly not found, at these sites leads to the conclusion that many of the sites were constructed as ritualistic sites. Many of the subject sites showed no indication of habitation, such as pottery shards or animal bones. This would tend to indicate a ceremonial site rather than a populated city. The design of a site, and the associated artwork, location, geoglyphs, and petroglyphs, all come together to lead one to conclude that certain sites were constructed on sacred locations as post-apocalyptic birthing sites. This type of site may have been necessary, after an apocalypse, to restore mankind's existence on earth. Many of the sites are said to have been mysteriously abandoned or covered with earth. Could it be that rather than being abandoned the sites had simply served their purpose after having restored the associated geoglyphical territory to its target population density? If that is the case, then there was no mass abandonment as is currently believed, but a slow and deliberate dispersion of children and parents throughout the territory leading to a target population density. After their intended use was fulfilled, they may have been hidden by some group that did not wish them to be found, or for reuse. Many tunnels have been filled and many structures covered.

It even appears some were destroyed by a powerful explosion.

As far as we were concerned, this remained a theory until the geoglyph on Easter Island was discovered and surveyed. To our amazement the geoglyph seemed to point out the same sites we had previously suspected as being birthing sites. Based on the established age of the controlling sites, the data pointed to ages beginning ca. 10,000 BCE. The latest age of one of the proposed birthing sites is ca. 1000 CE. The most recent sites seemed to be constructed using the same theme as the older sites, with one exception: they seemed to have been built to replenish a culture after a war or displacement rather than [after] a worldwide apocalypse. It has been shown that many sites, regardless of their purpose, were built on sacred ground which was identified thousands of years before the structure which is located there now.

Wikitravel.com

Moai, Easter Island

One of the prevailing themes related to birthing sites seems to be the need for an overseer, whether that be a man or god. Were the Moai statues there to replace the gods which served as the overlord during reproduction? It appears that the gods were there, and in their absence statues or images were produced to imitate them. A constant theme regarding birthing sites is the suggestion that sexual relations was a spectator sport, watched over by the gods. Is that why the Moai are facing toward the center of the island? As you will see, reproduction may not have been optional but was monitored by some type of overlord (a god).

AncientOrigins.net
Moai holding their stomachs

Effigies holding their stomachs appear at ancient birthing sites around the world. It is documented that the ancient Rapa Nui (Easter Islanders) believed in reincarnation and believed that people were reincarnated in their stomachs. If they believed that the reincarnation started in the male and was passed to the female, it would explain why both the males and females at birthing sites all over the world are seen holding their stomachs.

The Yonaguni Pyramid—ca. 8000 BCE

Probably the most profound validation that ancient man was using sacred sites on which to procreate and expand the human population lies about seventy-five miles east of Taiwan on Yonaguni Island. Yonaguni is the southernmost island in the Japanese empire. (For the full story, see **Narrative E.**)

Note: Not to scale

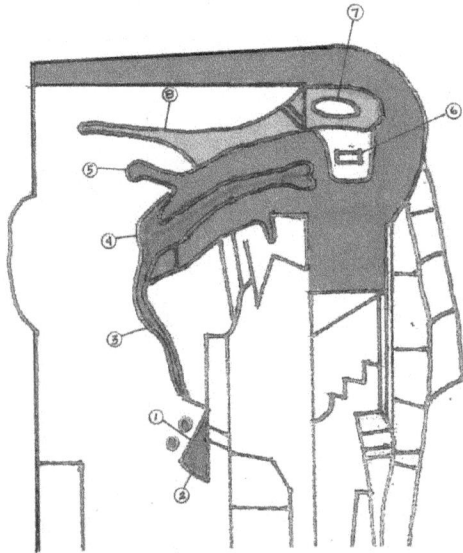

The Faram Research Foundation

Depiction of the male and female reproductive systems on the Yonaguni Pyramid, ca. 8000 BCE

Overlords of the Birthing Sites

On virtually all of the birthing sites there appears to be one or more effigies watching over the location. This would seem to indicate that the effigies represented the physical manifestation of the Gods as they watched over or managed the populace.

Graham Hancock Organization
Stone face on the Yonaguni Pyramid

Stone-face god overlooking Yonaguni pyramid

The birthing of a child, San Augustin, Columbia, ca. 3000 BCE

One of The Overlords watching over the ceremonies at Gobekli Tepi

Overlord, holding stomach, at Easter Island

Plaza of Faces at Kalasasaya Temple – Tiwanaku, Bolivia

Overlord in the background.

Fig. 13. Göbekli Tepe, engraving of a female person from layer II (foto Dieter Johannes, DAI).

Gobekli Tepe, ca. 10,000 BCE

The woman in the previous image is depicted giving birth. As you will see, birth is more commonly depicted by a stick figure with a bulge between the legs. It is interesting that this figure has one arm up and one arm down. Most birthing figures have either both arms up or both arms down.

However, there are the Kangjiashimenji Petroglyphs in western China that present the same body pose. In the following image is a scene from those ancient Chinese petroglyphs. Most scholars who have studied these images come to the logical conclusion that the figures indicate men, each with an erect penis. However, in our research we have come to the conclusion that the figures show women giving birth. With this many women giving birth at the same time, it would tend to indicate that the site was a post-apocalyptic birthing site similar to the others found around the world. If this is true, then the line with the bulge would be a stylized image of a woman giving birth, just as with the other sites.

The following three images show men who clearly have testicles. Based on images at other sites, the rest would be women giving birth. This would explain the appendage (baby) protruding from the rear of some of the women rather than from the front. One peculiar fact is that three of the figures seem to have both a penis and be giving birth. The many faces depicted here further validate that in post-apocalyptic times, sex and/or birth was either a spectator sport or was monitored. (See the following image.)

Mary Mycio wrote a fascinating article for the online magazine *Slate* (2013) called "Archeology Isn't for Prudes." It is reprinted below.

Jeannine Davis-Kimball
The Kangjiashimenji Petroglyphs, China

Jeannine Davis-Kimball
Petroglyphs in Hutubei, Xinjiang province, China

Chinese archeologist Wang Binghua discovered the petroglyphs in the late 1980s, and Jeannine Davis-Kimball,

223

an expert on Eurasian nomads, was the first Westerner to see them. Though she wrote about the petroglyphs in scholarly journals, they remained obscure. Google retrieves only a few results, depending on the spelling. The petroglyphs deserve more attention.

They range in size from more than nine feet tall to just a few inches. All perform the same ceremonial pose, holding their arms out and bent at the elbows. The right hand points up and the left hand points down.

While fascinating in themselves, the petroglyphs also reveal a great deal about the earliest human settlement in China's westernmost region. The intricately carved faces all display the long noses, thin mouths, and defined eye ridges of the Caucasian face. The people in the petroglyphs came from the West

While unprecedented in Central Asia, the iconography echoes images far to the west. Triangular female figures with the arms held like those in the petroglyphs often appear on Copper Age pottery from the Tripolye culture in what is now Ukraine. The animal symbols are also strikingly similar.

Could the cultures be related despite a distance of 1,600 miles and an untold number of years? The answer depends on who created the petroglyphs. While Chinese scholars attribute them to nomadic cultures from 1000 BCE, Davis-Kimball points out that nomads generally create portable art and not huge tableaus. The makers of the petroglyphs had to have been a sedentary people, since the elaborate artworks appear to have been carved over a period of centuries. This narrows the potential candidates down considerably. The only time in prehistory when sedentary people are known to have populated the region was during the Bronze Age, the millennium prior to 1000 BCE.

The faces of these settlers are known to the world from desiccated corpses, perfectly preserved down to their eyelashes and the weave of their clothes. These mummies have been excavated by the hundreds from Xinjiang's dry and salty desert sands since the 1980s.

The oldest and most intriguing bodies came from a twenty-foot-high, man-made sand mound about three hundred miles south of the petroglyphs. Known as Xiaohe, or Small River Cemetery No. 5 (SRC5), it was found in 1934 but then forgotten. The site is in a remote, restricted desert where China conducted nuclear tests. Rediscovered in 2000, the site had to be completely excavated in the following years to protect it from looters. Under the sand lay five layers of burials, from which thirty well-preserved desiccated corpses were recovered, the oldest dating to 2000 BCE.

The discovery proved politically explosive because most of the Bronze Age SRC5 mummies had long noses, eye ridges, and red and brown hair, none of which is typically Chinese. The Caucasian features seemed to contradict the official government view that the Han Chinese had the oldest historical claim to Xinjiang, dating to the second century BCE.

The question of which ethnic group lived here first is a serious issue today. Most of Xinjiang's inhabitants are not ethnically Chinese but Uyghur—they belong to a Turkic-speaking, Muslim nationality that numbers nine million and gives its name to the Xinjiang Uyghur Autonomous Region. They are indistinguishable from typical Europeans, and their ancestors first settled in Xinjiang in the ninth century. Uyghur nationalists, who want greater religious and cultural freedom and more autonomy from China, latched onto the ancient Caucasian mummies to claim deeper historical roots in the region.

The political conflict hampered research for a while. But when a 2010 genetics study concluded that the oldest mummies weren't Han Chinese but weren't Uyghur either, both sides backed down, leaving the subject to scientists and scholars where it belonged.

The cemetery where the mummies were found was unique in the world for its time. The site bristled with nearly two hundred poplar posts, up to twelve feet high, and it required extravagant amounts of lumber. Some of the posts, painted black and red, were either torpedo-like or resembled oversized oars. The bodies lay on the sand, covered with boat-like coffins wrapped in cattle hides.

Viktor Mair, a professor of Chinese language and literature at the University of Pennsylvania and one of the foremost experts on the mummies, writes that SRC5 was "a forest of phalluses and vulvas…blanketed in sexual symbolism." The torpedoes were phallic symbols marking all the female graves, while the "oars" marking the male burials represented vulvas. Many female burials contained carved phalluses at their sides, and the mound also contained large wooden sculptures with hyperbolized genitalia. "Such overt, pervasive attention to sexual reproduction is extremely rare in the world for a burial ground," according to Mair.

The fact that the world's most sexually explicit graveyard was located a few hundred miles from the most sexually explicit petroglyphs can't have been a coincidence.

The implications are tantalizing. Could the earliest scenes in the tableau represent fertility rituals originally brought from Europe by the migrants' ancestors in 3500 BCE?

(Author's note: It is still a mystery as to why some birthing images have both arms raised, both arms down, or, as in this case, one up and one down. This may indicate that the site is either a birthing site, a fertility site, or with one hand up and one hand down, both.)

Gobekli Tepe effigy

227

The previous image appears to be a father and a mother with a baby being born. Both the father and mother have had their faces removed. The reason why only the faces were removed stirs the imagination. The taller subject seems to have been wearing a helmet. Notice that the mother is holding her abdomen. The sacred serpent of the ancients adorns both sides of the statue.

AncientOrigins.net

Gobekli Tepe figure

Gobekli Tepe, ca. 10,000 BCE - Israel, ca. 600 BCE

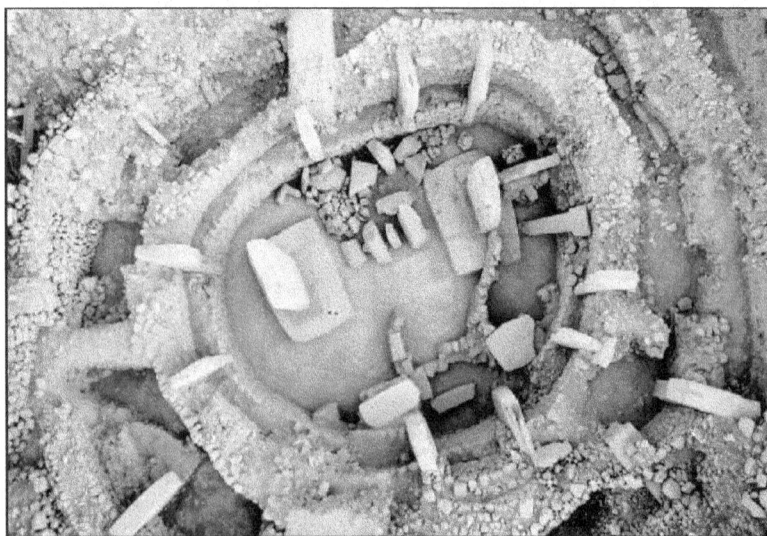

Gobekli Tepe birthing/conception ritual pit

Notice the pit in the previous image with seating all around. This configuration repeatedly appears at major birthing sites. The pillars depicted around the pit are aligned to geoglyphically show the area this particular birthing site is serving. There are many more pillars in the adjacent pits, which also contribute to outlining the territory through the use of the ancient science of geoglyphology.

Watch for the commonality of these same circular pits with seating all around the perimeter in the following images, from birthing sites around the world.

Fig. 13. Göbekli Tepe, engraving of a female person from layer II (foto Dieter Johannes, DAI).

Woman giving birth, Gobekli Tepe

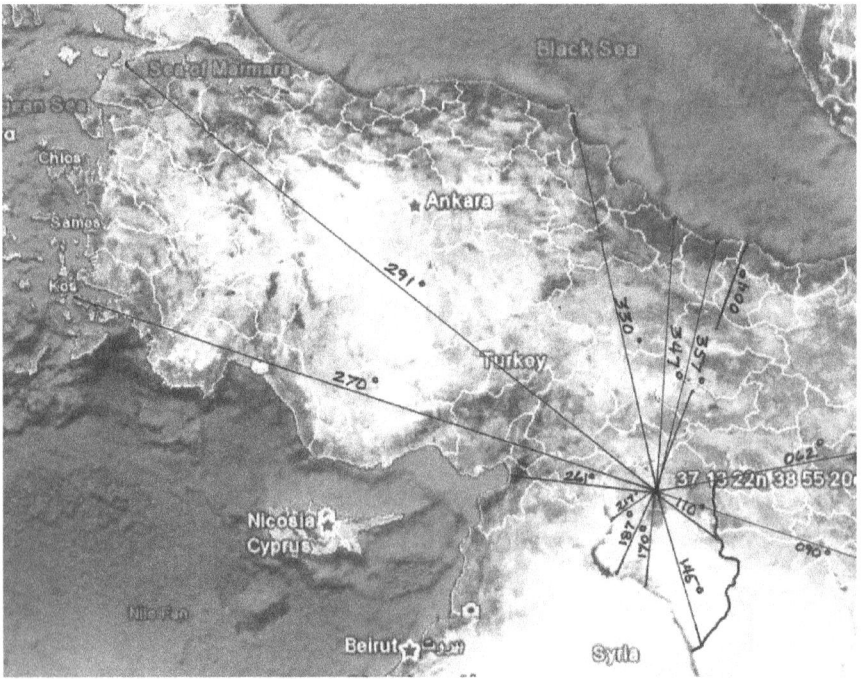

The Birthing Territory of Gobekli Tepe

This territory is based on a geoglyphic survey using the orientation of the existing exposed pillars at Gobekli Tepe. These comprise only 10% of the structures yet to be uncovered. (See narrative D.)

The "H" Connection

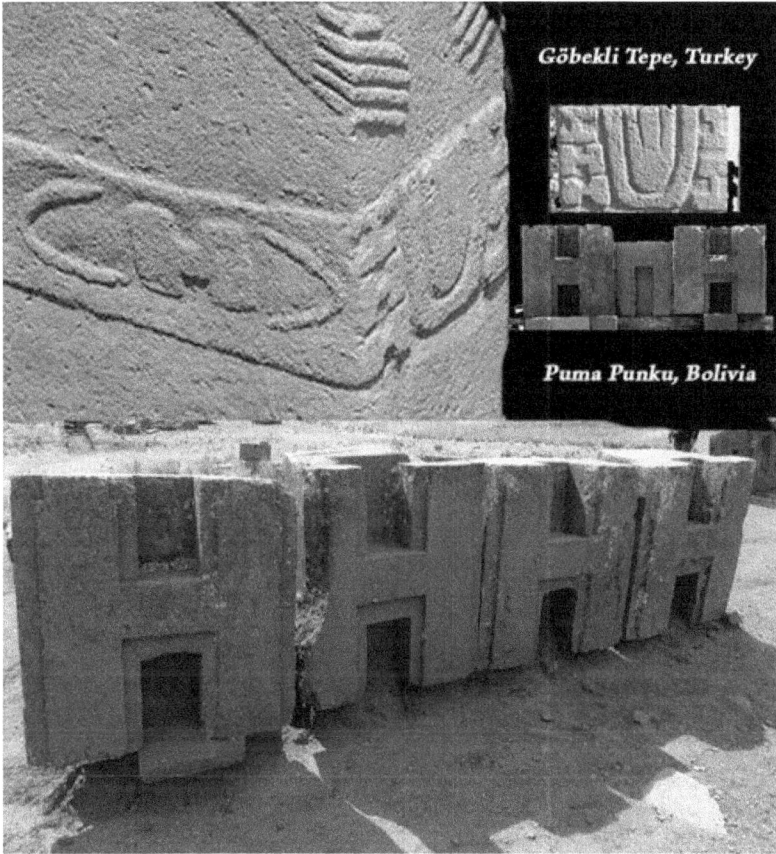

AncientOrigins.net

Graham Hancock says, "I've read about connections in symbolism between statues, H symbols, or baskets found at Easter Island, Sumer, Gobekli Tepe, and the Americas, particularly Puma Punku."

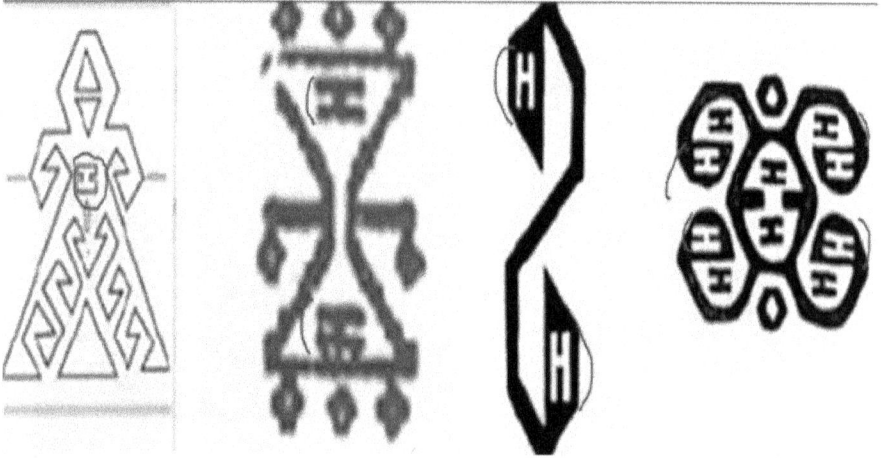

Image credit: Fatih Kekevi

Meaning of the "H" Symbol

Fatih Kekevi of Turkey explains that the above image is "a symbol seen in Kilim carpets and handkerchiefs in Turkey, Iran, Central Asia, and some Balkan countries. A young girl who wants to get married uses it. 'H' is a symbol of marriage, a wish for having baby (see H in the belly), to be tied as a couple, 'I' as a person, another 'I' as the other person, and '-' as the bond between the two. The symbol name is Saçbaği, "Hair Bound."

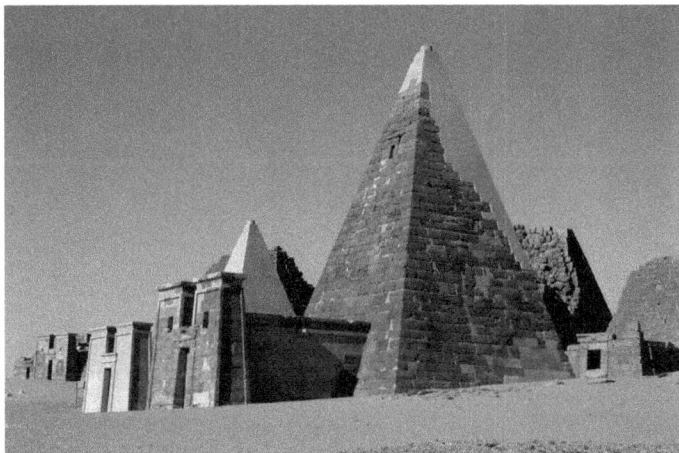

The pyramids of Kush, Egyptian Sudan with same uneven H symbol as Puma Punku

Once again we see pyramids with the "H" symbol adorning the entrance way. As mentioned previously, pyramids' circular pits and mountains tend to focus the earth's energy so that this energy can be used by man for beneficial purposes.

Ceremonial pit, Nevali Çori, Şanliurfa, Turkey
(Similar to Gobekli Tepe)

Fatih Kekevi

Left: A male, a female, and a newborn baby holding the water of life. The left statue is from Gobekli Tepe. Right: Umay Ana, mother goddess of Turks.

Fatih Kekevi

Hands on the stomach
Easter Island, Peru, Gobekli Tepe

Meaning, according to Fatih Kekevi of Turkey:
Hands at the belly: Reproduction and birth
Hands at the belt: Power of the leader
Both combined: A leader who will ensure the reproduction of the clan.

500 BCE – Ukraine

Ukraine

Is this one of the "overlords" surrounded by seven women?

Easter Island Rongorongo writing

Rongorongo writing has not yet been deciphered by the scientific community. However, it does contain the images of a subject with both hands up, legs spread, and an object between the legs.

Dogon Tribe, Africa

All images show birthing. The Dogon image shows the entire child with a red "changing the earth" symbol on the abdomen of the mother.

Chaco Canyon, New Mexico

Caral, Peru

Hawaii - A man with two women giving birth

Ed Wheelan, *Ancient Origins*, January 25, 2020

Sinai Desert cave, Egypt, ca. 10,000 BCE

Canada - Tlingit Chief with the four and eight-sided symbols and
the Birthing Symbol

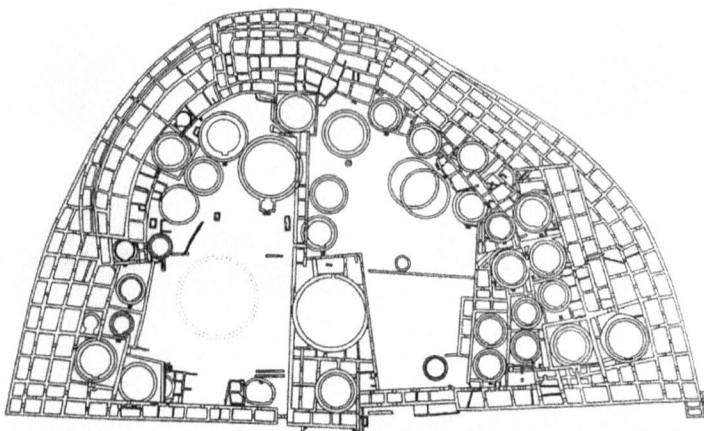

Chaco Canyon, New Mexico, ca. 1100 CE

Notice the pits with the seating all around. Also notice that the directional bearings are determined by geoglyphic circles in this image. The circles are intentionally arranged in a pattern to be deciphered by applying the ancient science of geoglyphology. By applying the protocols associated with geoglyphology to the circles, the territory served by this birthing site will be revealed. (See Narrative P.)

Chaco Canyon arena, New Mexico

As many already know, the earth generates electromagnetic waves, which can be useful in a person's well-being or spirituality. These forces can be harnessed and multiplied by the use of certain earthly structures. This natural phenominon can be tapped and used for many mind- and body-enhancing purposes. This natural energy can be harnessed by the body being within the earth, above the earth in a Dolmen, or in or on an artificial or naturial conical ediface such as a pyramid or mountain. Could this focused magnetic force increase the viability and well-being of an infant if conceived under the right circumstances in a sacred place?

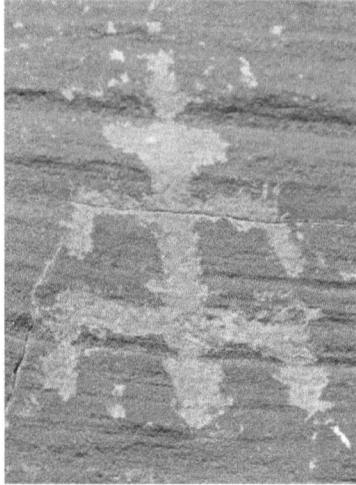

Ancient Origins
Child being born

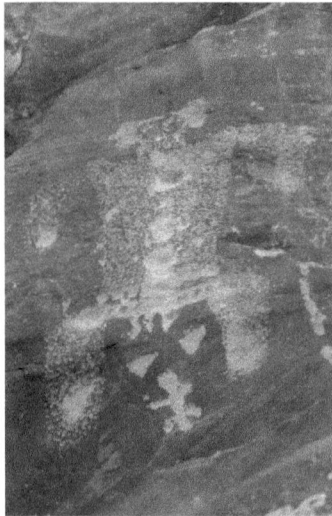

Peggy Mekemson
Woman giving birth with arms and legs pointed down

Gran Quivera birthing site, Salinas National Monument, New Mexico

Notice the Mini-Apartments, available at many birthing sites. It was typical for the ancients to build numerious small apartments at or near the birthing sites, presumably to accommodate woman waiting to become pregnant or to give birth.

Machu Picchu, Incan, ca. 1450 CE

Machu Picchu phallic figures

Easter Island
The same ear ornaments as at Machu Picchu

The Reclining Woman of Machu Picchu

246

More mini apartments at Machu Picchu

Machu Picchu sits on the top of one of the highest mountains in Peru. This would provide an increased amount of earth energy for birthing events. The recreation areas and the smaller number of apartments may indicate that this birthing location was for royalty only.

Caral, Peru, ca. 3000 BCE
Notice again the circle with the seating all around.

Caral, Peru

Phallic symbol in a Caral temple
Whale vertebra added to simulate pubic hair

Caral Peru
Freestanding phallic symbol

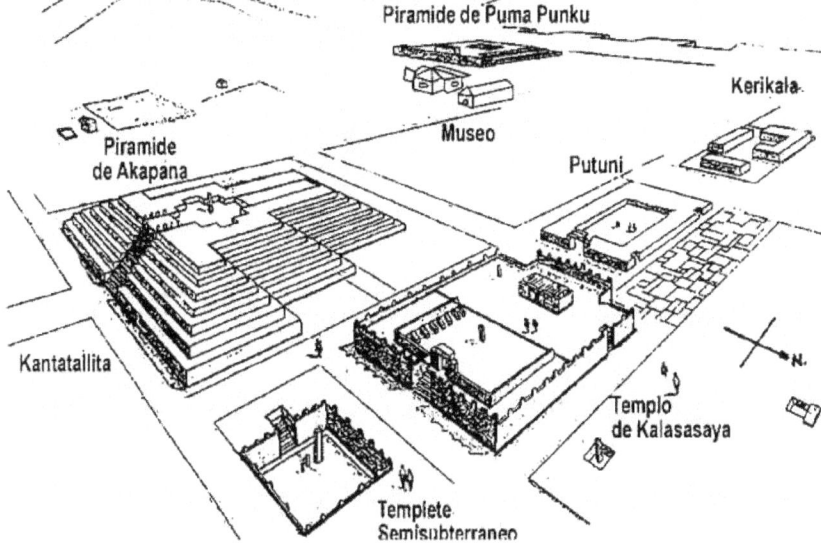

Ceremonial Site of Tiwanaku

Piramide de Puma Punku

Kerikala

Piramide de Akapana

Museo

Putuni

Kantatallita

Templo de Kalasasaya

Templete Semisubterraneo

Puma Punka . Kalasasaya . Akapana . Museum Bolivia

© KathyDoore.com/Tiwanaku

Tiwanaku, Bolivia, ca. 200 BCE

Here we have a square arena with the seats all around and posts in the center,similar to Gobekli Tepe. Also notice the eight-pointed star symbol on the top of one of the pyramids. This is the same symbol used by the Native Americans in the southwestern United States.

Plaza of Faces, Tiwanaku, Bolivia

Once again we have a group of gods overlooking a courtyard. This practice is similar to the Moai at Easter Island and similar sites that display gods overseeing a ceremonial enclosure of some sort.

Based on the weathering on the faces in the plaza, it would appear that the faces were made from various types of stone. If that is so, then it's possible that these faces were carved at the donor's homeland and brought to Tiwanaku for some type of ceremony. Once again we have an arena with faces directed inward, as if watching a ceremony, just as with the Moai at Easter Island and the other Birthing sites.

**Woman holding stomach with the godly event spiral on her belly
Romania, ca. 4000 BCE**

Visual-Arts-cork.com

Knowth, Ireland, petroglyph

This is a drawing of the previous image. Could this be male and female genitalia coming together to create another being from the cosmic aether?

Notice that there are two spirals in the image. The spirals are ancient godly symbols. A spiral starting with a left stroke symbolizes an earthy god or event. A spiral starting with a right stroke indicates a heavenly god. I find it interesting that there is a symbol for a holy earthly event between the two phallic symbols, while the heavenly god looks on. This is just one more clue that the ancient gods, or their representatives, were supposed to watch over repopulation in the rebuilding of mankind in post-apocalyptic times.

Gobekli Tepe with the left and right C symbol, as shown in the previous image. The "H", symbolizing birth and conception, appears in place of the spiral.

Nazca Birthing Symbol
(Photo credit: Yamagata University, Japan)

A Japanese university team researching the Nazca Lines in Peru has discovered an additional 143 geoglyphs. The Yamagata University research group led by Professor Masato Sakai announced the findings on Friday, November 15, 2019. The team had been looking for additional Nazca Lines for three years. The lines depict humans, birds, and four-legged animals such as cats. The size ranges from five meters to as large as a hundred meters. They are believed to have been created between 100 BCE and 300 CE. Notice how the previous image resembles the effigies at other sites with the woman having the arms up and legs down, with birthing between the legs. (See narrative J for another forgotten Nazca geoglyph.)

Nan Madol, Pacific

  Nan Madol has been an enigma for centuries. It is six hundred miles from the nearest land, yet it harbors one of the most mysterious cities in the world. The city was built from long cylinders of basalt stacked so as to form a wall. See image.

The History Channel, Ancient Aliens

Nan Madol, Pacific

Nan Madol is arranged, with its nonparallel walls, as a giant geoglyph.

Ancient Aliens

Magnetic Basalt logs arranged into a dolmen

Could this have been for concentrating energy for birthing rituals?

Salawasi Island, Indonesia

Elite Readers

Woman holding her stomach – c9000 BCE

According to archaeological finds, Salawasi Island has been inhabited for at least two hundred thousand years. Although an exact date has not been established, the monoliths on Salawasi are believed to be post–Ice Age. As is the case with most of the birthing sites, no evidence has been found of continual habitation.

Elite Readers

Salawasi Island, Indonesia

Notice that even the men are holding their stomachs, just as in Gobekli Tepe, Easter Island, and other sites. Ancient cultures believed that re-incarnation started in the male and was passed to the female.

Salawasi Island, Indonesia

These same strange faces are also located at Gobekli Tepe

Ancient Birthing Figurines

Venuses of Kostiensky, ca. 25,000 BCE

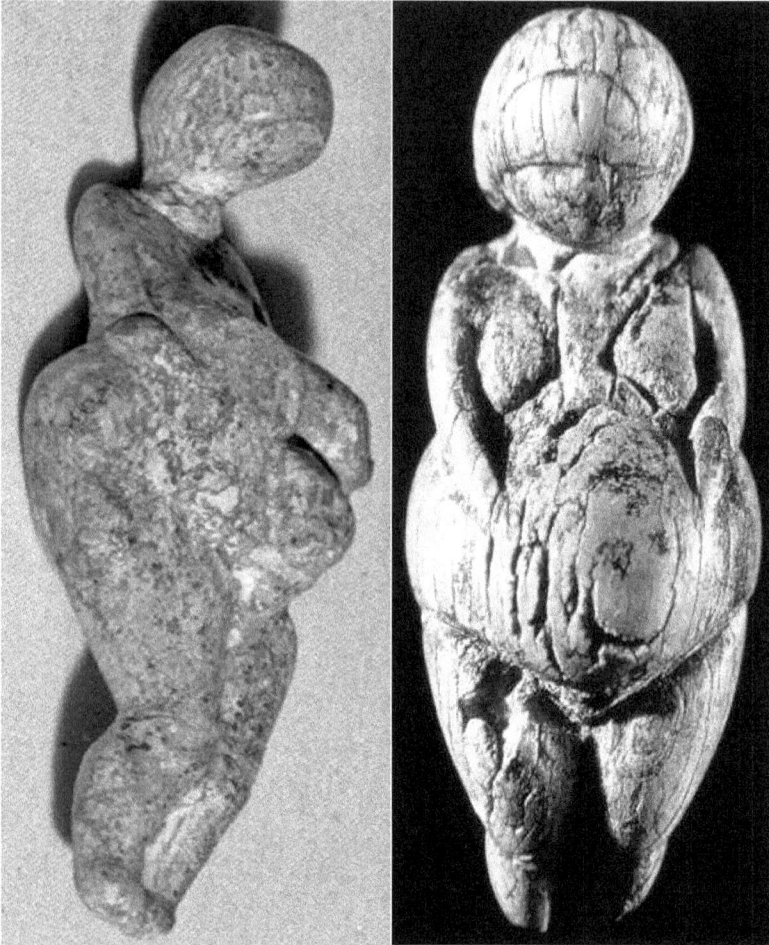

Russia

Notice that even these ancient figurines have their hands holding their belly.

Venus of Tursac, ca. 23,000 BCE

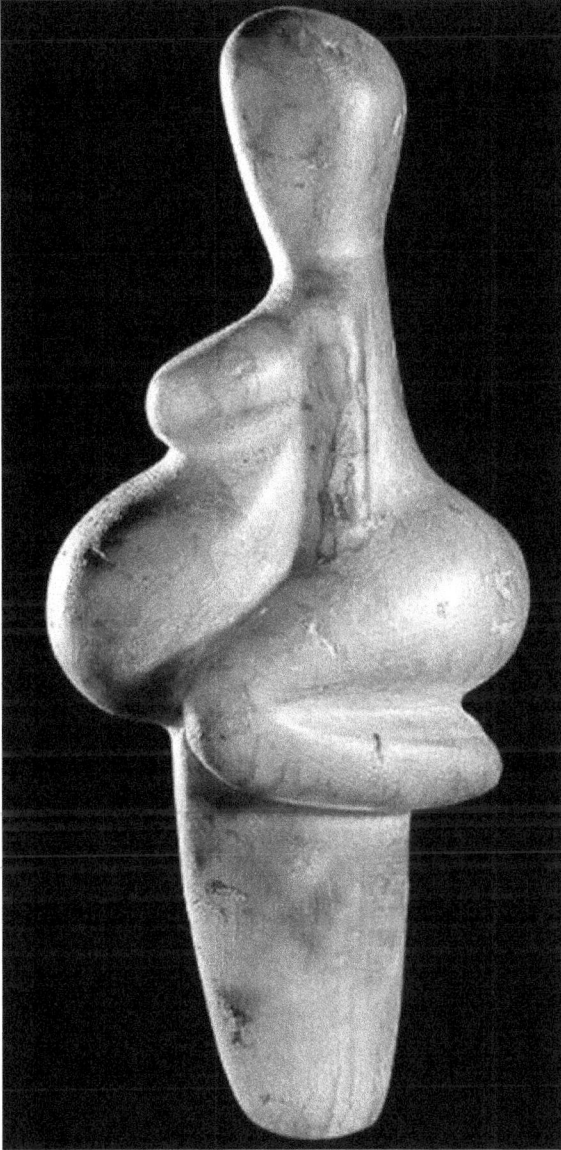

France

Venuses of Parabita, ca. 17,000 BCE

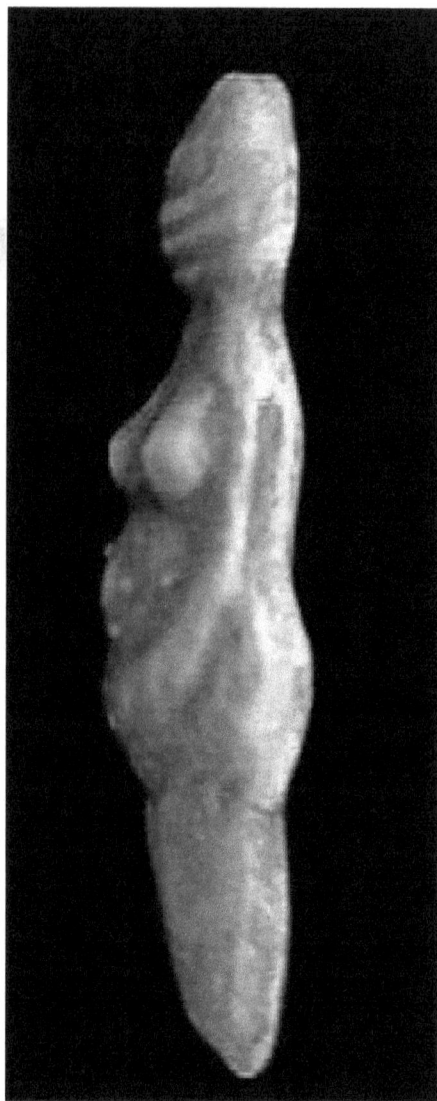

Italy

Avdeevo Venuses, ca. 28,000 BCE

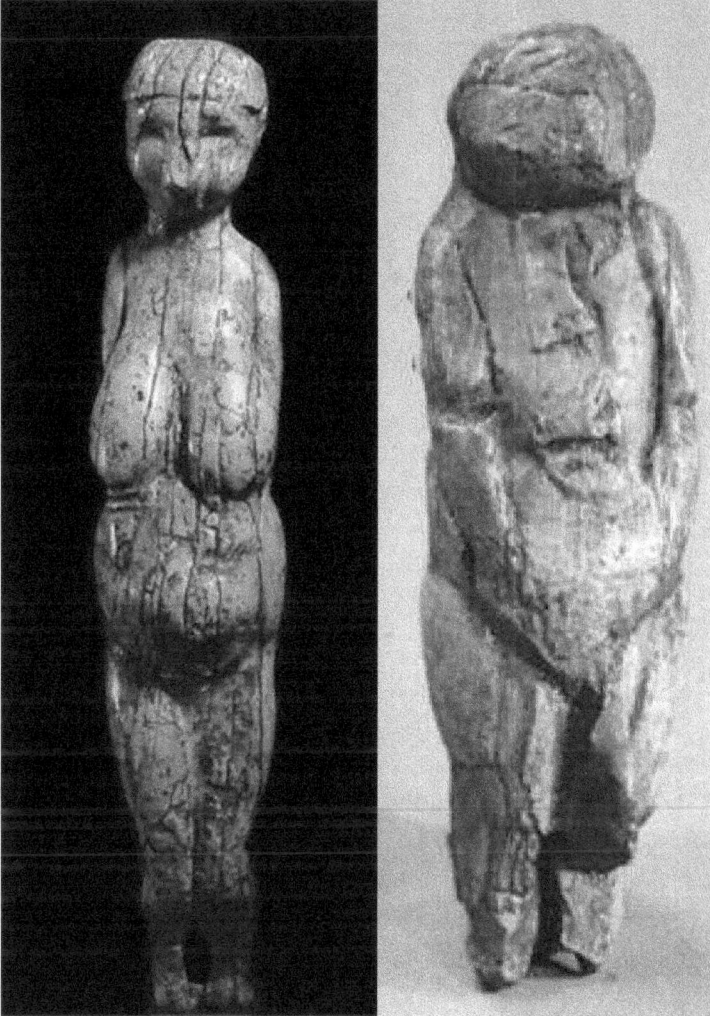

Russia

End Chapter 7

A. Beato – Courtesy of the Los Angeles Museum of Art

The Sphinx - Cairo, Egypt

As this is being written, there is a discussion among scientists that puts the previously taught age of the Sphinx, that being ca. 2500 BCE, into question. The following geoglyphological survey could answer that question and possibly push the date back over four thousand years.

Reproduction of the Nabta Playa geoglyph, southern Egypt

The Nabta Playa Geoglyph is the starting point for this discussion. The Nabta Playa site was discovered by accident by anthropology professor Fred Wendorf in 1974 and has been dated to 7500 BCE. Nabta Playa has been pivotal in providing information on pre-dynastic Egypt. In addition, there has been a discovery by the Faram Research Foundation that rivals all the previous discoveries at Nabta Playa. This observation may well provide a minimum age for the Sphinx.

While researching the geoglyph at Nabta Playa, we found that one of the main pointers on the geoglyph pointed to a place long forgotten by history. That place we named the Gulfo de Cintra geoglyphs.

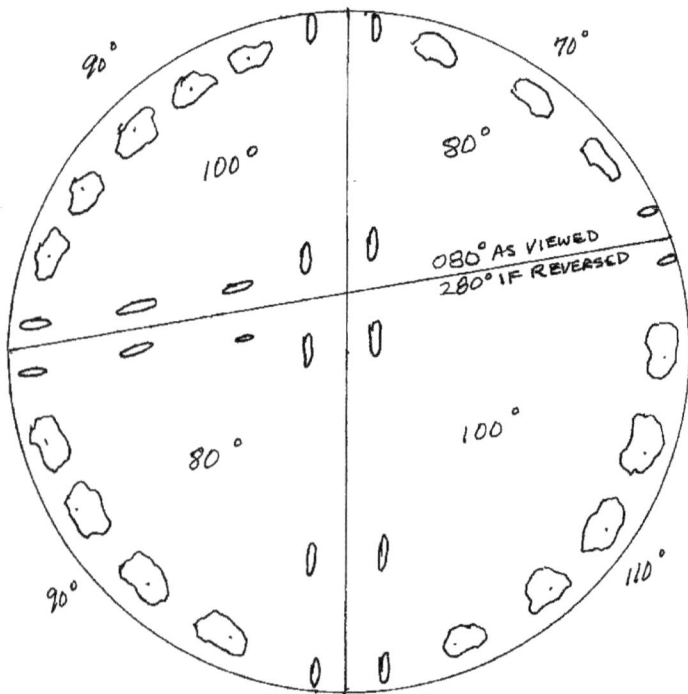

A Drawing of the Nabta Playa Stone Circle as seen from above

As was the case with an Aztec geoglyph in Mexico City, and after much trial and error, it was found that it was necessary to flip the Nabta Playa geoglyph over to get the true readings the creator of the geoglyph intended. The creators of important ancient geoglyphs sometimes used this method to ensure that their geoglyphs would not be decoded by the uninitiated. After flipping the geoglyph over, the original 80-degree bearing becomes the 280-degree bearing. By using this method, and following the 280-degree bearing, the incredible Gulfo de Cintra geoglyphs were located. Due to its obscured remoteness, the Gulfo de Cintra geoglyph would never have been located without the aid of Geoglyphology and the Nabta Playa geoglyph.

Pointer from Nabta Playa Geoglyph to the Gulfo de Cintra Geoglyphs

The Nabta Plata geoglyphs' age has been scientifically confirmed as 7500 BCE. Since Nabta Playa points out the Gulfo de Cintra geoglyph and Gulfo de Cintra points back to Nabta Playa it would be reasonable to assume that the Gulfo de Cintra geoglyphs are also nine thousand years old or older. Also, since the Nabta Playa geoglyph points to the Gulfo de Cintra geoglyph, and the Gulfo de Cintra geoglyph points back to the Nabta Playa geoglyph as well as to the Sphinx, one could assume that the Sphinx is also nine thousand years old or older.

The nine-thousand-year-old Gulfo de Cintra geoglyphs

The fact that these geoglyphs are still intact and above ground is incredible. As most people know, the wind in the desert can sometimes be destructive. The survival of the Gulfo de Cintra geoglyphs has come about as the result of a curious phenomenon. The tops of the geoglyphs are made of concrete circles. As luck would have it, the weight of the concrete has compacted the sand underneath so as to not allow the sand to be blown out from under the concrete. As a result, the consistent erosion has left the concrete on top of a tower of compacted sand.

A Similar, Naturally Occurring, Phenomena in Nevada, United States

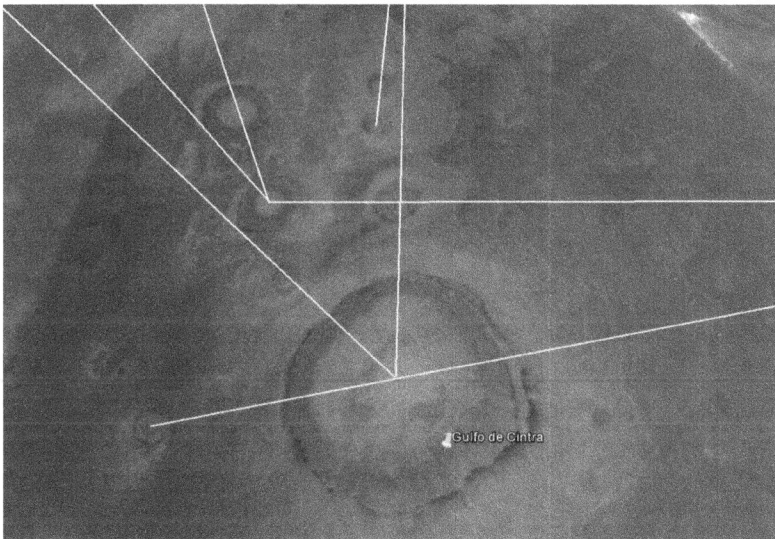

The Gulfo De Cintra Geoglyphs and Bearings From Above

Although the importance of some of the end points in the Gulfo de Cintra geoglyphs may seem obscure, you can be assured that they play a significant role in the worldwide geoglyphological picture.

The reference points used in geoglyphology exist around the world and are used repeatedly down through time as end points for geoglyphological surveys. Knowing where these key points exist is helpful in order to know if there is a built in error coded into a geoglyph. If there is an intentional error, it will normally be one or two degrees and will be uniform throughout the geoglyph. It has been suggested that the errors in the older geoglyphs could be the result of shifts in the magnetic pole which has occurred since the geoglyph was completed. This would be an illogical conclusion since all geoglyphs use true headings rather than magnetic headings.

For more than thirty thousand years, predetermined sites have been used as reference points in territorial surveys or as locations on which to build historically significant structures. The reference points used in geoglyphology have been used repeatedly down through time. This gives us two important clues. First, there has been a continuous worldwide culture in existence for at least thirty thousand years. Second, these reference points were surveyed and were important to our ancestors for millennia.

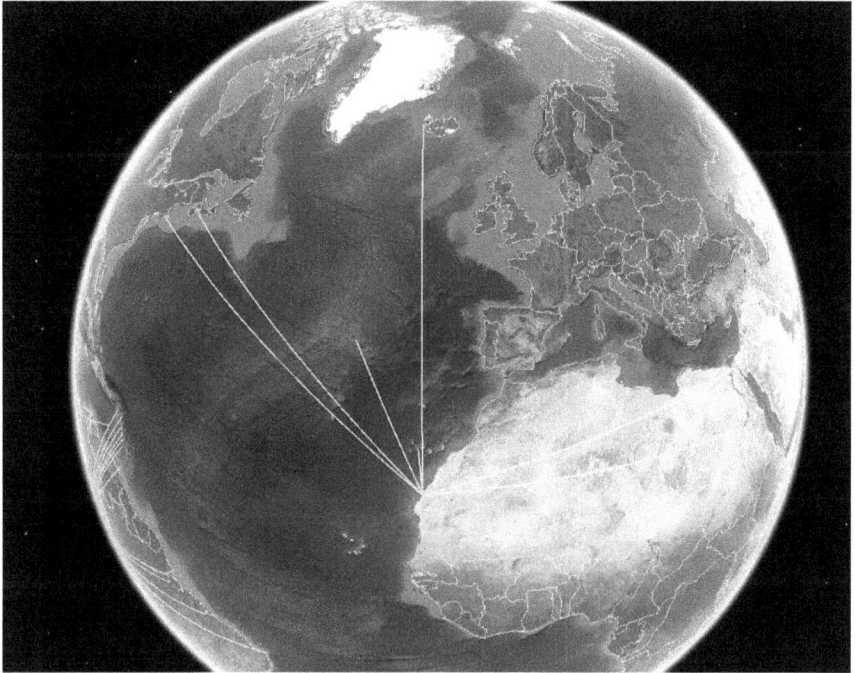

The Gulfo de Cintra Radials

The historical significance of the Gulfo de Cintra reference points, using modern names, cannot be understated. The endpoints of the Gulfo de Cintra geoglyphs follow:

1. **The Island of Gomera, Canary Islands.** This was the departure point of Columbus on his first trip to the Americas. Contrary to popular belief, his mission was to place geoglyphical survey markers in the Caribbean and document Portugal's gift of Mesoamerica to Spain. (See the book *La Merica*, 2013, also see Narrative O)

270

The Guimar Pyramids – Canary Islands

Countless Celtic geoglyphs depict the Canary Islands as the southernmost point in the Celtic territory. The Guimar Pyramids were constructed by Portugal ca. 1822 CE to validate the North American territory (United States) as it was when given to the Templars c1450 CE by Portugal. (See Narrative M)

2. **Nabta Playa.** Home to an enigmatic culture that lived there over nine thousand years ago. The Nabta Playa geoglyphs interact with the Gulfo de Cintra geoglyphs. (See narrative F.)

3. **The Sphinx.** Recently the Sphinx' true age has been challenged by renowned scientists. The city of Cairo did not exist until 969 CE. The Giza Pyramid supposedly did not exist until ca. 2500 BCE. So logic would dictate that Gulfo de Cintra geoglyph could not have been pointing out Cairo or the Giza pyramid.

4. **Southern Tip of Africa.** Once the southern tip of the ancient Euro-African territory ca. 32,000 BCE and the site of many ancient geoglyphs.

5. **The Azores.** Mythical location of Atlantis and located midway between Europe and the Americas.

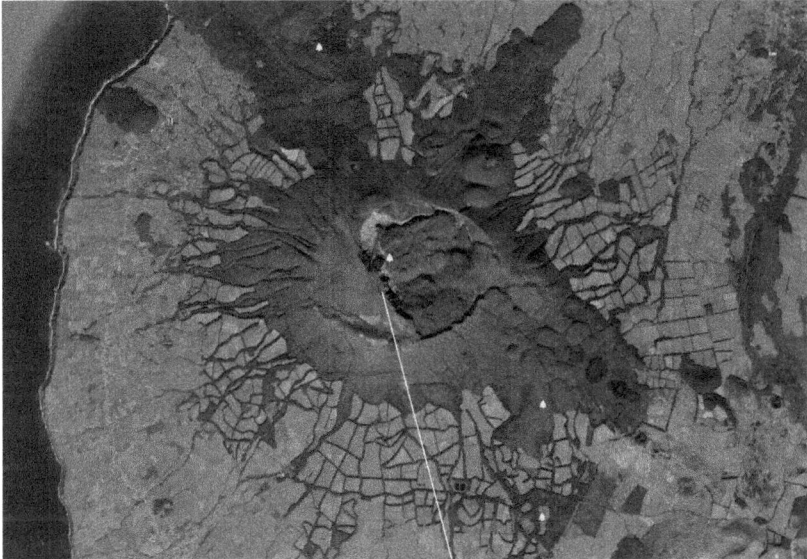

Google Earth – The Faram Research Foundation

Santa Barbara Volcano, Azores

7. **Snaefellsjokull Volcano, Iceland** – Reykjavik, Iceland is the midway port for ancient and historical (Celtic) travel between Europe and North America. (*La Merica*, 2013 Foundation Press)

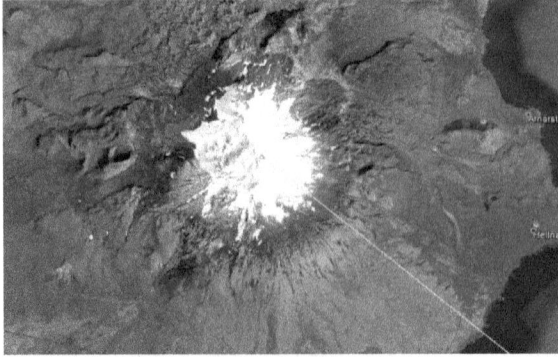

Snaefellsjokull Volcano, Iceland

8. Halifax, N.S. – The southern boundary point of the Viking Territory, as assigned by the Denmark – Norway Alliance, after the Vikings were banned from Norway for refusing to convert to Catholicism c1000 CE. (See Narrative L)

Star Fort Geoglyph in Halifax, N.S.

Star Forts are used as both geoglyphs and defensive positions. The star fort is the best configuration for a fort due to the overlapping fields of fire. There was most likely a previous geoglyph where the fort is now located. Don't forget, these locations were used repeatedly.

9. The Newport RI, USA – Location of the enigmatic Newport Tower which is the anchor point for the territory which would later become the United States. Although the Newport Tower was built between the 14th and 15th Century Newport RI, USA has been the endpoint for geoglyphs around the world for millennia. (See Narrative N)

The Newport Tower, RI

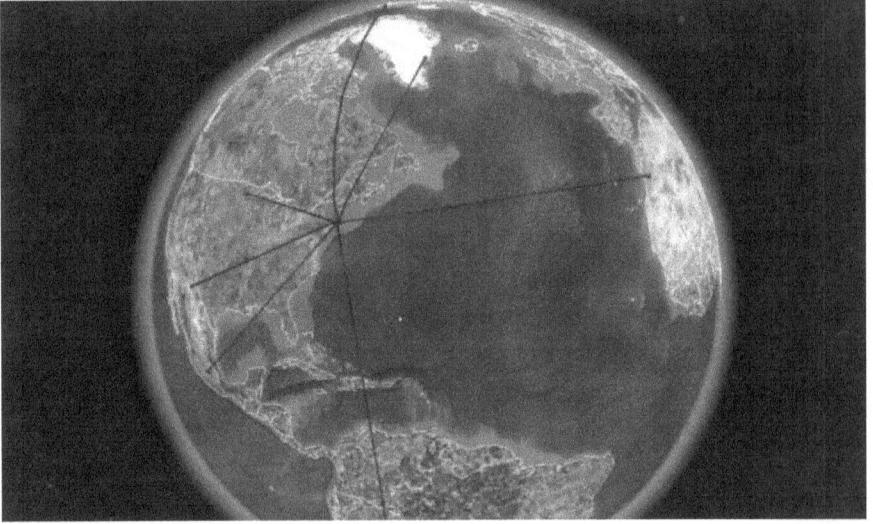

Ancient Geoglyphs around the world which point to Newport, R.I.

End Chapter 8

Narrative A

Bosnian Pyramids, Bosnia—ca. 31,000 BCE

Google Earth – The Faram Research Foundation
The three main Bosnian pyramids

The Earth Pyramid has since been named the Dragon
Pyramid. The location of the pyramids forms an equilateral triangle.

Stage One: The building of the Bosnian Pyramid of the Sun, ca. 31,000 BCE

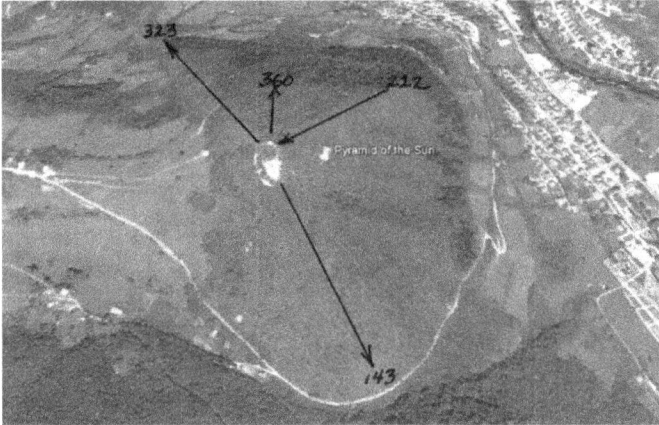

Bosnian Pyramid of the Sun bearings
(Based on the highest point on the ridges.)

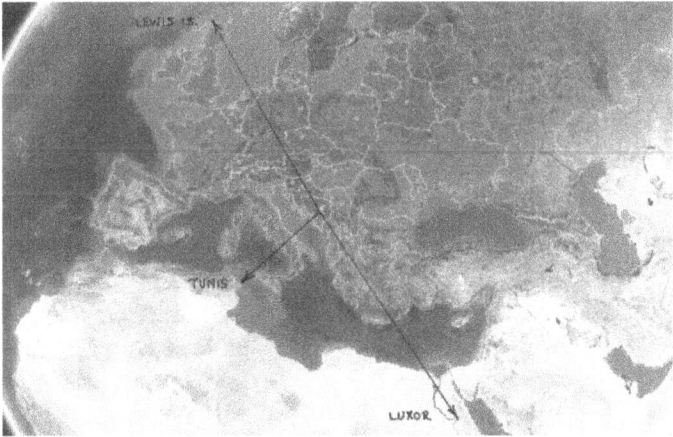

Bosnian Pyramid of the Sun radials

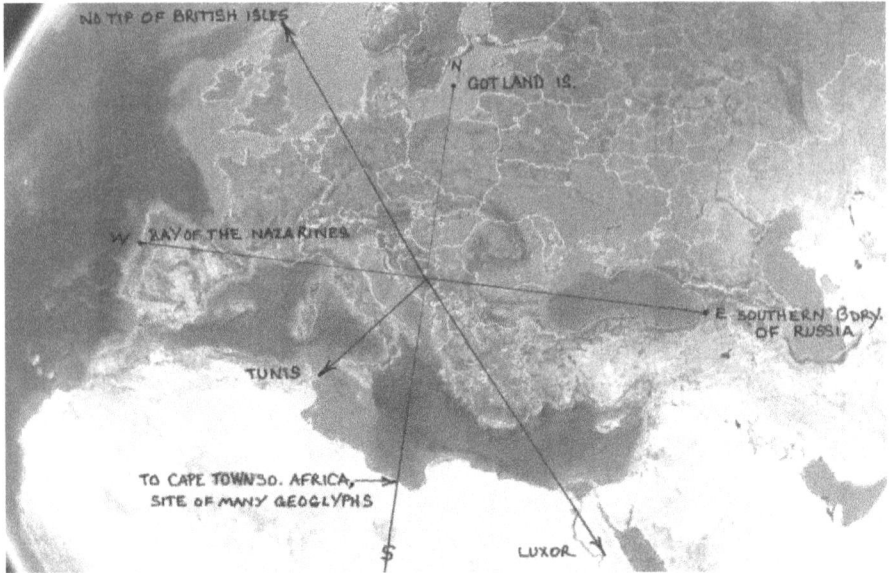

Bosnian Pyramid of the Sun territory, ca. 31,000 BCE

(After adding the four cardinal points of the compass)

NOTE: The Pyramid of the Sun territory at the time this pyramid was built included the continent of Africa. After the Ice Age, ca. 9500 BCE, the Pyramids of the Moon and Dragon were built and indicated that Africa was no longer included in the Bosnian territory. However, Africa did show up in a Semite geoglyph built ca. 1200 BCE. As a result of the apocalypse that occurred ca. 12,000 BCE, many new sites (geoglyphs) appeared on earth to map out the repopulation of the earth.

Stage Two: The Pyramids of the Moon and the Earth (Dragon), ca. 9500 BCE

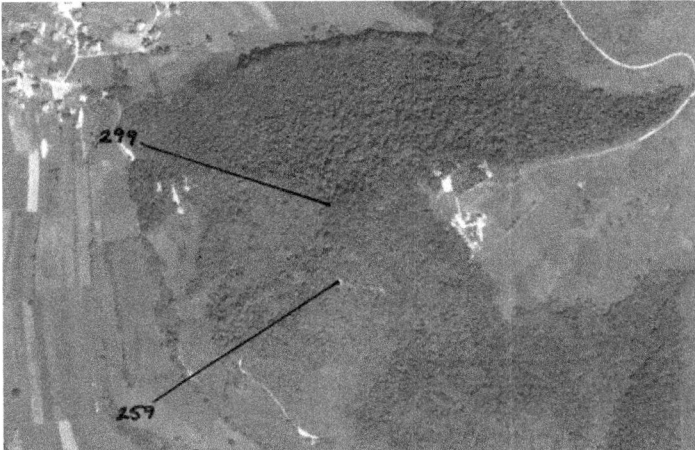

Bosnian Pyramid of the Moon bearings

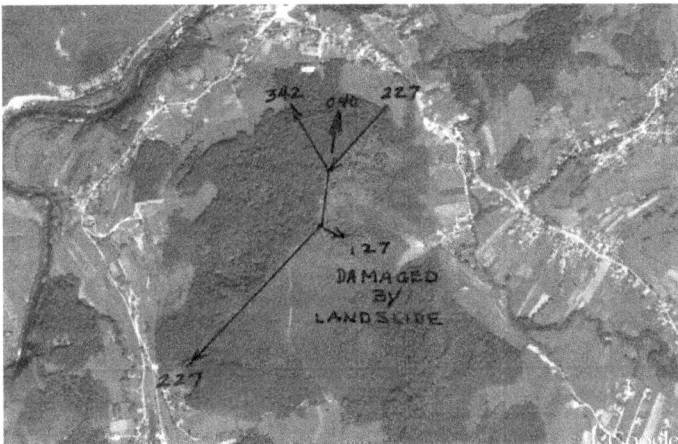

Bosnian Pyramid of the Dragon bearings

280

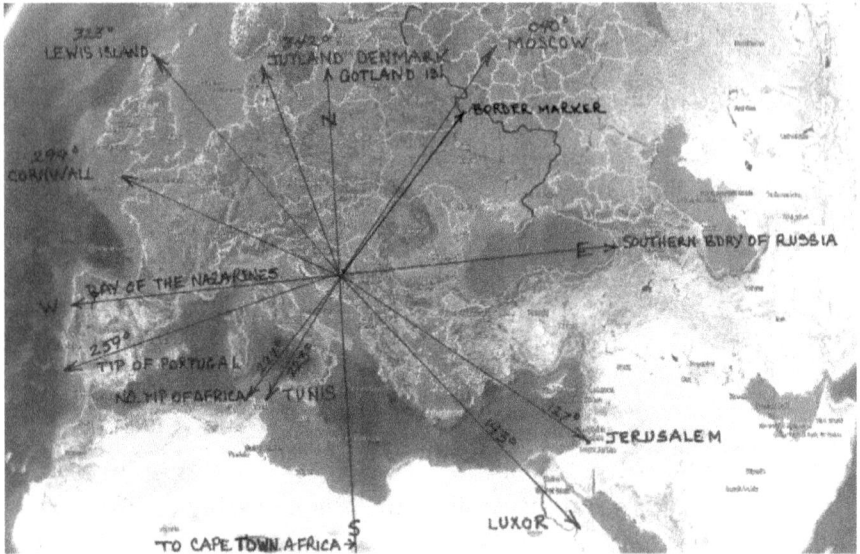

Google Earth – The Faram Research Foundation

**Radials, territory, and important points, defined by combining
the three Bosnian pyramid radials, ca. 9500 BCE**

As is the custom, major geoglyphs contain one radial that
points out the geoglyph defining the adjoining territory. In this case it
is the forty-degree radial that points to the Moscow City geoglyph.
The forty-degree radial does not define part of the territorial
boundaries depicted by the Bosnian pyramids, but it points out the
geoglyph that defines the territory next to it.

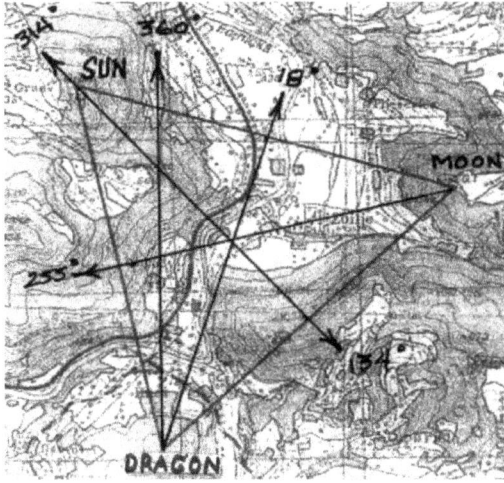

The triangle created by the three Bosnian pyramids (with resulting bearings displayed)

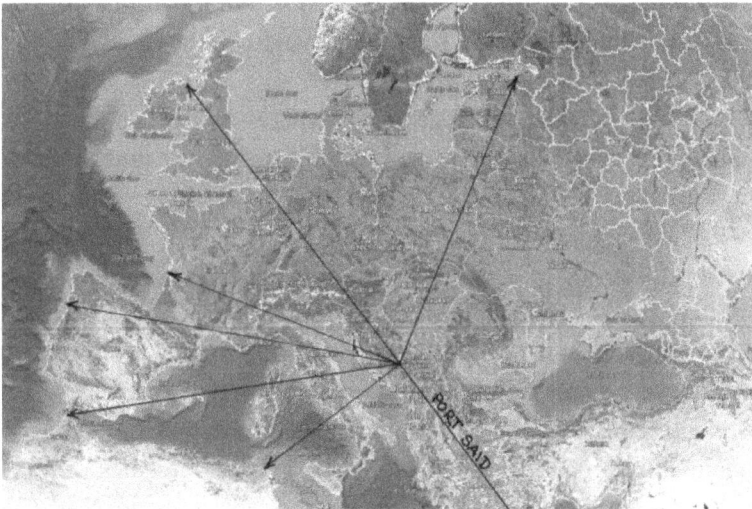

Radials of the Bosnian "triangle"

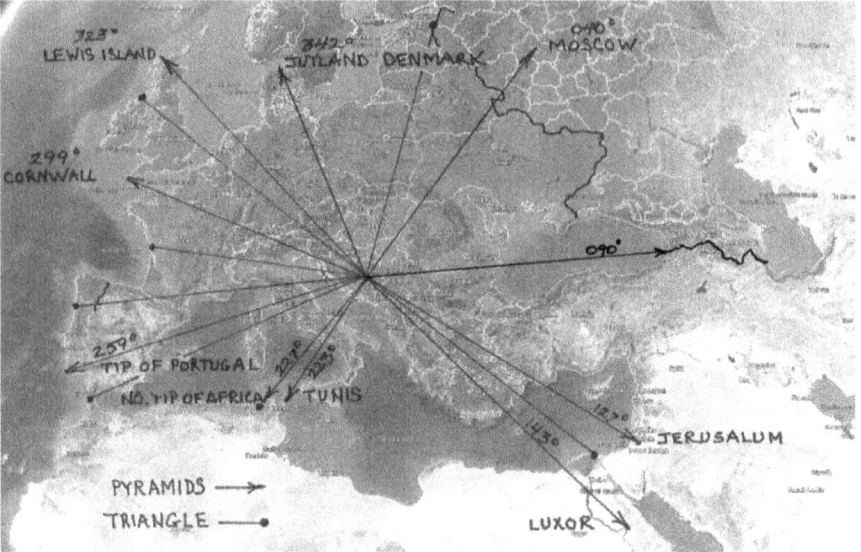

The combined radials of the 9500 BCE Bosnian Pyramids of the Moon, Dragon and the Bosnian triangle, ca. 9500 BCE

NOTE: This study indicates that what is now called the Russian/European border was already established by the time the Moon and Earth Pyramids were built, ca. 9500 BCE. You should be aware that ancient geoglyphs outline territories, many of which we still honor. Notice that the radials that define Africa as part of the European territory are now missing. As can be seen, Jerusalem was a point of interest even in 9500 BCE. This territory defines what later became the Celtic area of influence. Remember that even though a site is identified in historical times, it does not mean that the same site was not important thousands of years ago. Important sites were identified thousands of years ago and are used repeatedly down through time.

The Later Geoglyphs Built on Top of the Bosnian Pyramids, ca. 1300-1500 CE

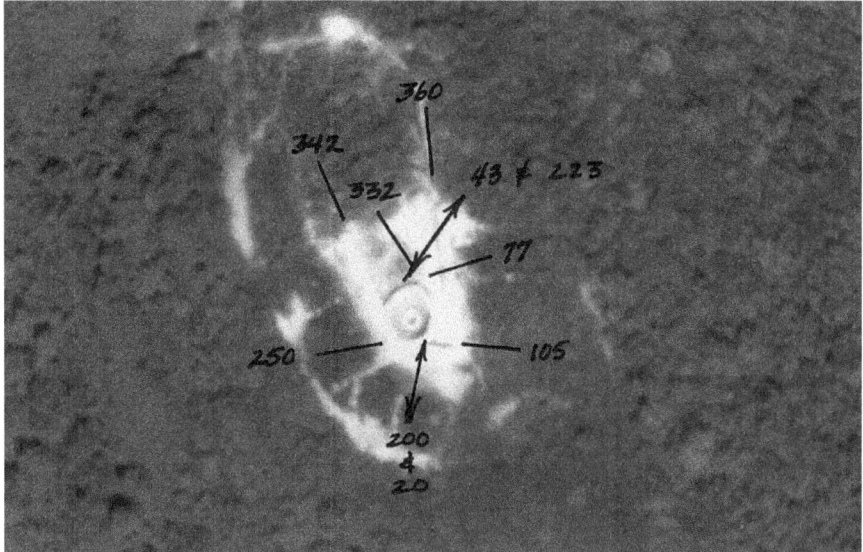

Bearings associated with the geoglyph (fort) on top of the Sun Pyramid

The culture that occupied Bosnia ca. 1500 CE added another structure at the top of the Sun Pyramid. That structure, like many other structures around the world, is also a geoglyph. The fort geoglyph on top of the Sun pyramid restated essentially the same territory as depicted by the Bosnian pyramids. The science of geoglyphology has been handed down for millennia by secret societies and governments of the world. This image is slightly blurred. The lines that generate the bearings can be seen by closer inspection on Google Earth.

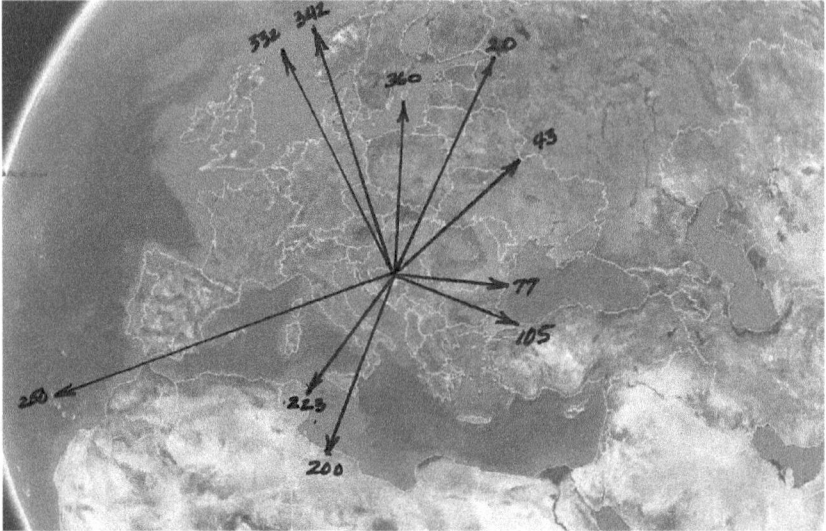

Radials associated with the geoglyph (fort) on top of the Sun Pyramid

Notice that the Canary Islands have now been added. The Canary Islands appear repeatedly in ancient geoglyphs as the southernmost point in the Celtic territory. The survey of the Bosnian pyramids indicates that prior to 29,000 BCE, the Celts and Russians, as we call them today, had already come to an agreement over where the border existed between Europe and Russia.

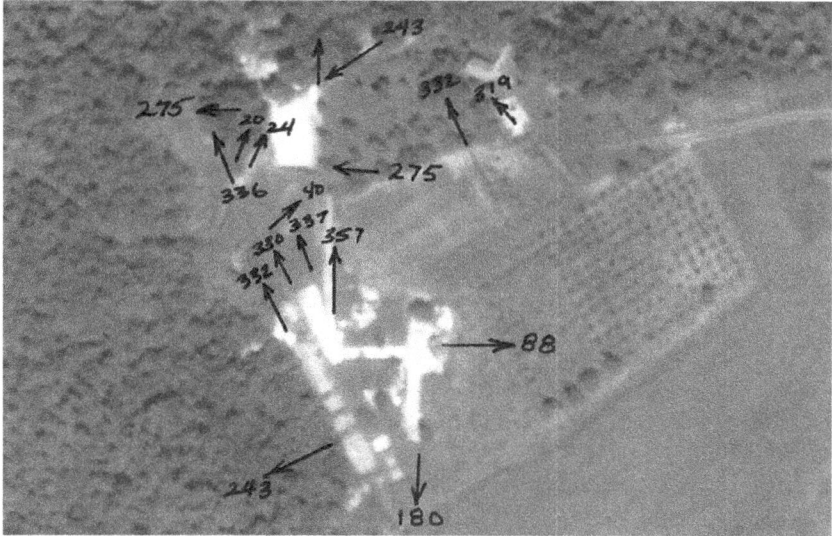

Bearings associated with the geoglyphs on top of the Moon Pyramid

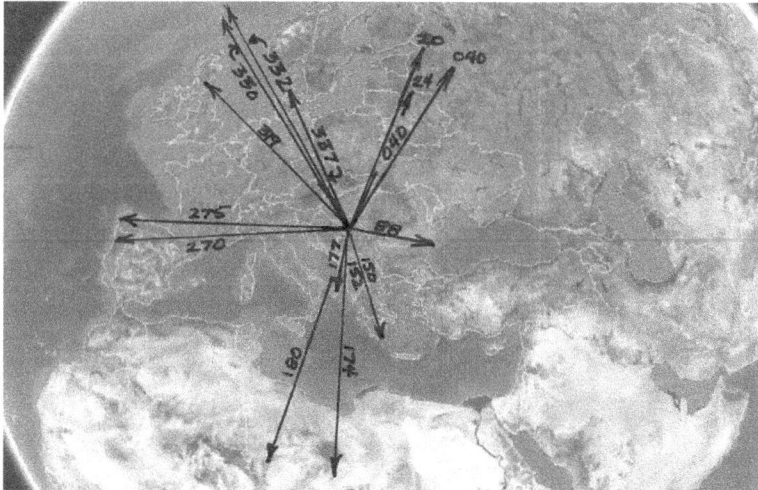

Bearings associated with the geoglyph on top of the Moon Pyramid (the 332- and 330-degree radials point to the north and south tip of the Shetland Islands)

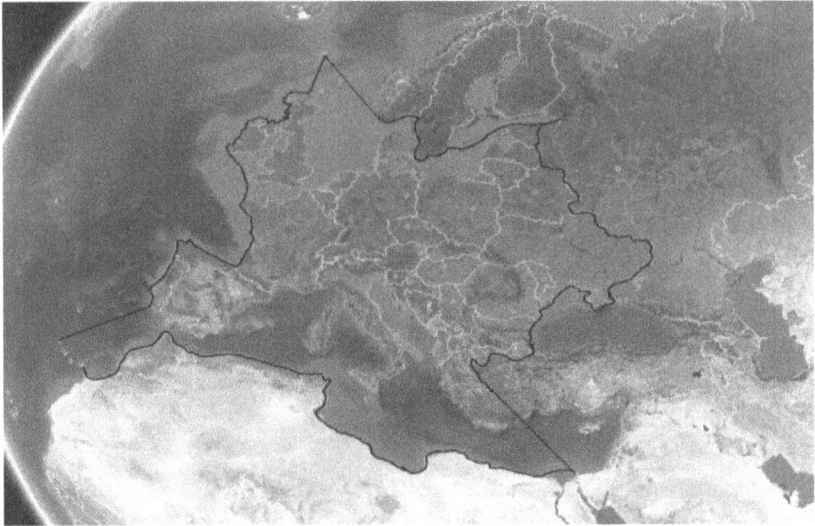

Territory defined by the two geoglyphs on top of the Bosnian pyramids

Notice that the territory not only includes Europe, as defined by the Bosnian Pyramid geoglyphs, but also includes what we now know as Celtic territory in Western Europe. The territory outlined here represents the pinnacle of the Celtic empire.

After WWII Russia invaded and captured much of Eastern Europe. Is it just a coincidence that when the Cold War was over, Russia retreated back to the exact boundary established ca. 31,000 BCE by the Bosnian pyramid geoglyphs?

Border Markings, Identified by the Pyramid Radials, Located on the Russian/European Border

Russia/European border marker 1

Russian/European border marker 2 (notice the Celtic cross)

End Narrative A

Narrative B

The Indonesian Pyramids, Java

Around the world there are thousands of pyramids, monoliths, and geoglyphs that, when the ancient science of geoglyphology is applied, form a network of territories that interlock like a puzzle. These territories are validated by the fact that they outline many countries that still follow their ancient boundaries. Research has shown that originally very large territories were defined by these geoglyphs and monoliths. As time passed and history dictated, many of these vast territories were subdivided into smaller parcels. These subdivisions tend to tell a story of historical progression that is not available from other sources. A short but informative article on geoglyphology can be found in narrative P for those desiring more information on geoglyphology.

The purpose of this narrative is to show that the Yonaguni pyramid, the Indonesian pyramids, and many points around the world are all tied together in a larger network that has been with us since the beginning of civilization. It must be remembered that even though a monolith or geoglyph points to a location where another geoglyph or monolith exists, it does not mean that they are age related. For example, you will see the twenty-thousand-year-old Sadahurip pyramid in Indonesia pointing to Caral, Peru, a five-thousand-year-old geoglyphical structure. One would have to ask how it can be possible that the pointer is older than the subject. The reason for this is that for thousands of years before any of these objects were created, these were sacred locations on which a structure may or may not have existed before. The same is true of the Newport Tower, Rhode Island, United States, location. The existing structure there was built only four to five hundred years ago. However, many ancient geoglyphs, some thousands of years old, point to that spot as an important location.

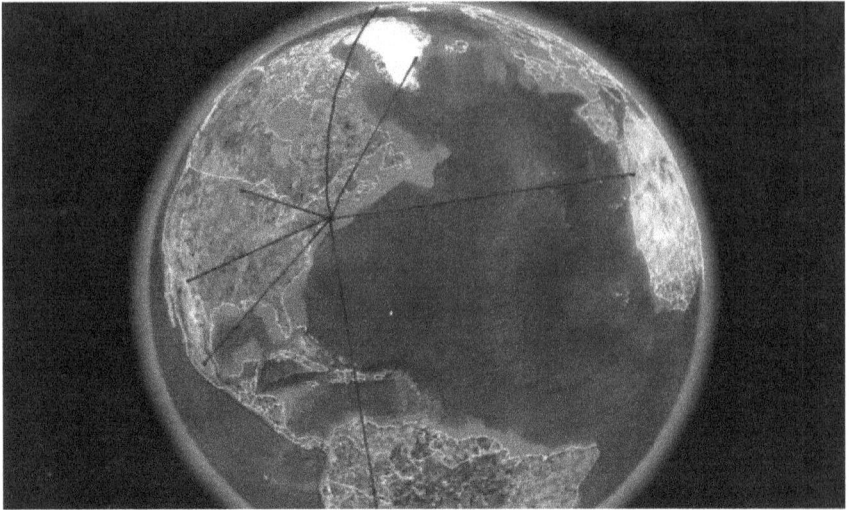

Known ancient geoglyphs that point to the Newport, Rhode Island, tower location

The Pyramids of Java, Indonesia

Map of Indonesia, with the Java pyramid area in the grey portion of the bottom string of islands.

Sadahurip pyramid, West Java, ca. 20,000 BCE

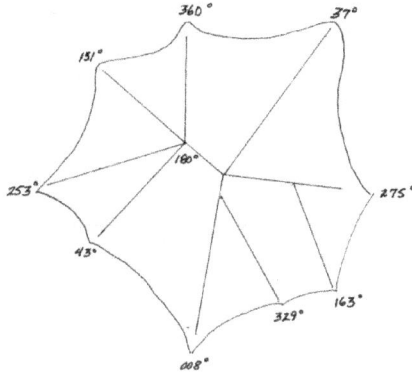

The Faram Research Foundation

Sadahurip pyramid ridges determined by a topographical survey.

Sadahurip pyramid radials and end points:

Upper Left—Western boundary of what is now the United States. This point is also identified by Stonehenge. Even though the rest of the US boundary has been modified several times, this point has remained as the western end of what became the US territorial boundary for over 20000 years.

Newport Tower—An important geoglyph in defining the later US boundaries. (See narrative N.)

Upper Right—Cape Hatteras

293

Chichen Itza—The main focus of the Mayan civilization and a defining point between the Aztec and Mayan territories.

The Two Sadahurip Pointers between Panama and Columbia—This was the original boundary between the Celtic/Templar and the Portuguese territory, prior to Mesoamerica being given to Spain. This exchange happened during the war between Spain and the Moors, which ended in 1492 CE. Portugal, the Celtic Templars, and Spain were allies during this Iberian war against the Moors. The real reason for the voyage of Columbus was to place geoglyphs (survey markers) in the Caribbean to establish Spain's claim to Mesoamerica. (See *La Merica* 2013).

The Red Line between Florida and Baja California—This is the boundary between the United States and Mesoamerica after Mesoamerica was given to Spain. This boundary was later changed by the Mexican–American War.

The Red Line That Crosses Panama—The northern boundary of Portuguese South America, as defined by the Caral, Peru, geoglyph.

Caral, Peru, ca. 5000 BCE—The Temple of Caral and its many angles are the geoglyph that defines the territory claimed by the predecessors of the Portuguese. This territory was handed down through the Phoenicians and Etruscans to the Portuguese. (See Narrative G.)

The Lalakon Pyramid, Java, Indonesia

The Lalakon pyramid, ca. 20,000 BCE

The Lalakon pyramid bearings

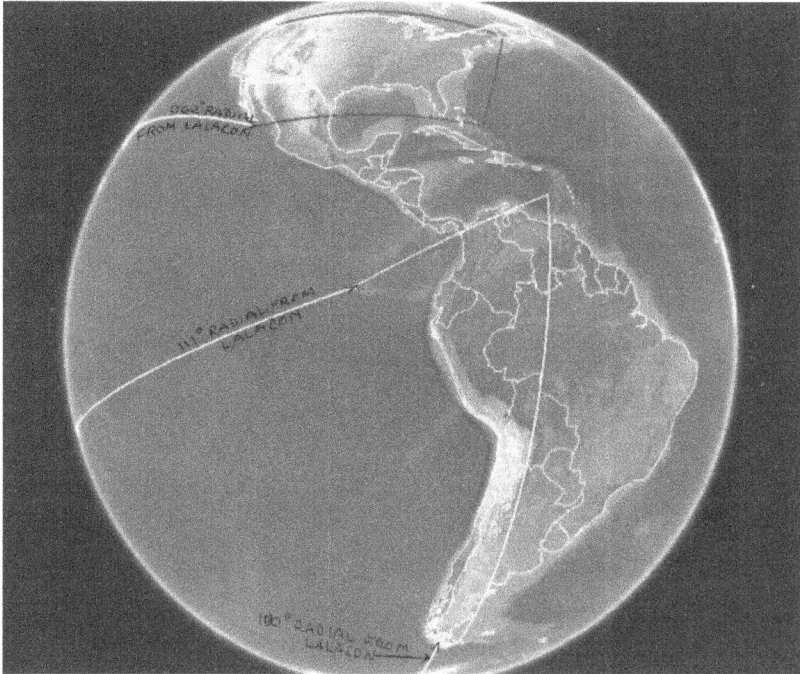

Google Earth – The Faram Research Foundation
The Lalakon pyramid radials

Notice that there are three radials that enter from the left. Those are three of the four radials generated by the Lalakon pyramid. Based on a totally separate set of geoglyphs, there are three territories shown above. They are the Templar/Freemason territory in black (North America), the Spanish territory in red (Mesoamerica), and the Portuguese territory in magenta (South America). This is a snapshot ca. 1500 CE. As mentioned before, the Lalakon radials are older than any structures or geoglyphs that currently exist on the sacred sites which Lalakon designates. The 298-degree radial, not shown, points to the Canary Islands in the Atlantic. The Canary Islands appear in most Portuguese/Celtic world geoglyphs as the southernmost point in their territory.

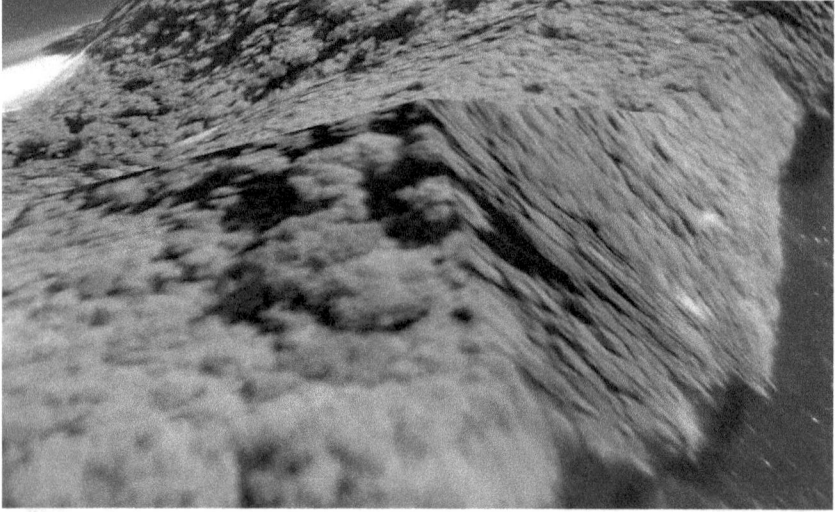

A new pyramid discovered in Indonesia, using geoglyphology

This pyramid was discovered by following one of the radials created by the Nan Madol geoglyphs in the Pacific.

It is clear that the ancient science of geoglyphology can be used to discover many aspects of the Old World not available from other sources.

End Narrative B

Narrative C

The Moscow Geoglyph, Russia, ca. 9500 BCE

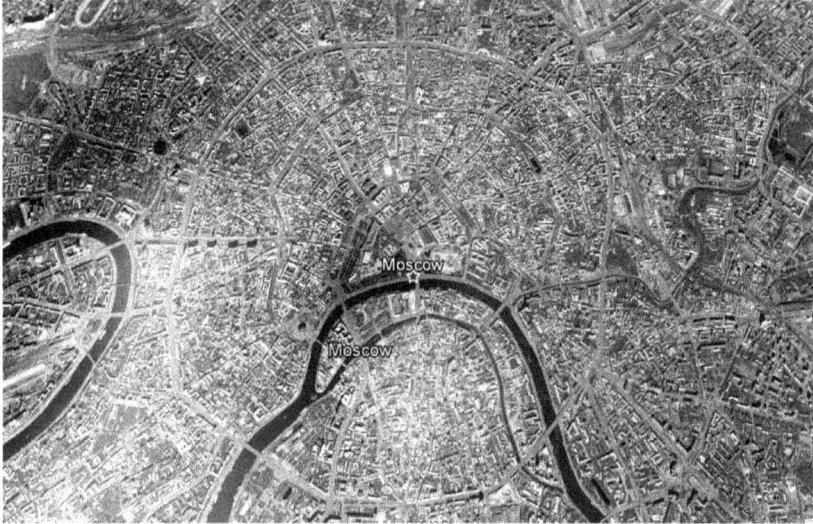

Google Earth – The Faram Research Foundation
Moscow street geoglyph

As is common in many other cities around the world, Washington, DC, for instance, the streets of Moscow form a geoglyph. The bearings of the streets, when extended, meet the protocols established by the ancients in the science of geoglyphology. As is common in many past surveys, the modern streets of Moscow most likely mimic an ancient geoglyph located in the same spot when the current city was built.

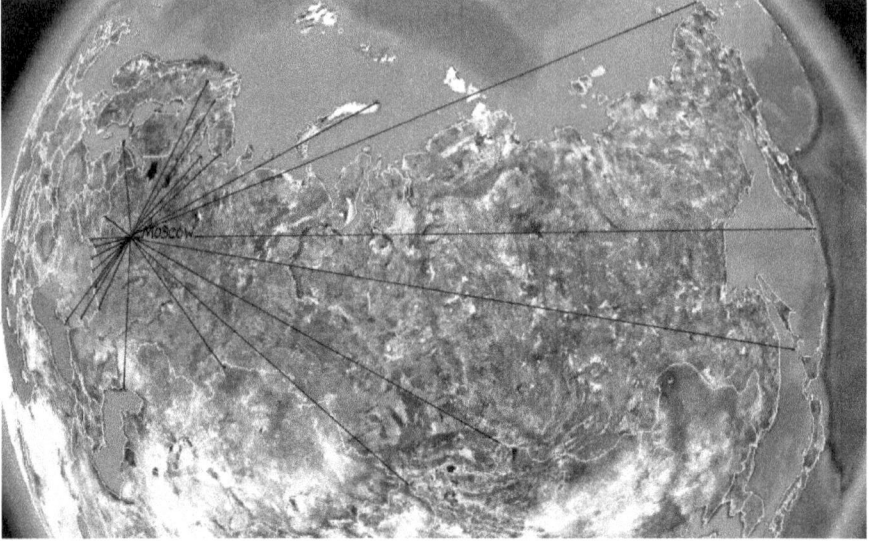

Moscow street geoglyph radial end points

Notice that the end points of the radials in western Russia follow the same border as Europe. (See Narrative A.) This means that the border between Europe and Russia was established at least thirty-one thousand years ago. It should be noted that this is the same boundary to which the Russians retreated after the Cold War.

End Narrative C

Narrative D

Gobekli Tepe, Turkey, ca. 10,000 BCE

Gobekli Tepe amulet with the tree of life and four-sided cross

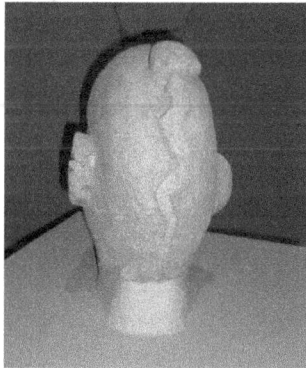

Gobekli Tepe head with sacred snake effigy

The snake, turtle, and several other symbols were sacred to the ancient spiritualists. In 300 CE the snake was demonized by the new Catholic Bible so as to be shunned by all who should dare to venerate it.

Ancient-Code

Gobekli Tepe arena, with seating all around

The pillars of pit D

The pillars at Gobekli Tepe point to specific geoglyphological spots in order to outline the territory allotted to the site by the ancients.

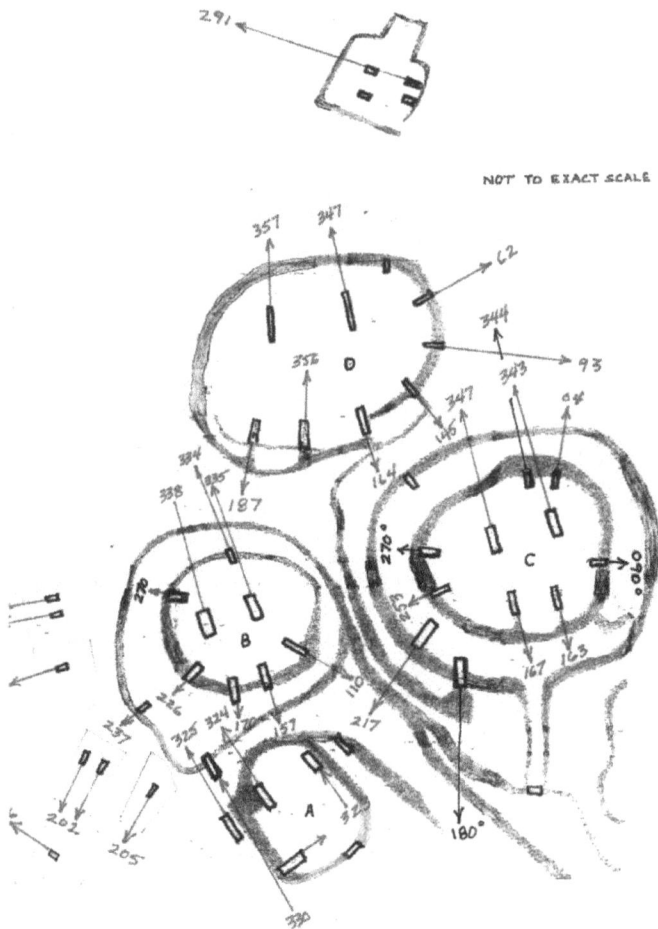

NOT TO EXACT SCALE

QCBERLI TEPE   37 13 22N 38 55 20E

The Faram Research Foundation

The bearings generated by the pillars of pits A–D

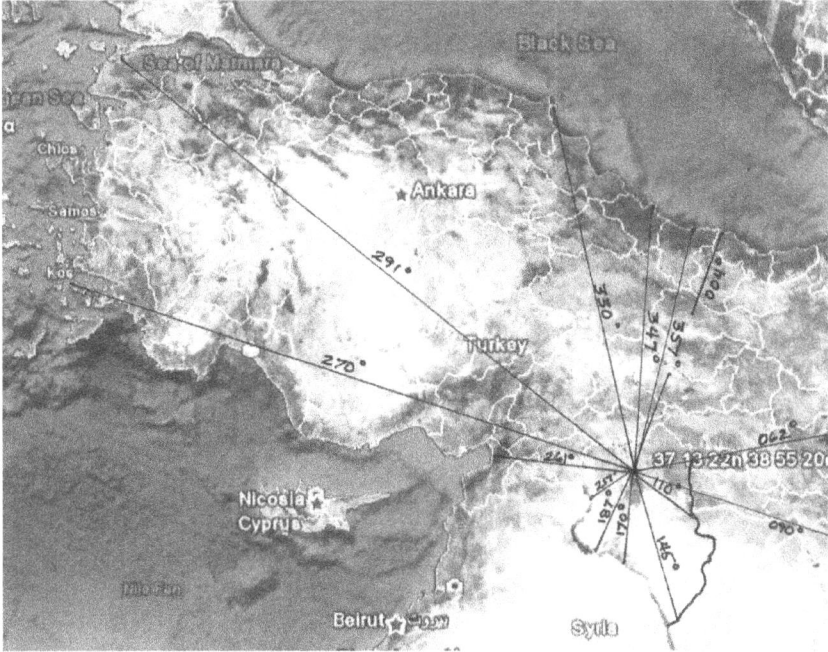

The territory outlined by the radials generated by the currently exposed Gobekli Tepe stone pillars

The Turkish peninsula has played a large part in the history of ancient secrets. Many cultures that possessed ancient knowledge passed through here, all leaving their mark on the landscape.

End Narrative D

Narrative E

The Yonaguni Pyramid, Japan, ca. 8000 BCE

Graham Hancock

The Yonaguni monolith/pyramid

Location

The Yonaguni pyramid is located just off shore on the south side of Yonaguni Island. Yonaguni-Jima is one of the Yaeyama Islands and the westernmost inhabited island of Japan. It is the last of the islands in the Ryukyu Islands chain and lies 108 kilometers (67 miles) from the east coast of Taiwan, between the East China Sea and the Pacific Ocean.

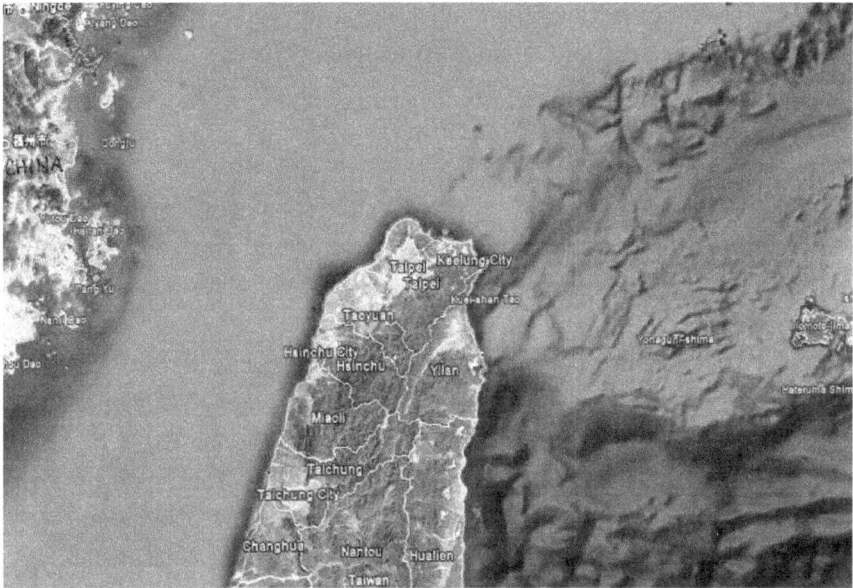

Yonaguni location, east of Taiwan

Geography

Taiwan is said to be visible from Yonaguni's Cape Irizaki on a clear day. The island is part of the Japanese archipelago and exists more than 640 miles from Kyushu, while only sixty-seven miles east of Taiwan.

History

During the last Ice Age, Yonaguni was part of the Chinese mainland. In the twelfth century, it was incorporated to the Ryukyu kingdom. In the seventeenth century, it was incorporated into the Japanese Han of Satsuma. By 1879 the island was formally incorporated into Japan.

Until the early twentieth century, Yonaguni was part of the larger Yaeyama village, which included the neighboring Yaeyama Islands. In 1948, it became an independent village. From 1945 to

1972, it was occupied by the United States and was then returned to Japan to form a part of Okinawa Prefecture.

The Yonaguni Pyramid/Monolith

In the 1980s, local divers discovered a striking underwater rock formation off the southernmost point of the island. This so-called Yonaguni pyramid has staircase-like terraces with flat sides and sharp corners.

The sea off Yonaguni is a popular diving location. Its popularity stems from its large population of hammerhead sharks. In 1987, while looking for a good place to observe the sharks, Kihachiro Aratake, a director of the Yonaguni-Cho Tourism Association, noticed some singular seabed formations resembling archaeological structures. Shortly thereafter, a group of scientists directed by Masaaki Kimura of the University of the Ryukyus visited the formations. Kimura is a strong advocate of the supposition that the formations are man-made.

While Kimura maintains that the site is evidence for an advanced prehistoric civilization, others argued that the structure was the result of natural phenomena. Research in the ensuing years has arrived at a consensus that the structure is indeed a man-made monolith carved from a natural formation.

The formation has since become a relatively popular attraction for divers, in spite of the strong currents. In 1997, Japanese industrialist Yasuo Watanabe sponsored an informal expedition comprising writers John Anthony West and Graham Hancock, photographer Santha Faiia, geologist Dr. Robert Schoch, a few sport divers and instructors, and a shooting crew for British Channel 4 and The Discovery Channel. Another notable visitor was free diver Jacques Mayol, who wrote a book on his dives at Yonaguni. A plaque in his honor was fixed to the undersea formations after his suicide in 2001.

Topography

The monument consists of medium to very fine sandstones and mudstones deposited about twenty million years ago. Most of the significant Yonaguni formations seem to be carved from one underlying rock mass. The flat parallel faces, sharp edges, and right and precise obtuse angles of the formation would indicate that the monolith was carved by man.

Other evidence, presented by those who consider the formation to be man-made, includes two round holes on the edge of the Triangle Pool feature. There also exists a straight row of smaller holes that have been interpreted as an abandoned attempt to split off a section of the rock by means of wedges, as in ancient quarries. Kimura has identified traces of drawings of animals and people engraved on the rocks, including a horse-like sign that he believes resembles a character from the Kaida script. Some have also interpreted a formation on the side of one of the monuments as a crude, Moai-like "face."

Supporters of the man-made origin also argue that, while many of the features seen at Yonaguni are also seen in natural sandstone formations throughout the world, the concentration of so many peculiar formations in such a small area is highly unlikely. They also point to the relative absence of loose blocks on the flat areas of the formation, which would be expected if they were formed solely by natural erosion and fracturing.

If any part of the monument was deliberately constructed or modified, it must have happened during the last Ice Age (ca. 12,000 BCE) when the sea level was much lower than it is today. During the Ice Age, the East China Sea was a narrow bay opening to the ocean at today's Tokara Gap. The Sea of Japan was an inland sea, and there was no Yellow Sea. People and animals could walk into the Ryukyu peninsula from the continent. Therefore, Yonaguni was the southern end of a land bridge that connected it to Taiwan, Ryukyu, Japan, and Asia.

The existence of an ancient stone-working tradition at Yonaguni and other Ryukyu islands is demonstrated by some old tombs and several stone vessels of uncertain age. The Yonaguni Monument is important in Graham Hancock's documentary *Quest for the Lost Civilization*. The monument was featured on episodes of *Ancient Aliens* and *History's Mysteries*, both on the History Channel.

In an interview, Professor Kimura was asked whether the ruins were artificial, and in what time period they were built.

"These are ruins, and to me, the fact has already been proved. The scientific conclusion is that the ruins are indeed artificial [man-made]. The School of Japanese Marine Geologists agreed on this outcome. We found that the ruins are at least six thousand years old. It could go back another four thousand years when we consider the length of time before they sank into the water.

During the past ten thousand years, the ocean water level rose about forty meters. From this fact, it is only natural to think that many ancient civilizations are now deep underwater. Professor Kimura states that even though there is scientific evidence to explain the ruins, it might be difficult to come to an agreement with the archaeologists, as doing so changes history.

Yonaguni pyramid model

310

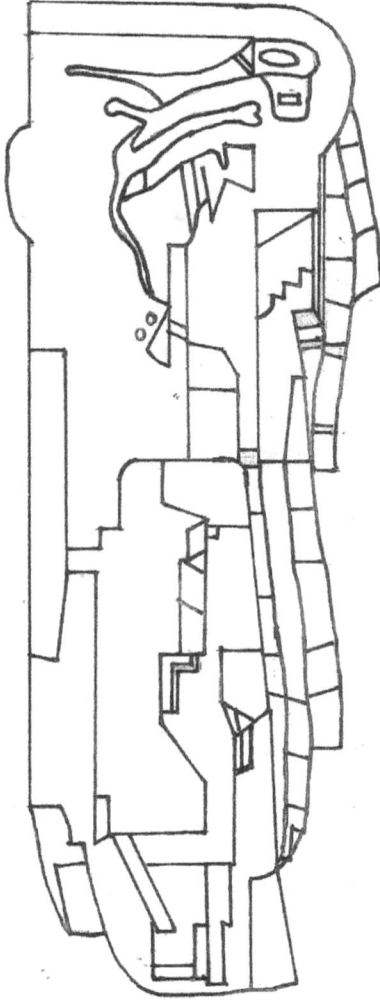

The Faram Research Foundation

Yonaguni pyramid view from above

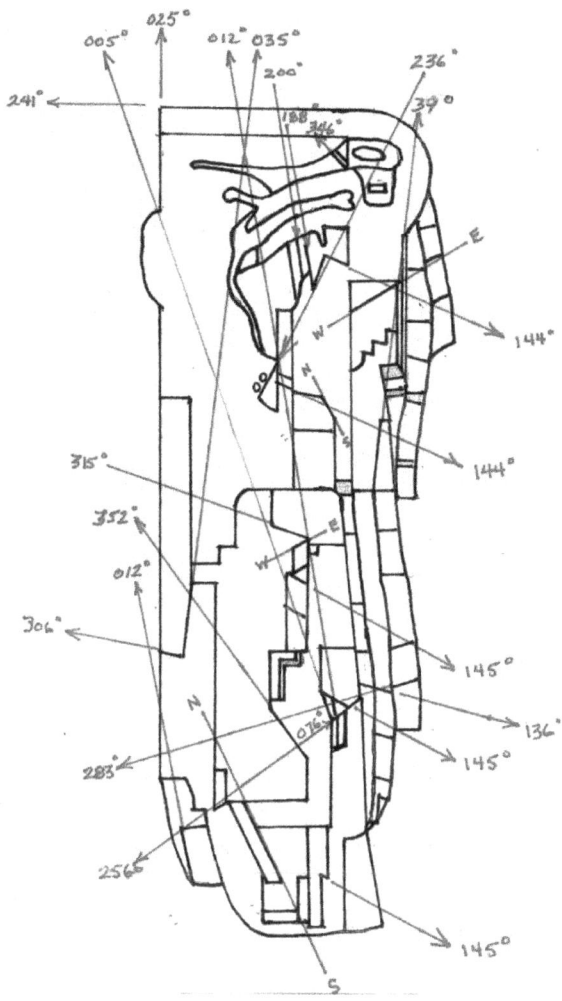

Note: Not to scale

The Faram Research Foundation

The bearings projected using the angles on the Yonaguni geoglyph

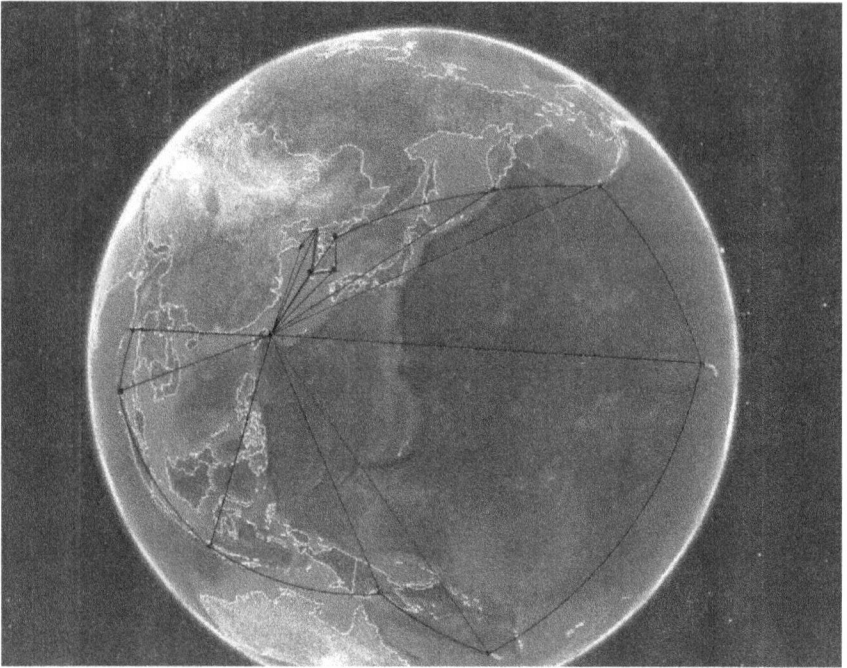

The territory outlined by the radials of the Yonaguni geoglyph

End points for the radials displayed in the above photo:

005-Degree Radial - Northwest tip of the Korean peninsula

012-Degree Radial - West side of Korea

013-Degree Radial - Northeast corner of the Korean peninsula

025-Degree Radial - East side of Korea

035-Degree Radial - Southern tip of Kamchatka peninsula, Russia/northern tip of the Japanese island string

039-Degree Radial - Attu Island, Alaska

076-Degree Radial - Hawaiian Islands

135-Degree Radial - Northern tip of New Caledonia

144-Degree Radial - South coast of Papua New Guinea

187-Degree Radial - West tip of Sumbawa Island

200-Degree Radial - South coast of Java

231-Degree Radial - The southern islands of Sumatra

239-Degree Radial - Banda Aceh, northern tip of Sumatra Island
241-Degree Radial - The lost geoglyphs of Fongbin, Taiwan
257-Degree Radial - Southern tip of Burma
283-Degree Radial - The geoglyphs and rock terracing, similar to Yonaguni, at Nanridao Island, China coast
306-Degree Radial - Bitou Point, north tip of Taiwan, both old and updated geoglyphs
315-Degree Radial - The glyphs at Fushancun, China coast. This glyph points to the northwest corner of the Korean peninsula and Fiji
346-Degree Radial - The many geoglyphs of Zhoushan Island, China coast

As with so many other geoglyphs around the world, the end points circumscribe the boundaries of what appears to be a territory or land claim. After the boundaries circumscribed by the Yonaguni geoglyph were plotted, it was noticed that the territory looked very familiar. After some research it was discovered that the territory outlined by the Yonaguni monolith matched the territory the Japanese conquered and occupied during WWII. It would appear that the Japanese were attempting to regain some ancient territory they had claimed thousands of years ago.

The Yonaguni geoglyph mimics many other ancient geoglyphs around the world that described territories, many of which are still honored to this day. Most of geoglyphs in this category originated around 8000–10,000 BCE. Based on initial investigations, it would seem that some entity awarded various peoples set boundaries within which they were to populate, grow, and prosper. What reinforces the belief that these were coordinated territories is that fact the original ancient territories fit together like a puzzle.

There is another fact that confirms that the Japanese were attempting to reclaim lost territory. In WWII the Japanese actually attacked and occupied Attu Island, at the tip of the Aleutian Islands in Alaska, even though it was of no use to them. Many have wondered to this day why that was done. If they were attempting to restore ancient boundaries, this would explain that seemingly irrational move. The land was retaken by the US Army in the Battle of Attu. Attu Island also shows up as the northern tip of the Easter Island geoglyph.

Google

The territory held by Japan during WWII
(Attu Island at the top)

The Fongbin, Taiwan, Geoglyphs
While plotting any geoglyph, it is our practice to search the destination point for other geoglyphs. There were several found using the Yonaguni radials; however, the most interesting were two geoglyphs, located together, that seem to be a precursor to the Yonaguni geoglyph. The two appear to have been constructed at

different periods in time and seem to have much in common with Yonaguni.

These geoglyphs were discovered by following the 241-degree radial from Yonaguni to the coast of Taiwan at a place named Fongbin.

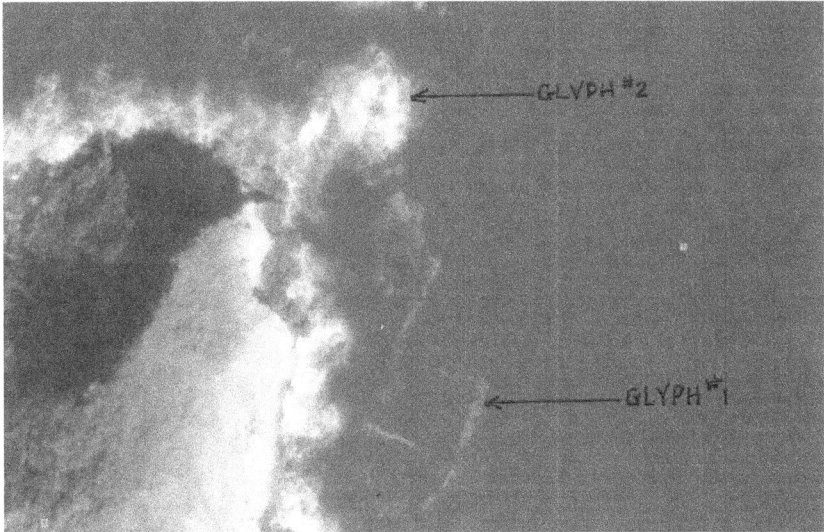

Google Earth – The Faram Research Foundation
The lost geoglyphs of Fongbin, Taiwan

As you can see from the list of radials emanating from the Yonaguni pyramid, the 241-degree radial points to a spot on the east coast of Taiwan known as Fongbin. In the photo above, you can see that these glyphs, like Yonaguni, are also covered by water. Interestingly enough, the Fongbin glyphs appear to circumscribe territories also.

From the islands identified by the Fongbin geoglyphs, it appears that they may have been built earlier than the Yonaguni glyph and therefore describe smaller territories. It is possible that the second Fongbin glyph was made to claim islands discovered after the first geoglyph was laid down.

Fongbin Geoglyph 1

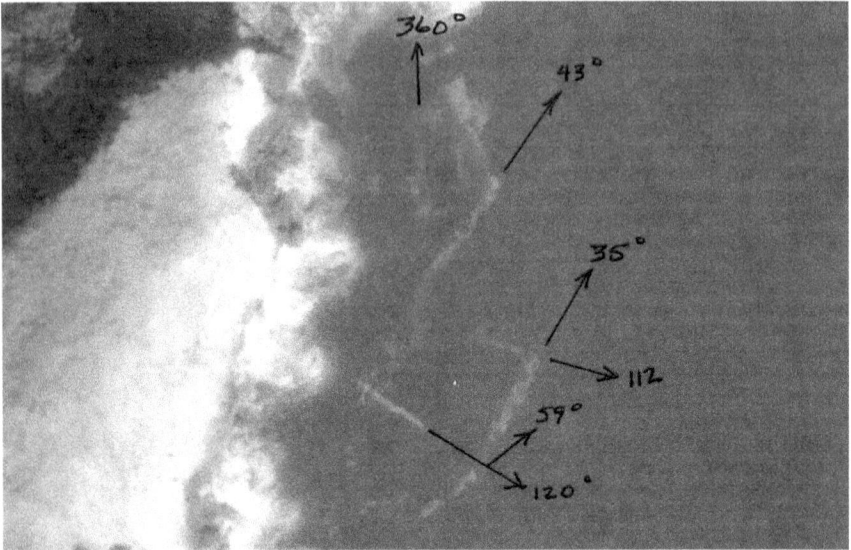

Bearings created by Fongbin glyph 1

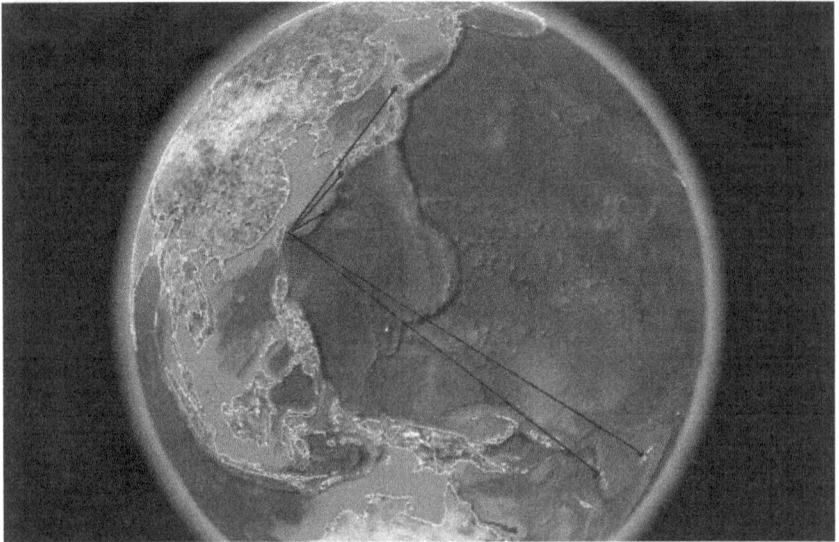

Radial end points of Fongbin glyph 1

317

End points for the radials displayed in the previous image:

035-Degree Radial - North tip of Japan

043-Degree Radial - South tip of Japan

059-Degree Radial - Okinawan Islands

112-Degree Radial - Samoa

120-Degree Radial - Fiji

Based on research, the type of geoglyphs used in glyph 1 above are from an earlier period than the ones used in glyph 2, which appears next.

Fongbin Geoglyph 2

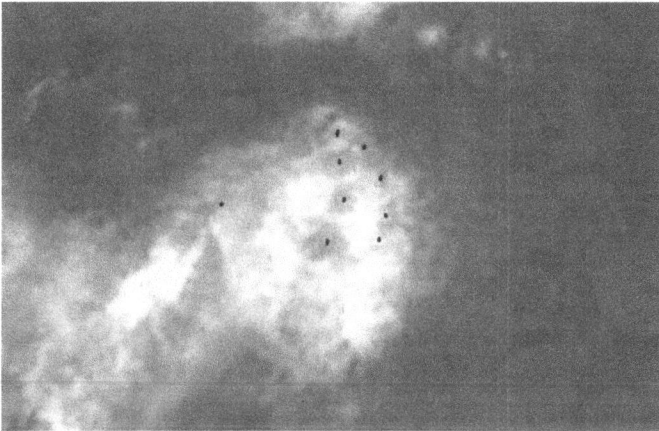

Google Earth – The Faram Research Foundation

Ground reference points that comprise Fongbin glyph 2

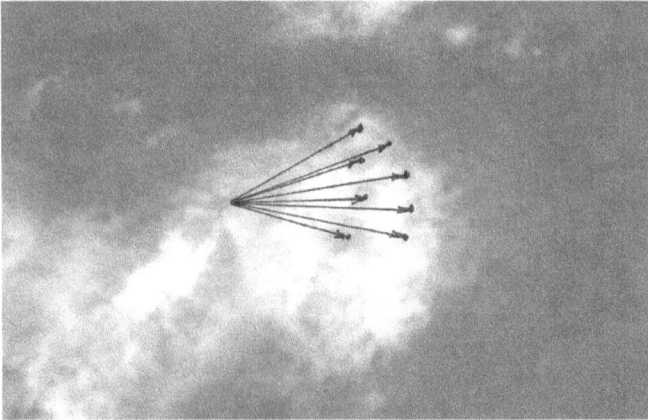

Bearings generated by Fongbin glyph 2

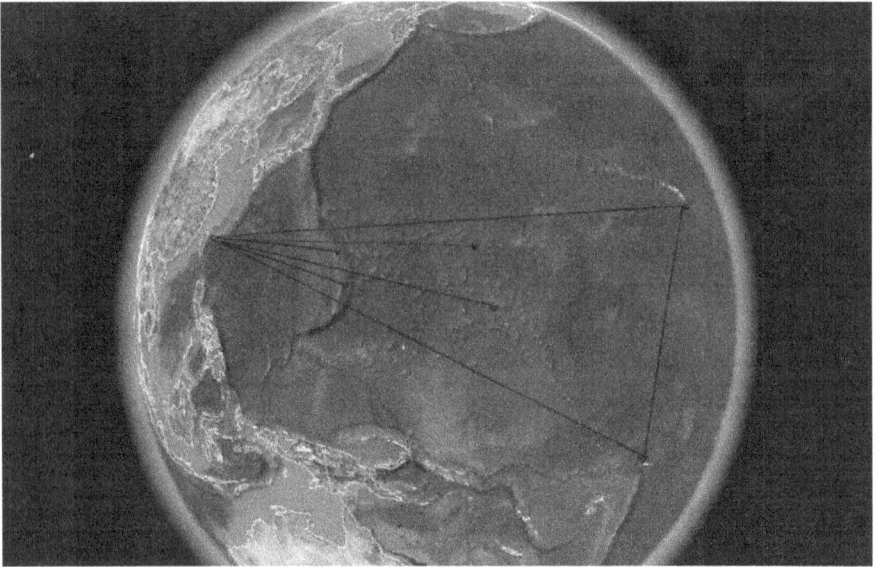

Radial end points of Fongbin glyph 2

End points for the bearings displayed in the above photo:
064-Degree Radial - Okinawa
075-Degree Radial - Hawaii

087-Degree Radial - Wake Island
092-Degree Radial - Kiribati (Christmas Island)
101-Degree Radial - Marshall Islands
110-Degree Radial - Guam
112-Degree Radial - Samoa

The above glyph consists of what is called a glyph array. It consists of a center point surrounded by points through which bearings can be calculated by drawing a line from the center point through the surrounding points. The discovery of the Fongbin geoglyphs, along with the Yonaguni geoglyph, appears to indicate additional exploration and expanding territorial boundaries over time, culminating in the larger territory defined by the Yonaguni geoglyph.

The Phallics of Yonaguni

Note: Not to scale

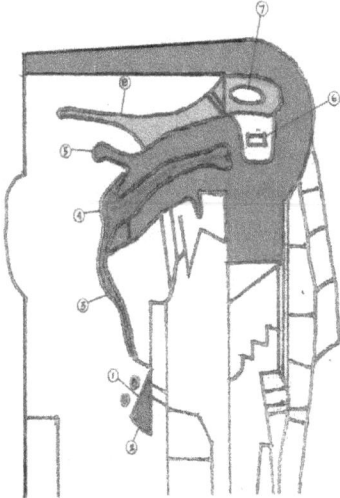

The Faram Research Foundation

The sculpture on the north end of the Yonaguni monolith

Needless to say it was a surprise to see a phallic sculpture depicted on a ten-thousand-year-old monolith. The glyph is obviously a depiction of the male and female reproductive systems. After studying the artwork, I came to the conclusion that the monolith, in addition to being a world-class survey marker, must have also been used as a ceremonial location. It appears that the purple area and the green areas were carved out as corridors where one or two people could walk. If this was the case, and based on the layout of the carving, the following scenario is proposed.

A person, presumably a man, enters the maze between the granite balls (1), representing the testicles, and enters the sunken triangular pool (2), representing the prostate, and bathes. He then walks down the corridor symbolizing the vas deferens (3) and enters the penis (4), walking past a representation of the female clitoris (5). The penis terminates at what looks like a ceremonial altar (6). At some time during the ritual, another individual, presumably a woman, would enter the maze at position (8), presumably representing the entrance to the fallopian tube, travel down the tube to position (7), representing the exit from the fallopian tube, and bathe in the sunken bath. The individuals would then meet at the ceremonial altar (6). This would have simulated the complete cycle of conception.

This may mean that this was a ceremonial site, similar to others discovered around the world that also outline ancient territories. These territories may have been the area these people claimed as their own and/or were charged with repopulating. Monoliths around the world indicate that there was an organized effort to repopulate the earth after the last great apocalypse. These ancient territories are mentioned in Plato's work *Critias* (see chapter 7).

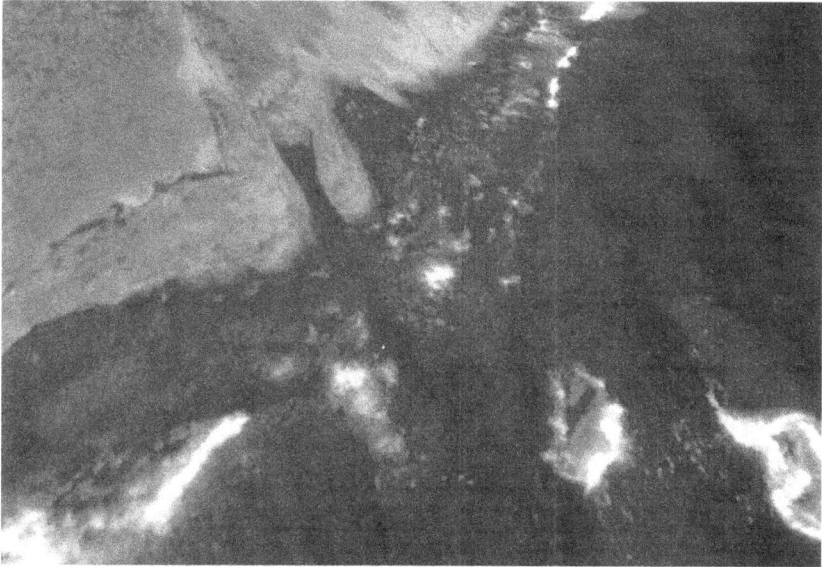

Google Earth – The Faram Research Foundation
The notch above the Yonaguni monolith

The above photo shows a notch carved out of the hill right above the Yonaguni structure. Could this have been a stairway leading down to the ceremonial location? Obviously this raises many interesting questions, not the least of which is how did a ten-thousand-year-old civilization know so much about the human reproductive process, and what was the purpose of the ceremony?

This discovery, when studied alongside the layout of other monoliths around the world, presents an interesting hypothesis. They all seem to share certain common traits that would lead one to believe that they were ceremonial sites, possibly used for fertility rites. Commonalities:

1. Many of the ancient geoglyphs show no signs of human habitation. In other words, there were no signs of burials, tools, or animal bones. This is the case when the site is a ceremonial site and the users of the site live elsewhere.

2. At or near the sites, there appears an altar or circular enclosure that could have been used for a ceremony.

3. Many of the altars or enclosures appear to have been placed to provide vantage points and seating from which others could view the ceremony.

4. Many of the ancient sites are constructed in a manner that forms geoglyphs that appear to outline the boundaries of what may have been an assigned territory.

5. The territorial boundaries of the geoglyphs studied thus far around the world do not appear to overlap. This would give credibility to the argument of a worldwide network with assigned territories somewhere in the ancient past.

Could this be an extremely advanced ancient human culture attempting to repopulate the world after the Ice Age? The gradual expansion of the territory represented by the Fongbin and Yonaguni geoglyphs suggest that the monoliths were built over time. One has to ask how they knew the geography of the earth so well, and how they were able to plot courses halfway around the world with the precision of a GPS.

A possible answer may be explained by the worldwide, prehistorical obsession with astronomy. It is now known that man has been traveling the globe for millennia. It would be self-serving to think that over tens of thousands of years, man could not have gained the astronomical ability and geographic information to map the world. With such knowledge they could have plotted courses and bearings as well as our current global positioning systems do. Barring the intellectual advancement of humans leaves an interesting alternative: Did humans have help?

End Narrative E

Narrative F

The Nabta Playa and Gulfo de Cintra Geoglyphs, Egypt, ca. 7000 BCE

Google – Public Domain

The Nabta Playa geoglyph, Egypt, ca. 7000 BCE

The stone circle at Nabta is special in several ways. First, it is the only reported megalithic circle in Egypt, but perhaps more importantly, it was situated on the Tropic of Cancer (presumably deliberately), which makes it one of the first known examples of an astronomic observatory in the world.

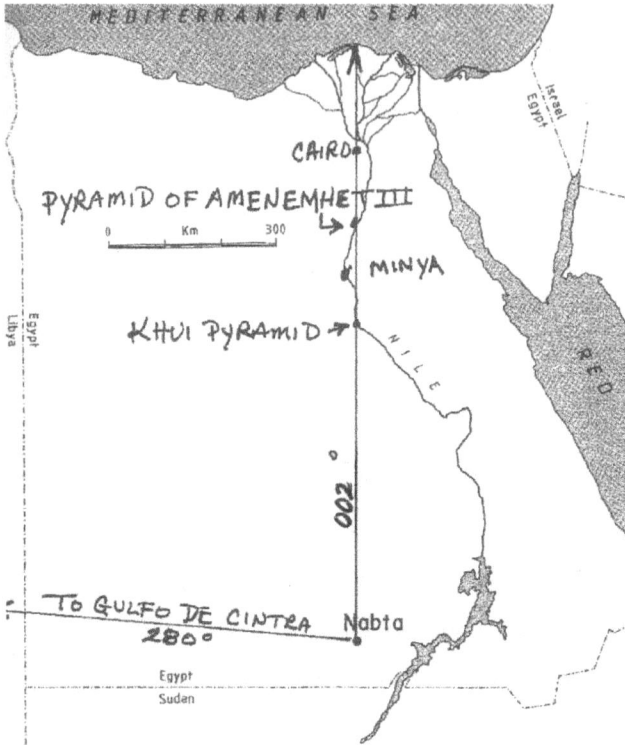

The Nabta Playa location in Egypt

The Faram Research Foundation

Located one hundred kilometers west of Abu Simbel in southernmost Egypt, Nabta Playa is a large, internally drained basin that, during the early Holocene Period (ca. 8000–3500 BCE) was a large and important ceremonial center for prehistoric people. It was intermittently and seasonally filled with water, which encouraged people to come there. Today it contains dozens, perhaps hundreds, of archaeological sites. People came from many regions to Nabta Playa to record astronomical events, erect alignments of megaliths, and build impressive stone structures.

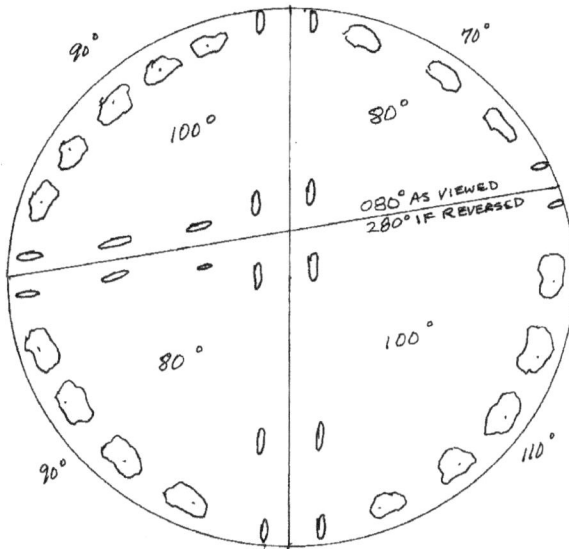

A Drawing of the Nabta Playa Stone Circle as seen from above

The Faram Research Foundation

"This is the oldest documented astronomical alignment of megaliths in the world," said archaeoastronomer J. M. Malville, quoted in Mwt Seshatms Nkatraet Ma'Atnefert. "A lot of effort went into the construction of a purely symbolic and ceremonial site. The stone slabs, some of which are nine feet high, were dragged to the site from a mile or more distant.

The ruins lie on the shoreline of an ancient lake that began filling with water about eleven thousand years ago when the African summer monsoon shifted north. It was used by nomads until about 4,800 years ago, when the monsoon moved southwest and the area again became "hyper arid and uninhabitable."

Five megalithic alignments at Nabta radiate outward from a central collection of megalithic structures. Beneath one structure was a sculptured rock resembling a cow standing upright, Malville said.

326

The team also excavated several cattle burials at Nabta, including an articulated skeleton buried in a roofed, clay-lined chamber.

Neolithic herders that began coming to Nabta about ten thousand years ago, probably from central Africa, used cattle in their rituals just as the African Masai do today, Malville said. No human remains have yet been found at Nabta. (Author's note: As mentioned previously, ceremonial sites seldom have signs of human habitation.)

The twelve-foot-diameter stone circle contains four sets of upright slabs. Two sets were aligned in a north–south direction, while the second pair of slabs provides a line of sight toward the summer solstice horizon.

Because of Nabta's proximity to the Tropic of Cancer, the noon sun is at its zenith about three weeks before and three weeks after the summer solstice, preventing upright objects from casting shadows. "These vertical sighting stones in the circle correspond to the zenith sun during the summer solstice," said Malville. "For many cultures in the tropics, the zenith sun has been a major event for millennia."

An east–west alignment also is present between one megalithic structure and two stone megaliths about a mile distant. There also are two other geometric lines involving about a dozen additional stone monuments that lead both north–east and south–east from the same megalith. We still don't understand the significance of these lines," Malville said.

The Gulfo de Cintra Geoglyph

Although the recently discovered Nabta Playa geoglyph contained astronomical attributes, it has been the noted that most geoglyphs contain both an astronomical and a geoglyphological component.

As we surveyed the Nabta Playa geoglyph, we could not find the surveyed components that met the protocols set down by the ancients for the science of geoglyphology. It was then that we decided to flip the geoglyph over and see if that would provide a solution. This has only been necessary two previous times, one of which was the Mexico City geoglyph, which existed at the time Cortes invaded Mexico City.

Sure enough, flipping the geoglyph worked. Now, instead of the east/west radial reading 80 degrees, the radial now read 280 degrees. Following the 280-degree radial west takes us directly at the Gulfo de Cintra geoglyphs.

The Gulfo de Cintra geoglyphs are so remote, they would have never been located without the application of the geoglyphology contained in the Nabta Playa geoglyphs. These geoglyphs are important for many reasons:

1. They prove that there was a worldwide network nine thousand years ago.

2. They prove that the location of the Sphnix was an important location nine thousand years ago. (Note: The geoglyph could not have been pointing to the city of Cairo, nor the pyramid of Giza since neither had been built yet.)

3. These geoglyphs further validate that geoglyphological protocols have been passed down through the ages.

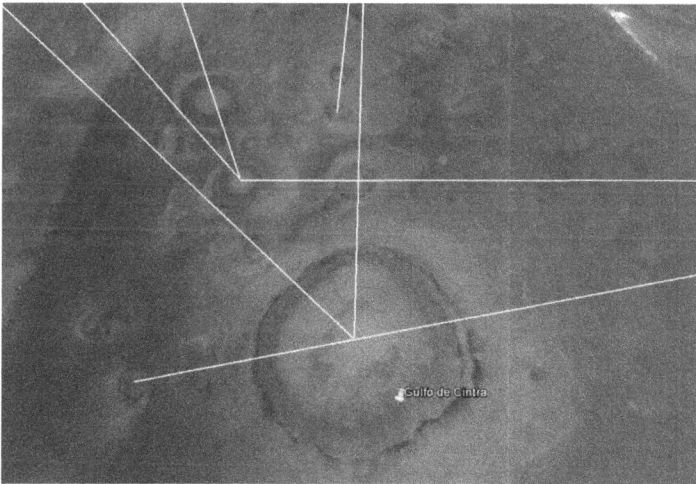

Google Earth – The Faram Research Foundation
The Gulfo De Cintra geoglyph bearings

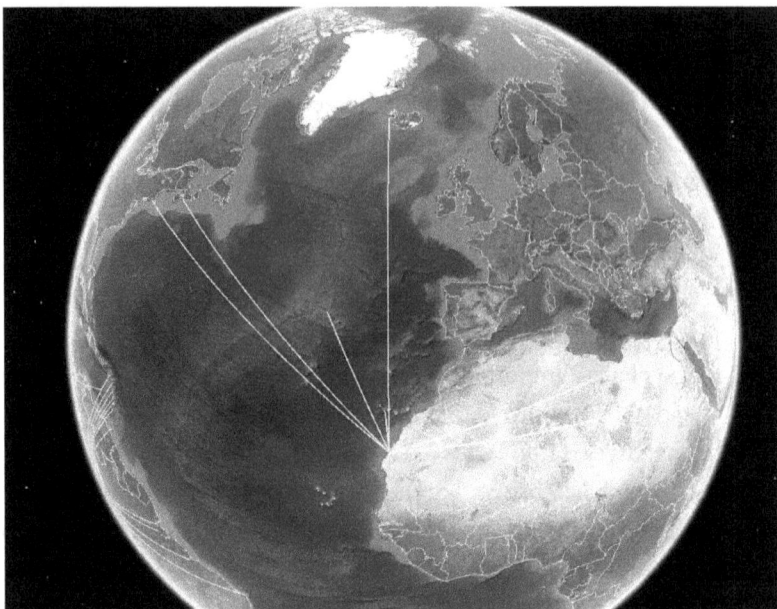

The Gulfo de Cintra Radials

End points of the Gulfo de Cintra Geoglyph:

1.) Newport, RI USA

2.) Halifax, NS

3.) Snaefellsjokull Volcano, Iceland

4.) The Sphinx

5.) Nabta Playa, Egypt

6.) Gomera, Canary Islands

7.) Santa Barbara Volcano, Azores

The Gulfo de Cintra geoglyph points directly back to Nabta Playa, which in itself is validation that the two are related and that the two geoglyphs have been decoded correctly.

The history associated with the end points in this geoglyph is quite significant. It should be recognized that significant and sacred reference points were established eons ago by the ancients. These points have remained in use down through thousands of years and are still referenced today by informed individuals building geoglyphs. It should be noted that the same cultures that handed down the ancient spirituality also handed down the protocols of geoglyphology and the location of the corresponding end points.

End Narative F

The Caral Geoglyph, Peru, ca. 5000 BCE

On April 27, 2001, the *Journal of Science* printed a stunning announcement. According to Dr. Ruth Shady Solis, "The emergence of urban life and complex agriculture in the New World occurred nearly a millennium earlier than previously believed."

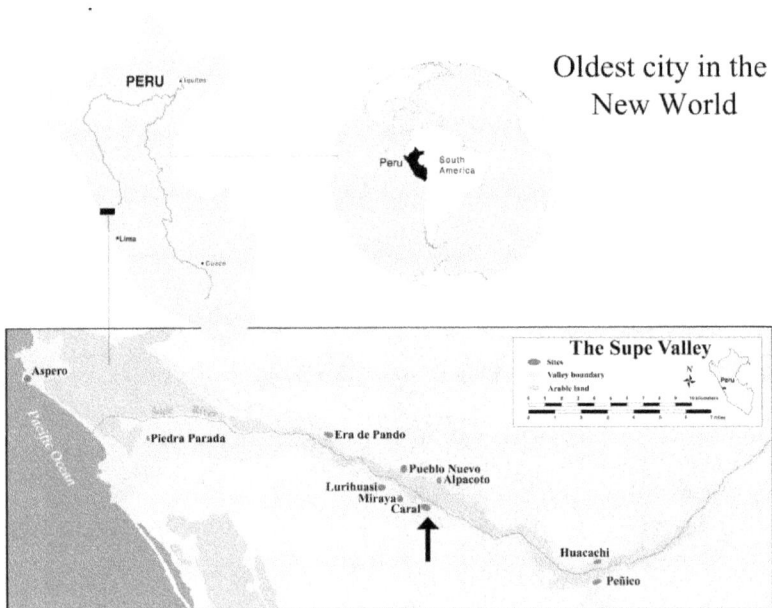

Oldest city in the New World

Map of central zone at Caral. Courtesy of the Field Museum

Radiocarbon dates from the ancient city of Caral, in the Supe Valley of Peru, show that monumental architecture was under construction as early as 2627 BCE until about 2000 BCE. This was even before ceramics and maize were introduced to the region. Also remarkable is the enormous size of the urban complex: sixty-five hectares in the central zone itself, encompassing six large platform mounds (or "pyramids"), many smaller platform mounds, two sunken circular plazas, and diverse architectural features including residential districts. Caral is by far the largest recorded site in the Andean region with dates older than 3000 BCE and appears to be the model for the urban design adopted by Andean civilizations that rose and fell over the span of four millennia.

The Ancient City of Caral and Its Importance
Excavations at Caral have been undertaken by Jonathan Haas from Chicago's Field Museum, Ruth Shady Solis of the Anthropology Museum at the Universidad Nacional Mayor de San Marcos and the Field Museum, and Winifred Creamer, Northern Illinois University and the Field Museum. It was featured in a *Science* article in April 2001, after a long and careful investigation into the radiocarbon dates from the site.

The interesting thing about Caral and the rest of the Supe Valley sites is that it illustrates the problems archaeologists have dealing within so-called "urban settlements" and "state societies." Building monumental architecture such as pyramids and irrigation canals and cities takes sophisticated planning. When archaeologists first came upon the cities of our ancient pasts, they began developing theories of why states rise. One of the most prevalent theories was that it takes a combination of factors to create the political climate that creates public works, and that usually means full-scale agriculture, craft specialization, a writing system, ceramic production, social stratification, even metallurgy.

But the Supe Valley sites, and other early urban settlements such as Catalhoyuk in Turkey ca. 6300–5500 BCE, apparently arose without all of these elements.

Although we can't know the political structure of the people who built Caral, to date, no ceramics, evidence of metallurgy, or writing have been found. Caral was first discovered by archaeologists about 1905 and has been explored only intermittently. Until lately, anthropologists have largely ignored Caral, considering it puzzling, Dr. Haas said.

Pottery has never been found at the site, and its absence would ordinarily suggest that the civilization existed before 1800 BCE. But Dr. Haas said that for many experts the sheer size of the place—and the level of societal complexity that it implies—meant that it had to be newer. The consensus, he said, was that "something that big cannot be that early." So the lack of ceramics, by this way of thinking, was only an anomaly. Since those statements the city of Caral has been carbon-dated to 2627 BCE.

The sacred city of Caral-Supe (Peru), the oldest center of civilization in the Americas, was inscribed on UNESCO's World Heritage List by the World Heritage Committee, chaired by Maria Jesus San Segundo, the ambassador and permanent delegate of Spain to UNESCO.

Geoglyphs of the Ancient City of Caral, Peru

Google Earth – The Faram Research Foundation
The Caral, Peru, complex

The *Science* article (2001, pp. 723–726) further explains,

Caral was inhabited between roughly 2600 BCE and 2000 BCE, enclosing an area of more than sixty hectors. Caral was described by its excavators as the oldest urban center in the Americas, a claim that was later challenged as other ancient sites were found nearby. Accommodating more than three thousand inhabitants, it is now the best studied and one of the largest Norte Chico sites known.

There are over nineteen other pyramid complexes scattered across a thirty-five-square-mile (eighty-square-kilometer) area of the Supe Valley. The date of 2627 BCE is based on carbon-dating reed and woven carrying bags that were found in situ. These bags were used to carry the stones that were used for the construction of the pyramids. The material is an excellent candidate for dating, thus allowing for a high precision. The site may date even earlier, as samples from the oldest parts of the excavation have yet to be dated. The town had a population of approximately three thousand people. But there are nineteen other sites in the area, allowing for a possible total population of twenty thousand people for the Supe Valley. All of these sites in the Supe Valley share similarities with Caral. They had small platforms or stone circles with nonparallel walls. Nonparallel walls of a city are the hallmark of the city being designed to geoglyphically document the territory claimed by the builders. Dr. Shady believes that Caral was the focus of this civilization, which itself was part of an even vaster complex, trading with the coastal communities and the regions further inland—as far as the Amazon.

Dr. Shady's belief in a civilization stretching east to the mouth of the Amazon River is substantiated in this study. Other studies confirm that the civilization, of which Caral was part, used the Amazon River for transportation from its headwaters to the mouth of the river. Interesting is the fact that the world's largest open-pit gold mine lies at the headwaters of the Amazon River. There is a clear path around a mountain from the goldmine to Machu Picchu. Headlines have been appearing recently about geoglyphs being found all through the Amazon jungle as land is cleared for farming.

The Caral complex was split into the five main sections addressed in the following photos. The radials described below the photos are the end points for the given radial.

It is our experience that the creators of geoglyphs will present some sign that verifies that the purpose of a geoglyph was solved correctly. In the case of the Caral glyphs, that verification is the 360/180-degree line that begins in the center of the meteor crater, as defined by the Antilles Islands, and proceeds south in a line that passes through the circle glyph, identified by the Caral 116- and 117-degree radials, and terminates precisely at the tip of South America. By outlining the crater with the Antilles Islands end points, the originators demonstrated not only their accuracy but their knowledge of the topography. Another confirmation is the equilateral triangle formed by the Galapagos Islands, the center of the Columbian meteor crater, and the man-made circle glyph identified by where the Caral 116- and 117-degree radials cross.

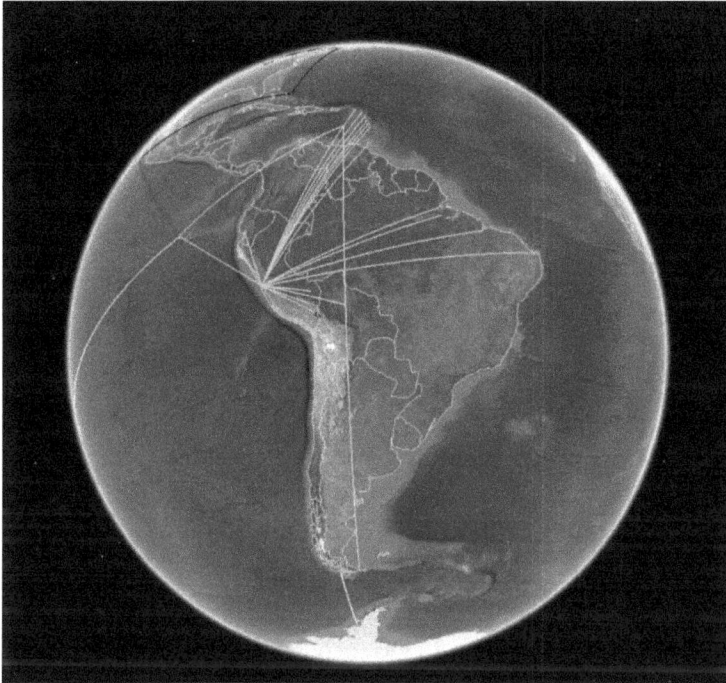

Google Earth – The Faram Research Foundation

Radials defined by the glyphs in the city of Caral

Google Earth – The Faram Research Foundation

Caral, Peru, plate 1, western complex

End points for the bearings displayed in the above photo:
028-Degree Radial - Saint Kitts Island, Antilles
029-Degree Radial - Montserrat Island, Antilles
040-Degree Radial - Entrance to Orinoco River, Venezuela
118-Degree Radial - Headwaters of the Amazon
308-Degree Radial - Galapagos Islands

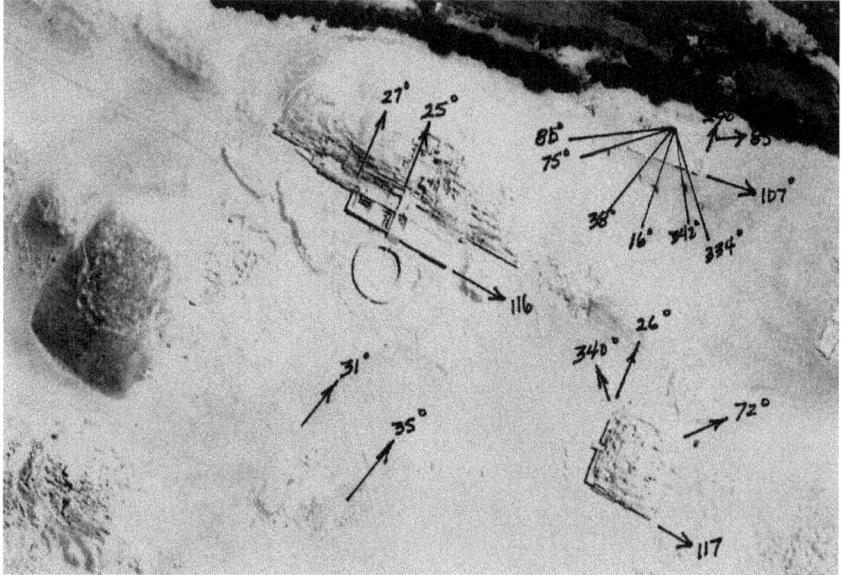

Google Earth – The Faram Research Foundation

Caral, Peru, plate 2, western center complex

End points for the bearings displayed in the above photo:

016-Degree Radial - Dominican Republic

025-Degree Radial - Roques Island, Venezuela

026-Degree Radial - Anguilla Island, Antilles

027-Degree Radial - Saint Kits Island, Antilles

029-Degree Radial - Montserrat Island, Antilles

031-Degree Radial - Dominica Island, Antilles

035-Degree Radial - Granada Island, Antilles

038-Degree Radial - Trinidad Island, Antilles

072-Degree Radial - Entrance to Amazon River, Brazil

075-Degree Radial - The ancient Altamera canals, Amazon, Brazil

085-Degree Radial - East tip of South America

107-Degree Radial - Largest open-pit gold mine in the world
(13°00′36″ S, 70°32′34″ W)

116-Degree Radial - North rim of Santa Rosa geoglyph, Bolivia

117-Degree Radial - South rim of Santa Rosa geoglyph, Bolivia

334-Degree Radial - Entrance to Gulf of Guayaquil, Ecuador

340-Degree Radial - Chichen Itza, Mexico
342-Degree Radial - Puna Island, Gulf of Guayaquil, Ecuador

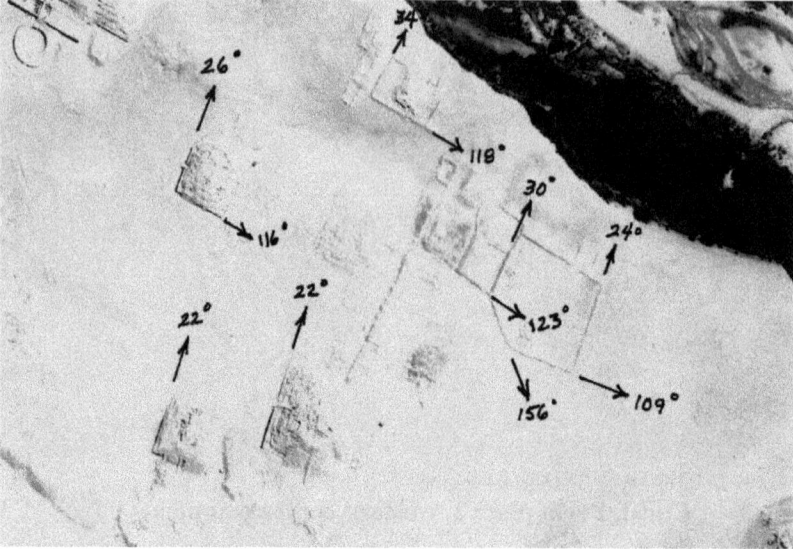

Caral, Peru, plate 3, eastern center complex

End points for the bearings displayed in the preceding photo:

022-Degree Radial - East end of Puerto Rico
024-Degree Radial - East end of Virgin Islands, Antilles
026-Degree Radial - Anguilla Island, Antilles
030-Degree Radial - Guadalupe Island, Antilles
034-Degree Radial - Santa Lucia Island, Antilles
109-Degree Radial - Largest open-pit gold mine in the world
(13°00′36″ S, 70°32′34″ W)
116-Degree Radial - Machu Picchu
123-Degree Radial - Lake Titicaca, Peru/Bolivia
156-Degree Radial - Bahia Blanca, Argentina, with geoglyphs

Google Earth – The Faram Research Foundation

Caral, Peru, plate 4, eastern complex

End points for the bearings displayed in the above photo:

020-Degree Radial - Puerto Rico

023-Degree Radial - Saint Thomas Island, Antilles

026-Degree Radial - Saint Martin Island, Antilles

031-Degree Radial - Guadalupe Island, Antilles

292-Degree Radial - Reciprocal 112, ten-thousand-year-old mining site called La Oroya (11°31'25" S, 75°54'29" W)

304-Degree Radial - Ancient city of Barranca, Peru, possibly earlier than Caral (10°44'35" S, 77°44'53" W)

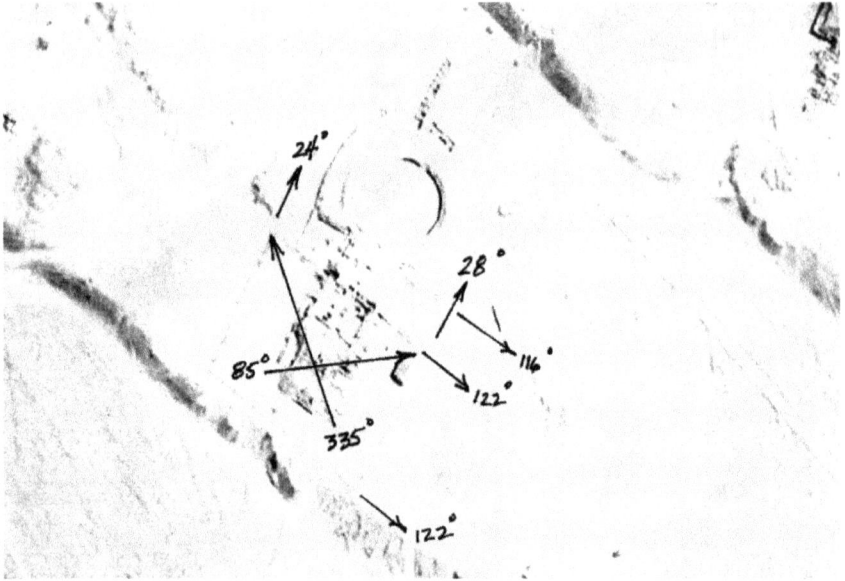

Caral, Peru, plate 5, southeastern complex

End points for the bearings displayed in the above photo:

024-Degree Radial - East end of Virgin Islands

028-Degree Radial - Saint Kitts Island, Antilles

085-Degree Radial - East tip of South America

116-Degree Radial - Machu Picchu, Peru

122-Degree Radial - Lake Titicaca, Peru/Bolivia

335-Degree Radial - Entrance to Gulf of Guayaquil, Ecuador

(3°44′55″ S, 80°41′42″ W)

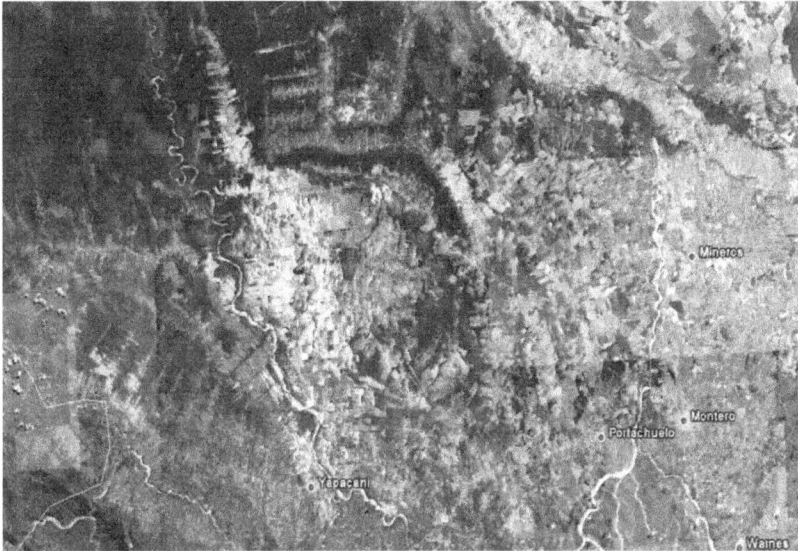

The Santa Rosa circular glyph (17°10.04′48″ S, 63°43′20.57″ W)

The Santa Rosa geoglyph is twenty-two miles across and was defined by the Caral 116-degree radial touching the northeast side and the 117-degree radial touching the southwest side. The topography of the glyph does not seem to lend itself to volcanic or meteorite action but appears to be man-made. Farming and the river have divided the glyph on the west side. Therefore part of the glyph is west of the river. This glyph was strategically placed to form the geometric designs that are depicted in the following photo.

The Caral Triangle, as outlined by the end points of the Caral radials

The southern tip of the triangle is located at the Santa Rosa geoglyph, mentioned in the previous image.

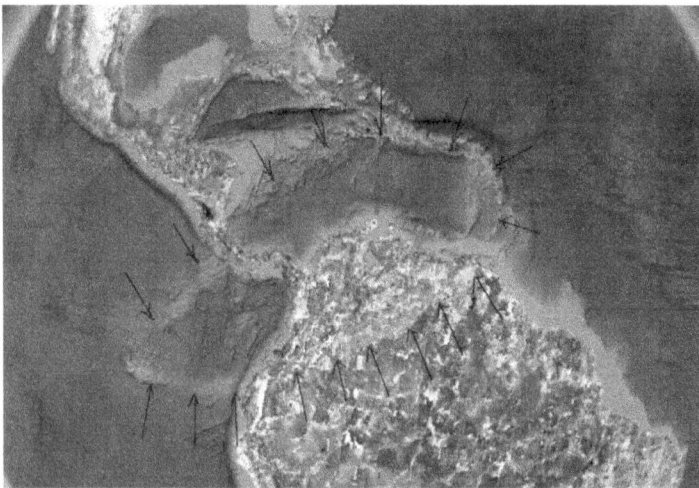

An outline of the Colombian crater

The Columbian crater is defined in the previous photo by the arrows that appear around the perimeter. The tectonic plate that runs along Mesoamerica has most likely caused the rift to rise, thereby reconnecting North and South America. The boundary of the impact crater is illustrated by the two different colors of earth that exist along the crater edge. The center of the circular part of the crater, on the east side, is the end point of the line that runs through the Santa Rosa circle to the precise tip of South America.

The results of this study suggest the following:

The archaeological findings in Caral seem to coincide with many other major complexes, such as the Yonaguni pyramid in Japan, Mohenjo Daro in Pakistan, Gobekli Tepe in Turkey, and numerous other monuments and monoliths around the world. Their commonality stems from many factors, the most common trait being that in the lower layers of the digs, there appears to be little if any evidence of permanent habitation. This is evidenced by the absence of primarily tools and pottery. Another thing they share in common is their construction includes amphitheaters or overlooks in the landscape, which would allow for the observation of some type of ceremony. Sexual connotations are suggested by the many phallic symbols on Yonaguni Island and other major sites. (See narrative E.) This theme is accentuated by the discovery of large quantities of an aphrodisiac in the ruins of Caral.

The second feature they all share is that, using the ancient science of geoglyphology, they all denote territories very similar to the territories mentioned by Plato in *Critias*. This would imply that rather than the structures being the start of civilization, the original inhabitants were the remnants of one of the earth's many cataclysms. They may have been very advanced people, without the tools of their previous culture, beginning the repopulation of the earth. The geoglyphic nature of these structures could indicate an assignment of territories and the rebirth of our current civilization.

End Narrative G

Narrative H

The Carnac Stones – ca. 4100 BCE

Google Earth – The Faram Research Foundation
The Carnac Stone Rows

The Carnac stones have been one of the most puzzling

archaeological artifacts in the world for hundreds of years.

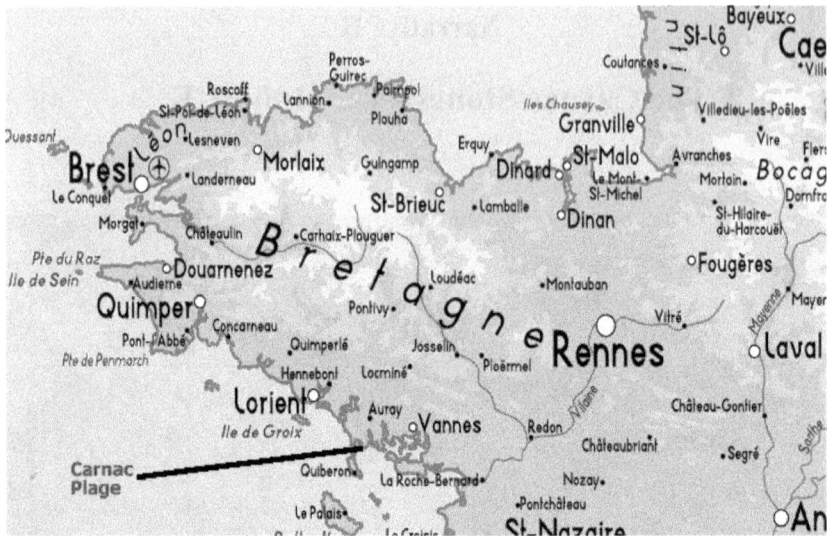

Carnac stones' location, Brittany, France

As Wikipedia explains, "The megalithic stones are an exceptionally dense collection of sites around the village of Carnac in Brittany, consisting of alignments, dolmens, tumuli, and single menhirs. More than three thousand prehistoric standing stones were hewn from local rock and erected by the pre-Celtic people of Brittany. This is the largest such collection of stones in the world. Most of the stones are within the Breton village of Carnac, but some to the east are within La Trinité-sur-Mer. The stones were erected at some stage during the Neolithic period, probably around 3300 BCE, but some may date to as early as 4500 BCE."

Scientists and scholars have been attempting to decode the Carnac stones for hundreds of years. All these attempts were destined to fail until, in 2004, an ancient science named geoglyphology was rediscovered. (Geo = earth, glyph = a writing or symbol, ology = to study.) Without the protocols that were built into the ancient science, any attempts to decode the Carnac stones were an exercise in futility. This stemmed from the fact that the codes for using the Carnac stones came from geoglyphological protocols.

After many years of study, the protocols used in the ancient science were learned and successfully applied to the many geoglyphs located around the world. During this research it was learned that geoglyphs were used to outline territories that the culture that made the geoglyph claimed for themselves. Needless to say, mastering this ancient science and being able to follow cultures and their territories opened up a whole new window into the history of the world.

Google

Carnac stone rows

The question up to this point has been why a culture would move and align so many stones in what was previously considered an abstract manner. Over the past ten years of studying geoglyphs around the globe, it was discovered that pyramids, stone monoliths, and other geoglyphs were placed, in addition to several other uses, to map out territories the builders considered their own. Ancient Japanese texts state that each territory was originally assigned to ancient scholars who were charged with teaching man the ancient spirituality, sciences, and philosophy. In ancient times these were all part of the human experience. Since modern man has separated the human experience into science and religion, we no longer see the connection between them.

While hundreds of conventional geoglyphs have been located and surveyed around the world, Carnac is in a class of its own. While Carnac uses the same protocols as other geoglyphs, the way they are applied is unique to the Carnac stones. While most geoglyphic surveys are performed by running lines through or parallel to tangible objects, Carnac requires that these principles be applied to the spaces between the stones rather than the stones themselves. As you see in the following image, the puzzle is solved by running lines through the center of the spaces between the stones in order to decode the puzzle. There is only one pair of stones that, when a line is drawn between them, will position the line directly in the center of the space. Once these lines are determined, the rest of the survey continues just as in other territorial geoglyphs.

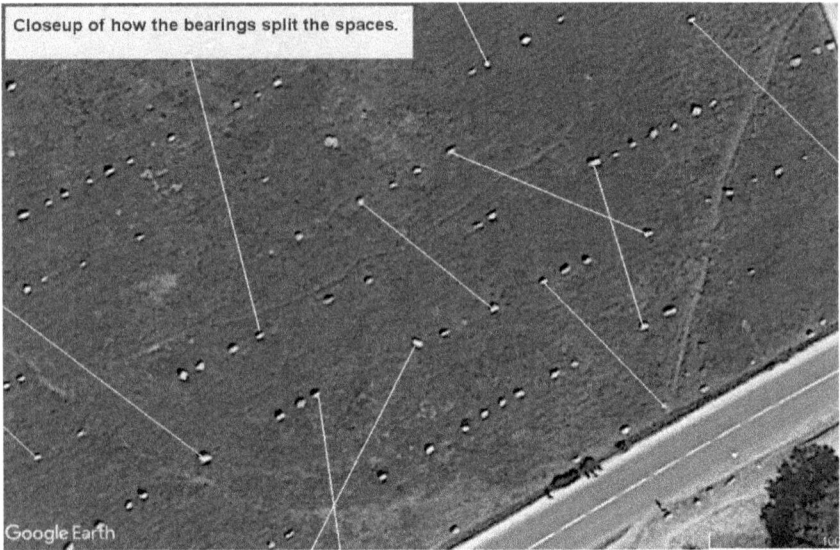

Closeup of how the bearings split the spaces.

Google Earth – The Faram Research Foundation

View of lines splitting the spaces between the stones

This image illustrates the difference between a normal geoglyph and the Carnac geoglyphs. Normally a bearing is derived from running a line between two rocks or points. In this case the puzzle can only be solved by finding the two stones that will inscribe a line through the center of the spaces.

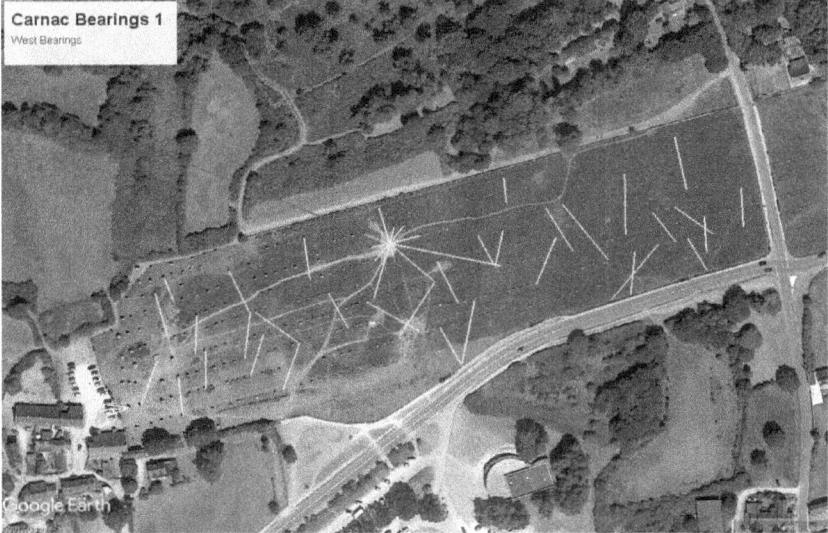

Google Earth – The Faram Research Foundation

Carnac bearings, west side

Google Earth – The Faram Research Foundation

Carnac bearings, east side

Google Earth – The Faram Research Foundation

Carnac bearing and radial origination points

In the previous image there are two magenta radials (radials being extensions of the bearings). The west radial points to Edinburgh, Scotland, and the east magenta line points to Stonehenge. Since both end points are historically related to the Celts, one would have to assume that the Celtic culture had its roots somewhere before 3400 BCE. One would also have to assume that these ancient cultures had a detailed knowledge of the earth long before history tells us.

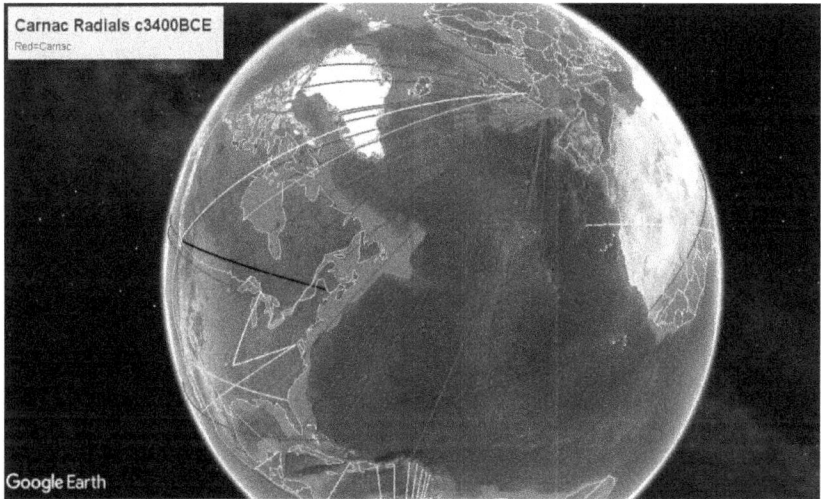

Google Earth – The Faram Research Foundation
Carnac radials, ca. 3400 BCE

The Stonehenge and the Carnac monoliths were constructed at about the same time, ca. 3400 BCE. What the original Stonehenge depicted is difficult to say, since a portion of the outer rings were destroyed, and then later, ca. 1100 CE, the existing center stones were placed on the ground within the circle. The new geoglyphs at Stonehenge designate the Celtic territory that existed at the time the new stones were laid. Between the time of construction of Carnac and Stonehenge (ca. 3400 BCE) and the changes to Stonehenge (ca. 1100 CE), two major events occurred that allow us to validate the territorial changes that are exhibited in the later Stonehenge geoglyphs.

In 700 CE the Galician Celts moved from Galicia to Denmark to escape the Moors' invasion of Iberia. This is verified by recorded history and by the fact that there are more Galician artifacts in Denmark than there are in Galicia. The Danish Celts then recruited the Vikings to help them liberate east Britain from the Saxons. When the Vikings were barred from Norway ca. 1000 CE for refusing to convert to Catholicism, they were granted the islands of Iceland and Greenland by the Denmark–Norway Alliance. This is also evidenced by these islands not being included in the Stonehenge territorial geoglyph constructed ca. 1100 CE. Notice in the next image that the territory was revised between the building of Carnac and the revision of Stonehenge.

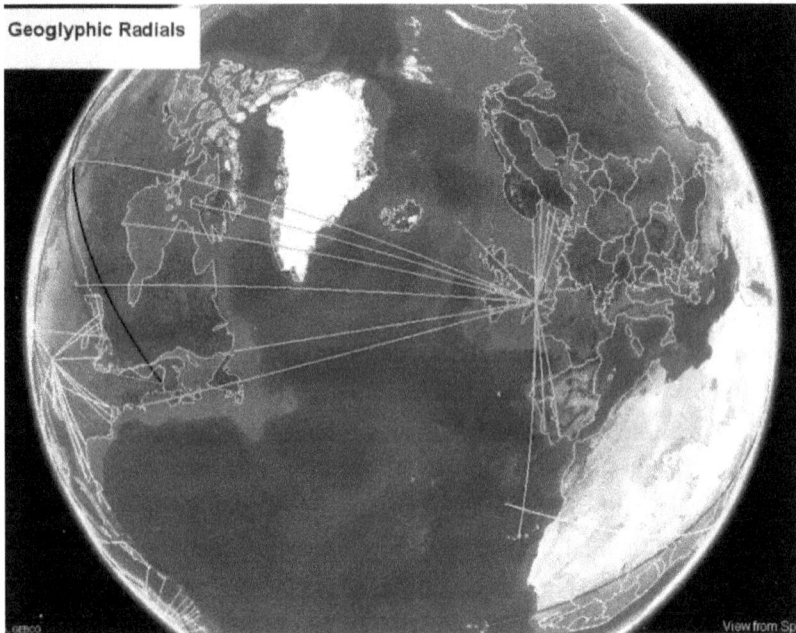

Google Earth – The Faram Research Foundation
Newer Stonehenge radials, ca. 1100 BCE

The Stonehenge radials depicted in the previous and following images were generated from the smaller stones, placed at a later date, on the ground within the Stonehenge circle.

Notice the four-sided cross. The practice of constructing major geoglyphs so as to portray a four-sided cross is common in many of the older geoglyphs around the world. This fact alone proves that a secret worldwide network existed.

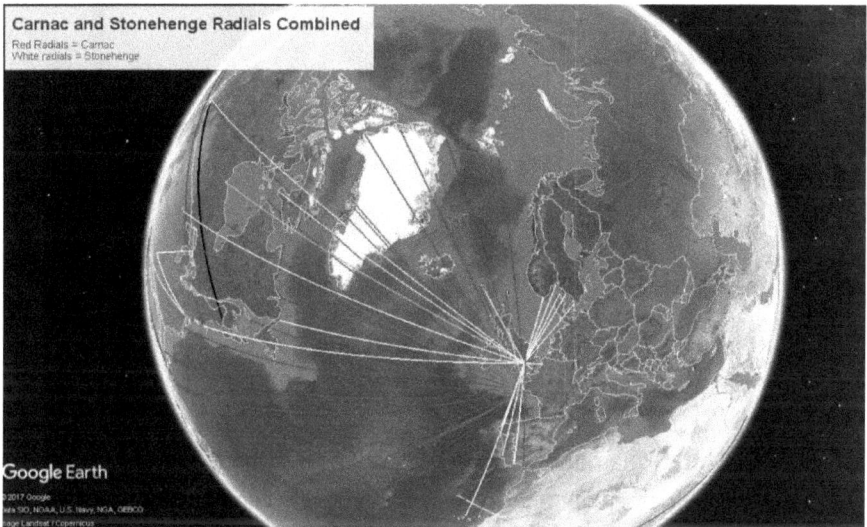

Google Earth – The Faram Research Foundation
Carnac and newer Stonehenge (lighter) radials combined

Notice that both the Carnac and Stonehenge radials point to the western end point of the current US boundary with Canada. Also notice that Stonehenge points to the two geoglyphical landmarks that define the rest of the US territory, Inspiration Peak and the Newport Tower locations. (See Narrative N.)

In the preceding image, notice that the later Stonehenge light-colored radials no longer encroach on the territory given to the Vikings ca. 1000 CE. The Viking territory was outlined by the

Tiniteqilaq, Greenland, geoglyph. (See the following image and Narrative L.)

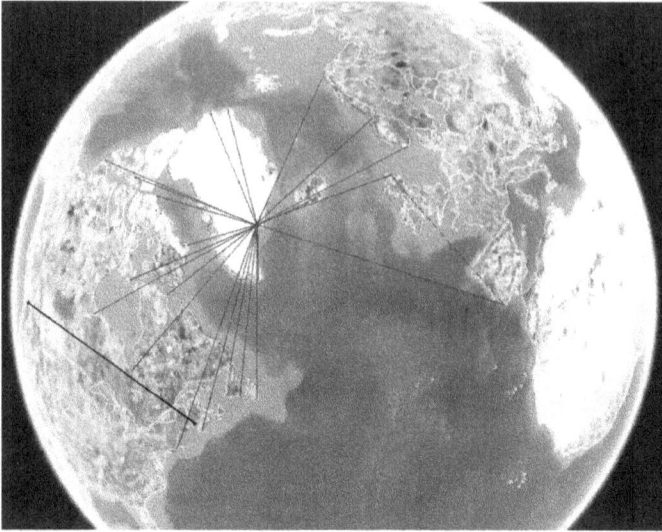

Google Earth – The Faram Research Foundation

Radials of the Viking territory as defined by the Tiniteqalaaq, Greenland, geoglyph, ca. 1100 CE

Note: The radial pointing to Newport, Rhode Island, is not part of the territory but a pointer to the Newport Tower geoglyph, one of the geoglyphs defining the adjoining Templar/Celtic territory. Since the Vikings and the Celts were allies at the time, the Vikings were given the Tiniteqalaaq territory by the Denmark–Norway Alliance, and they were allowed to reside in the friendly territories of Scotland, Ireland, and the Farallon Islands.

The Vikings/Norse were kicked out of the Scotish Hebrides Islands in 1313 CE when it was learned that the Norse were colonizing Celtic territories in North America. (See the book *La Merica*, 2013) The Vikings had been allies of the Celts and were given refuge in the Scotish Hebrides in c1000 CE when they were banished from Norway for refusing to convert to Catholicism. Henry Sinclair's voyage to America in 1398 CE was intended to stop this invasion. Sinclair's troops/Templars accompanied him to the Americas. (See Narrative L.)

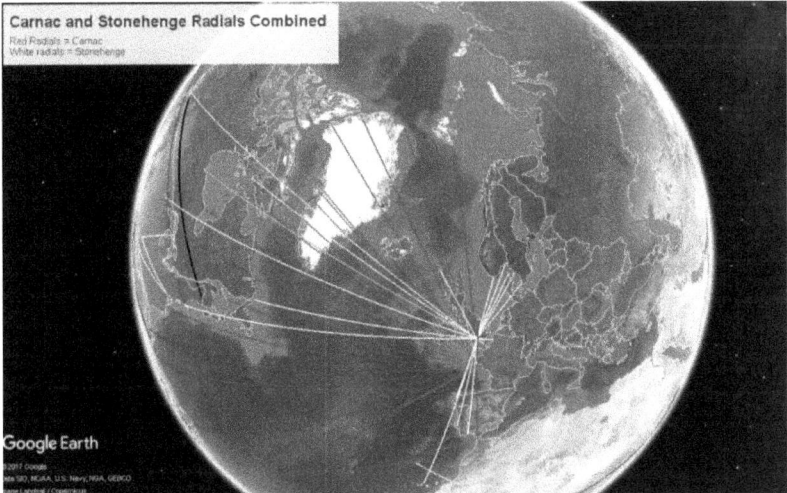

Google Earth – The Faram Research Foundation
Stonehenge and Carnac radials combined

It is obvious that between the time Carnac was constructed and the time Stonehenge was modified, there was a loss of part of the Carnac territory. As you can see, the territory around Iceland, Greenland, and Canada is omitted from the Stonehenge geoglyph. By the time the later (smaller) stones were installed at Stonehenge, geoglyphs worldwide were being used to dissect the original territories and establish new ones. (See Narrative I)

Until the Canary Islands were turned over to Spain ca. 1822 CE, every Celtic/Portuguese territorial geoglyph pointed to the Canary Islands as the southern limit of the Celtic territory. Just before the Canary Islands were turned over to Spain, the Guimar pyramids were built to document the territory that was given to the Templars ca. 1400 CE by Portugal. That territory is basically what we now call the United States. (See Narrative N.)

End Narrative H

Narrative I

Stonehenge, United Kingdom, ca. 2500 BCE

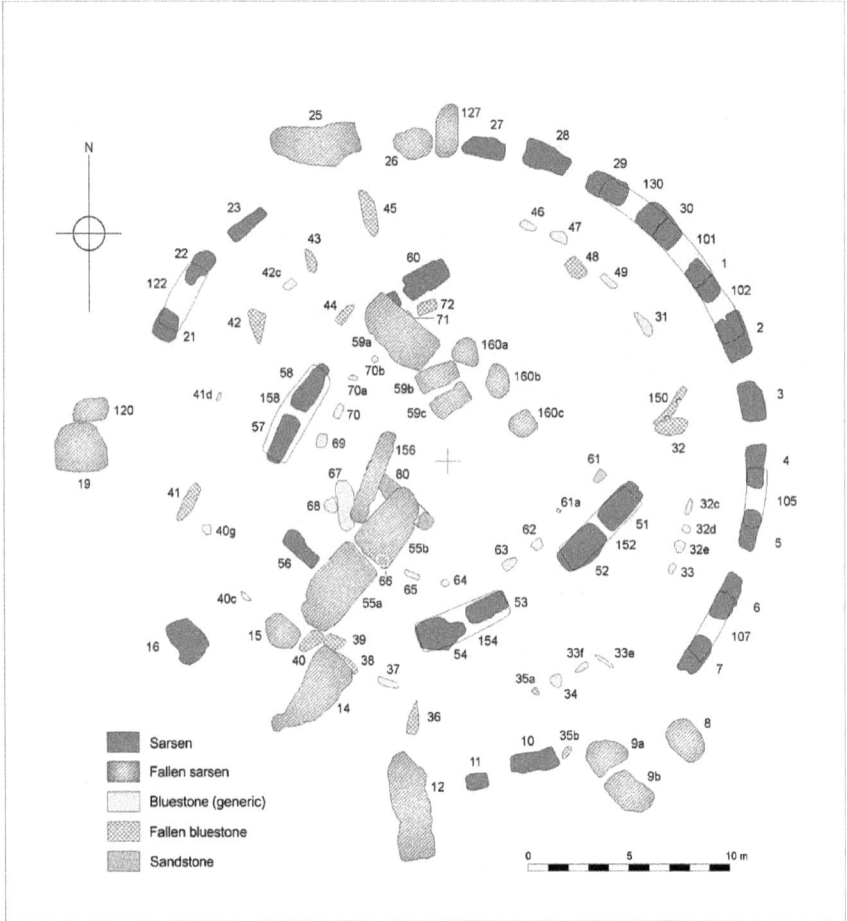

Drawing by Anthony Johnson

Stonehenge after smaller stones were added

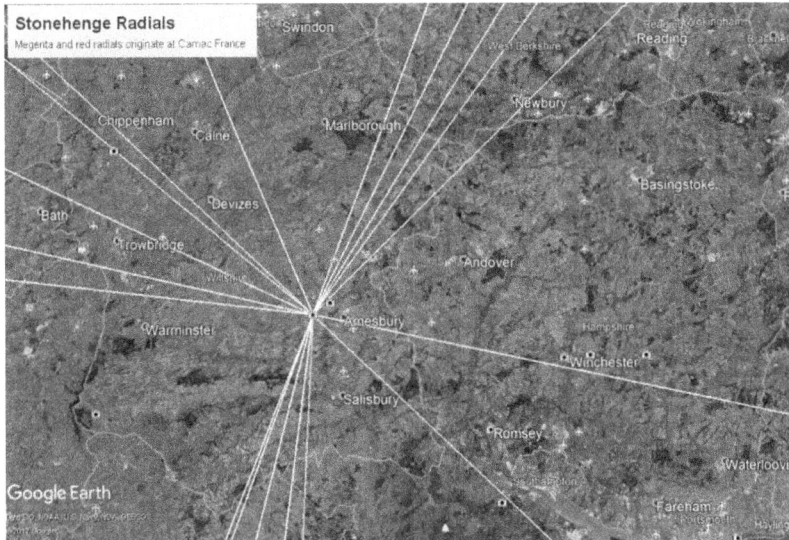

Stonehenge Bearings
Notice the Celtic cross

It was a common practice for the ancients to construct their important geoglyphs in such a manner as to form a symblance of a four-sided cross. This further ties the builders of these geoglyphs to the ancients.

Stonehenge radial end points

Although the Stonehenge radials only designate the Celtic territory as viewed from Stonehenge, it does point out key Celtic sites which became important in defining the territory that would become the United States. These important markers are the current western end of the US–Canada border, Inspiration Peak in Minnesota, and the Newport, RI site.

End Narrative I

Narrative J

The Nazca Star, Peru, ca. 500 BCE

Google Earth – The Faram Research Foundation

"The Nazca Star"
Nazca, Peru

Recently many previously unknown geoglyphs have been found in proximity to previously recognized and published Nazca Lines. These new discoveries have been published in periodicals around the world.

Reuters ran a story on May 29, 2018, with the headline "Archaeologists Discover New Geoglyphs near Nazca Lines in Peru." The story said, "Archaeologists using drones have discovered more than twenty-five geoglyphs etched into a swath of coastal desert in southern Peru near the Nazca Lines, a culture ministry official said Monday." A few days later, on June 1, the *Daily Express News* announced, "Nazca Lines shocking discovery: twenty-five mysterious new glyphs found—but who left them?" Reporter Sebastian Kettley wrote, "The Nazca Lines in Peru stunned archaeologists again this week after more than twenty-five new glyphs were found in the ancient Nazca Desert. But who left these mysterious lines on the ground?"

The Nazca Lines are a series of large ancient geoglyphs in the Nazca Desert, in southern Peru. Some of the figures are up to 1,200 feet long. Scholars believe the Nazca Lines were created by the Nazca culture between 500 BCE and 500 CE. Most are simple straight lines, while others form geometric shapes. Many are zoomorphic designs of animals and human figures.

The designs are shallow lines made in the ground by scraping away naturally occurring reddish pebbles, exposing the whitish ground beneath. Due to the dry, windless climate of the plateau, the lines have been preserved naturally.

The lines and figures can be seen from an aircraft, from the surrounding foothills, and from other high places. Most scholars agree that the designs were created by the Nazca culture; however, at this point most scientists disagree on who engineered the lines or why they were constructed. In addition to the other geoglyphs that have been recently found, there is one that has been hiding in plain sight. That geoglyph has been named the Nazca Star.

Nazca star (left) in relation to previously recognized lines (right)

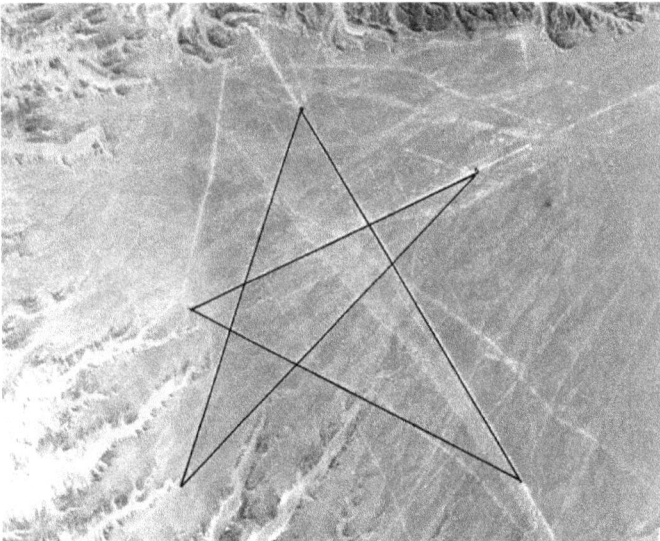

The Nazca Star highlighted

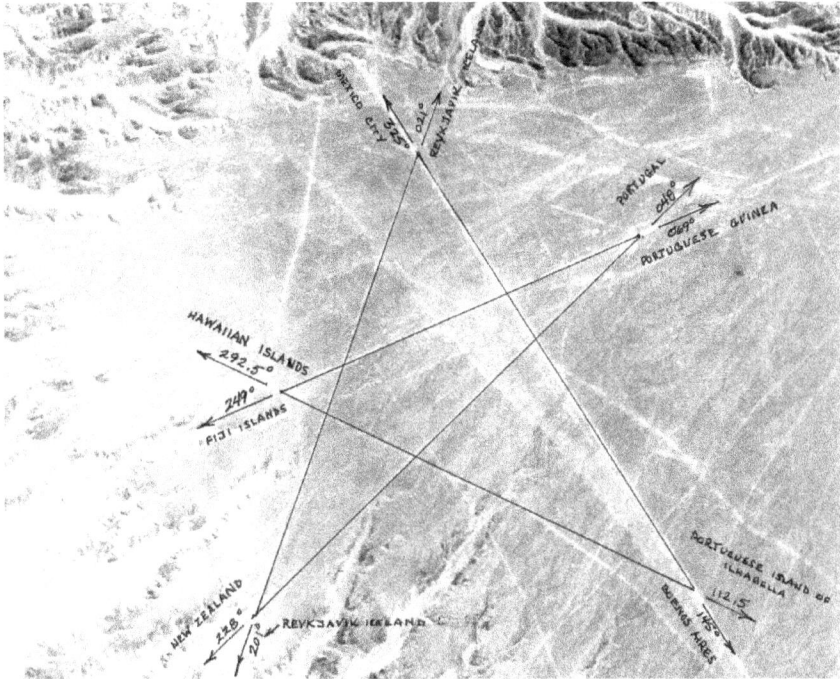

Google Earth – The Faram Research Foundation

Nazca Star projected end points

These end points were located using Google Earth and the protocols contained within the ancient science of geoglyphology. The end-point names are the names currently in use. The end points in this geoglyph, and in others around the world, were established thousands of years before this geoglyph and were used repetitively by the ancients. All of the end points mentioned have significant relevance in the world of geoglyphology.

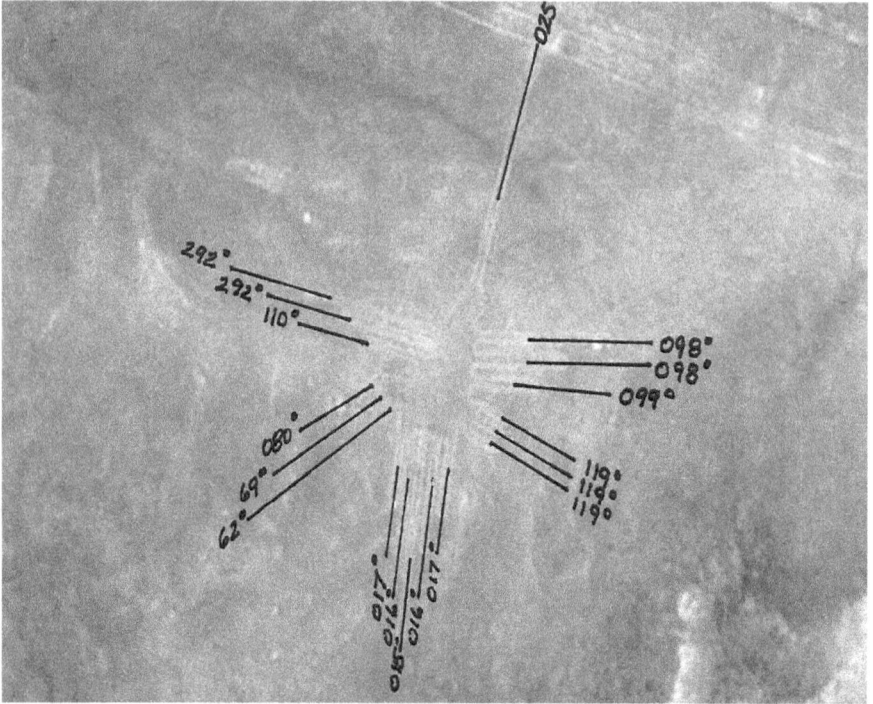

Nazca Hummingbird bearings

In this image you see the iconic Nazca Hummingbird geoglyph. Using the ancient science of geoglyphology, the hummingbird geoglyph, as well as the other zoomorphic geoglyphs at Nazca, were found to be geoglyphological survey markers. This can be proven by determining the orientation of the radials using Google Earth and extending them using the protocols established in the ancient science of geoglyphology. Not by coincidence, both the Nazca Star and the Nazca Hummingbird display the 292-degree bearing. The 292-degree radial points to Hawaii. The other bearings displayed by the hummingbird geoglyph point to other important landmarks. These same landmarks are used frequently around the world to establish other territorial boundaries. The twenty-five-degree radial of the hummingbird geoglyph points to the Faroe

Islands, which played a major role in Celtic and Norse history. Since this image was made public, the hummingbird has been blurred out on Google Earth and a hand-drawn image placed over it that may or may not be accurate.

You must be wondering how the Pacific islands of Hawaii, Fiji, and New Zealand figure into the territory that is outlined by the Nazca Star geoglyph. Geoglyphs around the world point out Hawaii as the dividing point between the territory claimed by ancient Japan and the territory claimed by the ancient Celts, Portuguese, Etruscans, Phoenicians, and their predecessors.

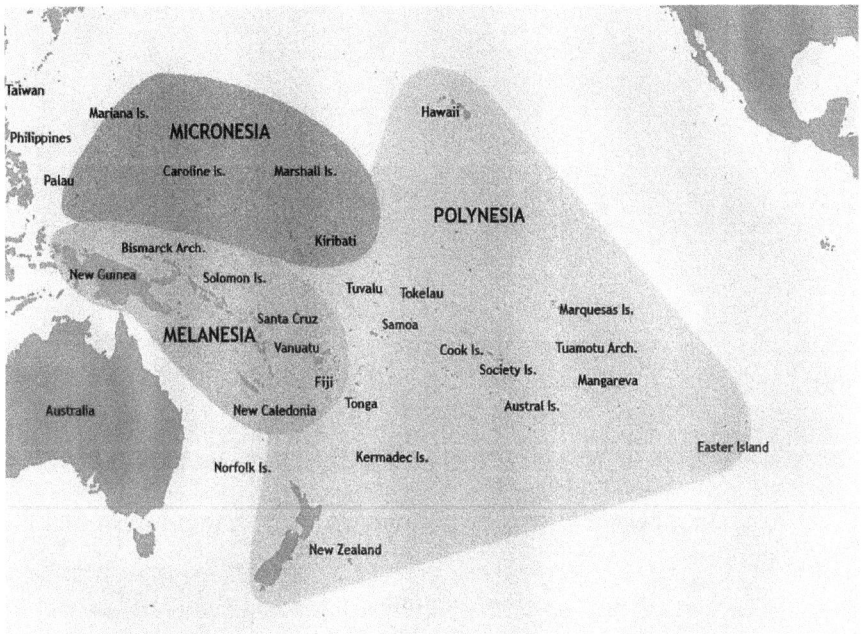

Google

Map of Polynesia

This map shows the ancient territory known as Polynesia. You will notice three of the end points described by the Nazca Star geoglyph coincide with the western boundary of the Polynesian territory, Hawaii, Fiji, and New Zealand. The Polynesian boundary exists just outside the ancient Japanese boundary described in narrative E. It should also be noted that the enigmatic Easter Island completes the triangle known as the Polynesian territory.

The Ancient Japanese Territory

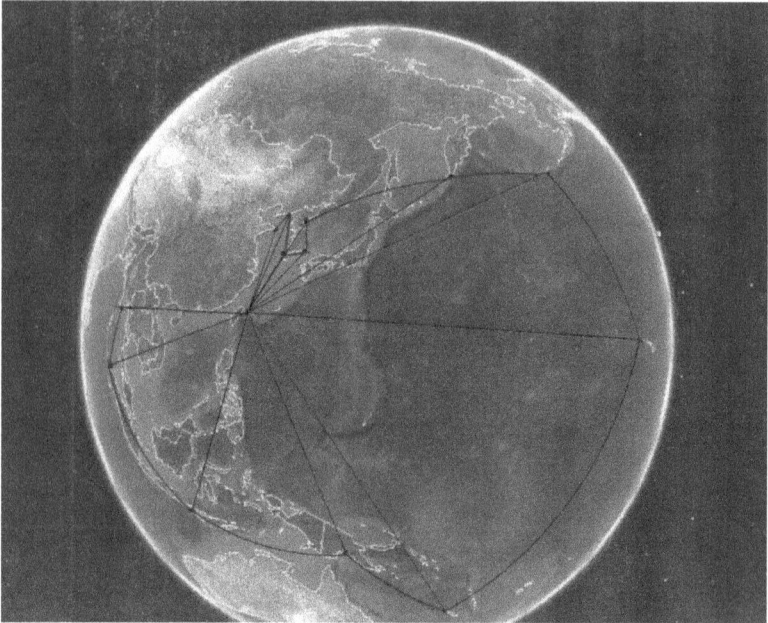

Google Earth – The Faram Research Foundation

Ancient Japanese territory as defined by the Yonaguni pyramid, ca. 8000 BCE.

(See Narrative E)

Japanese keyhole geoglyph

This territorial geoglyph, like the Yonaguni pyramid, is located in Japan. Both geoglyphs designate basically the same territory, constructed in different time periods, that was claimed by ancient Japan.

(Note: The ancients used some type of chemical on the flora to preserve these geoglyphs. The chemicals used lasted hundreds of years. This occurs all over the world.)

Geoglyph Bearings

(Note: The original survey was conducted at much higher magnification. All bearings are not displayed in this image.)

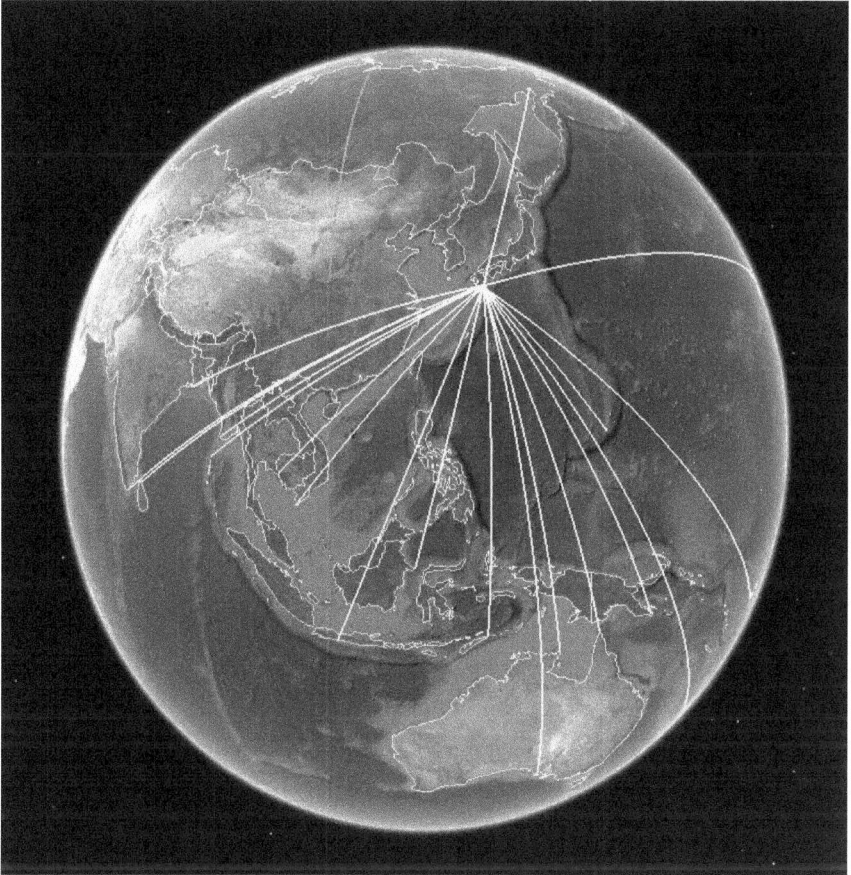

Japanese keyhole geoglyph end points (west side view)

Notice that in the keyhole geoglyph Australia has been added to the territory that was described by the Yonaguni geoglyph.

Google Earth – The Faram Research Foundation
Japanese geoglyph end points (east side view)

As you can see, the area claimed by Japan was expanded between the time the Yonaguni pyramid was cut and the time this geoglyph was laid out. It appears that Australia and some Middle Eastern land were added. What is important to note is that the western end points of Hawaii, Fiji, and New Zealand match the same end points in the Nazca Star geoglyph. This and similar findings bear out our research showing that at some time in the past, the earth was divided up into territories. These territories existed all over the world and fit together like a giant jigsaw puzzle. It should be noted that many of the ancient territorial geoglyphs still designate the boundaries of modern countries.

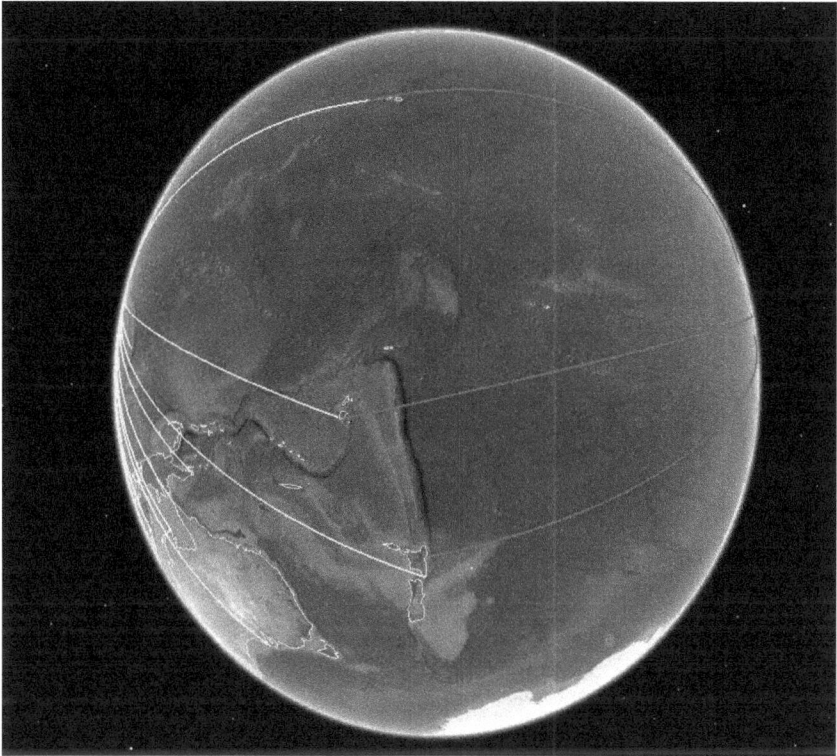

Google Earth – The Faram Research Foundation
Japanese and Nazca Star geoglyph coinciding end points

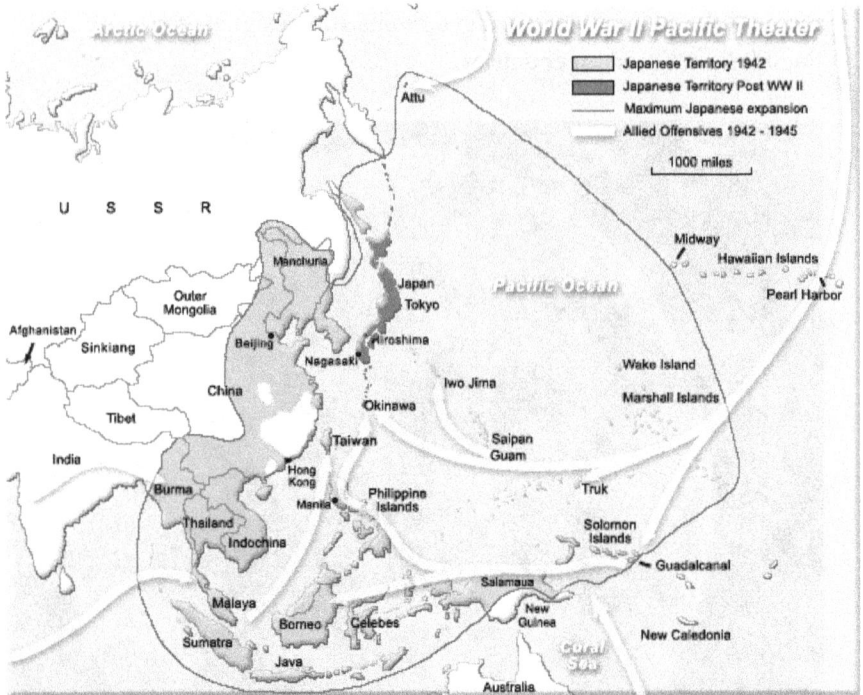

Territory attacked or held by the Japanese in WWII

This map designates the territory the Japanese were attempting to reclaim in WWII. The territory matches the territorial claim as stated in the Yonaguni pyramid geoglyph. As we all know, Hawaii, the easternmost point in the ancient Japanese territory and the westernmost point in the Nazca Star geoglyph territory, was attacked by Japan but not captured. This fact seems to validate the ancient Japanese claim demonstrated by the Yonaguni pyramid. The Japanese also attacked Attu Island in Alaska. Attu Island is the northernmost point depicted in the Yonaguni territory and has no resources. Why would the Japanese attack a worthless island far away from their homeland? Can all these circumstances be coincidental?

European Presence in the Americas

Research has shown that ports currently known as Lisbon, Portugal; Vera Cruz, Mexico; and Buenos Aires, Brazil, all played an important part in the ancient history in the Atlantic. The Nazca Star makes reference to all three of the ancient ports. Vera Cruz is recognized as the port serving Mexico City.

Historians agree that Portugal and its predecessors at one time held a dominant nautical position in the Atlantic Ocean. Can the obvious references to ancient places currently held by the Portuguese indicate a pre-Columbian presence in the Americas? In the Juan de la Cosa map of 1500 CE, survey markers are denoted by a dot within a circle at the head of all the major rivers in South America and southern North America.

Placing a survey marker at the head of a river was the way explorers claimed the land bordering the river. Could all the rivers in South America and southern North America have been explored in the eight years between 1492, when Columbus reportedly discovered the Americas, and 1500, when the map was drawn?

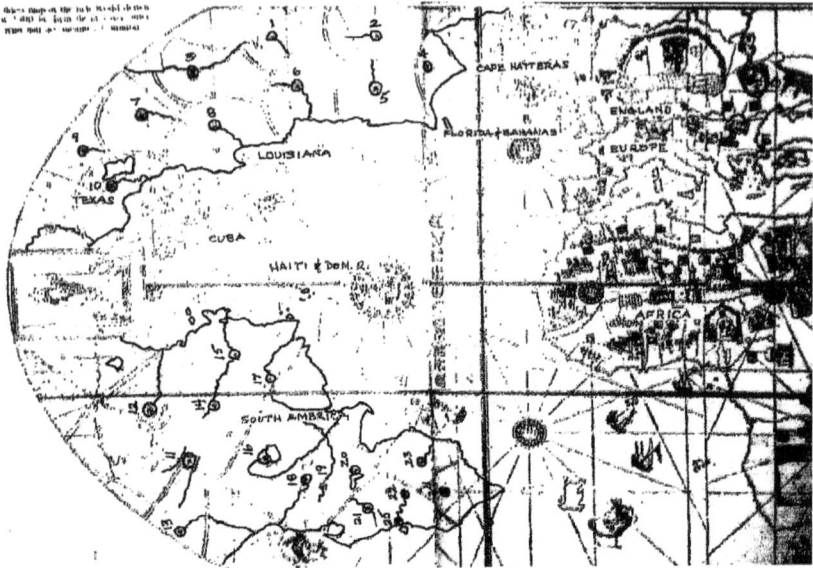

The Juan de la Cosa map of 1500

The geoglyphs and associated rivers that appear on the Juan de la Cosa map have been highlighted for better visibility. The geoglyphs appear on his map as a dot within a circle. A satellite photo of each survey marker can be found in the book *Ancient Signposts* (2011).

It is interesting that Juan de la Cosa, a Galician and the illustrator of the map, was also the owner and navigator of the *Santa María*, on which Columbus made his first voyage to the Americas. De la Cosa's navigation took Columbus's fleet to the precise eastern point where ancient geoglyphs indicate that the border of the ancient Mesoamerican and North American territories met.

It is a well-known fact that the crew of the *Santa María* was considering mutiny three days before they reached their destination. How did Alonso Pinzón, captain of the *Pinta*, know to tell the crew that if they did not reach land within three days, they would turn back? They reached land on the third day. History tells us that at the same time, they made a course correction. Why would they make a course correction unless they already had a map showing their destination? There currently exist territorial survey markers (geoglyphs) near the point where Columbus landed. These survey markers outline the territory in the Caribbean and Mesoamerica that was claimed by Spain after the war with the Moors, which ended in the spring of 1492.

Google Earth – The Faram Research Foundation
The Amerigo Vespucci map, 1507

It would be interesting to know how Alaska and the associated Pacific islands (right side of map) appeared on a map made in 1507 CE. One would have to assume that the entire Pacific had been explored prior to 1507. Historical records tell us that Russia and Japan fought over Alaska thousands of years ago. You may have noticed that a pointer to Alaska, present on the Yonaguni territorial map, is missing in the map of the later Japanese keyhole geoglyph.

374

This transition coincides with Japanese history. European maps showing previous habitation in the Americas suddenly appear ca. 1500, after the voyage of Columbus. The creators of many ancient maps were not aware of the consequences of including pre-Columbian exploration on their maps.

If Europeans were in ancient America, it would be logical that they would lay claim to their territory by placing a survey marker there. One of those markers would appear to be the Nazca Star.

Conclusions:

The Nazca Star is a newly discovered geoglyph, validated by similar geoglyphs around the world.

The Nazca Star and other Nazca geoglyphs have unique properties that can be validated by the protocols contained in the ancient science of geoglyphology.

The end points pointed out by the Nazca Star seem to have a logical place in ancient history.

The end points established by the Nazca Star, other geoglyphs, and evidence from around the world seem to point in the direction of a culture that had sophisticated navigational skills and existed throughout history.

End Narrative J

Narrative K

The Badlands Guardian, Canada

The following is a study of the Aztec Indian Head located at Medicine Hat, Canada, more commonly known as the "Badlands Guardian."

Google Earth – The Faram Research Foundation
Image of the Badlands Guardian before it was defaced

This survey was commissioned by Earth's International Research Society (EIRS) with reference to the Indian Head anomaly located forty miles east of Medicine Hat, Canada (50 0' 38.20N 110 6 48.32W). The Indian Head geoglyph, which is quite prominent from the air, has been the subject of speculation for many years. During our initial study, it was realized that there was more than one caricature located in that vicinity. After further inspection it was learned that the caricatures that existed at the site were related to the Mesoamerican cultures that existed ca. 900 BCE to ca. 1500 CE. Until now it was inconceivable that such a geoglyph could exist this far north of Mesoamerica. In addition to the caricatures, there also existed raised earthen lines throughout the surrounding flat lands. From past experience it was realized that we were not only dealing with facial features but with linear geoglyphs, left there to tell a story. That story comes to life in this presentation.

This study involves the use of geoglyphology. Although geoglyphology has only recently come to the forefront, it has been used by ancient civilizations for over thirty-two thousand years to outline territories, tell of travels, and preserve history for those who are fortunate enough to decode it. The practice of using the geometry of ancient geoglyphs to release the hidden details of their origins is not a new practice, and evidence of its use can be found throughout the world. This practice has been handed down through secret societies since long before the building of the Egyptian pyramids. I call the rediscovery and application of this ancient science geoglyphology. This study will terminate with conclusions based on the evidence collected from this site and from expertise gathered from the investigation of similar sites around the world.

In the field of geoglyphology, we are plotting lines in a spherical world and then displaying the results on a flat plane. It is difficult to grasp the concept of combining spherical geometry with plane geometry. That is why modern geoglyphology could not have been proposed without the advent of software that computes using spherical geometry and then displays the results on a flat plane. This type of precise mapping precludes the initial plotting of these bearings on a flat map. Maps become distorted when converted from a sphere to a flat map. Any lines that are depicted in this article on a flat, non-satellite map were first plotted using the Google Earth software and then drawn on the flat map after the end points were determined. Even then, the proper curvature is missing. The compelling question is, what knowledge did the ancients possess, in past millennia, which allowed them to accomplish these precise calculations? Our sophisticated mathematical software and satellite imagery are no more accurate than the calculations done by the ancients.

Google Earth – The Faram Research Foundation
Main caricature: an Aztec chieftain

This carving is so precise that the neck of the subject's garment, the shoulder seams, the wrinkles in his neck, and both shoulders can be seen. The thing that looks like an earphone is a road leading to an oil well.

Aztec chieftain stone image from Mexico

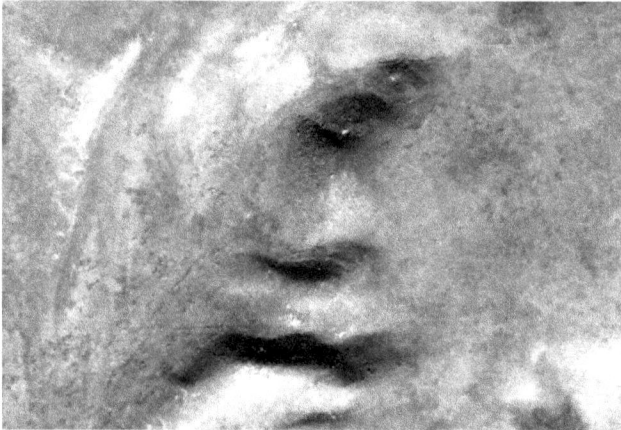

Olmec image located in the Aztec chief's headdress

It was traditional to have a ceremonial hood draped over one eye.

Olmec stone head

Edward H. Merrin of the Merrin Gallery (1968) explains,
The Olmec culture was the first true civilization of
Mesoamerica. Olmec culture developed along the Gulf Coast of
Mexico, but its influence spread much farther inland to the valley of
Mexico City, where the Olmec art style was adopted by the other
cultures. The Olmec created monumental works such as stone reliefs
depicting humans and supernatural beings and colossal heads of
ballplayer kings as well as smaller, precious works such as jade
masks, tools, figures, and ornaments. Terracotta vessels, small solid
terracotta figurines, and larger hollow ones were among the works
produced at the inland Olmec sites. The finest Olmec works are

united by their superb artistry. That this early culture, the mother of the Mesoamerican cultures which followed, could produce such refined works continues to astonish.

Timeline for Mesoamerican Cultures
Olmec—1500–450 BCE
Teotihuac—100 BCE–700 CE
Tollee—100 BCE–1180 CE
Maya—1500 BCE–1500 CE
Aztec—1325–1519 CE

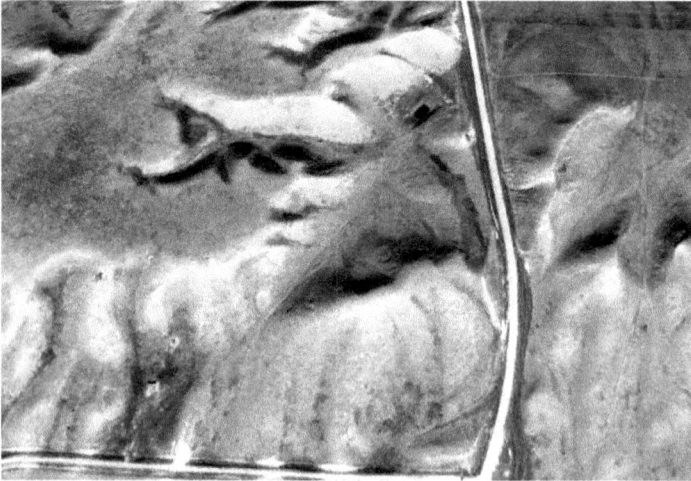

Google Earth – The Faram Research Foundation

Mayan with feathered serpent head dress, Located west of the Aztec caricature

Print of Mayan headgear similar to the one depicted in the previous image

The headgear presented in the preceding Mayan caricature incorporates the snake god called Quetzalcoatl. Quetzalcoatl is a Mesoamerican deity whose name comes from the Nahuatl language and means "feathered serpent." The worship of a feathered serpent deity is first documented in Teotihuacan in the first century BC, and veneration of the figure appears to have spread throughout Mesoamerica by the Late Classic period (600–900 AD).

Among the Aztecs, whose beliefs are the best documented in the historical sources, Quetzalcoatl was related to gods of the wind, of Venus, of the dawn, of merchants, and of arts, crafts, and knowledge. He was also the patron god of the Aztec priesthood, learning, and knowledge.

To the Aztecs, Quetzalcoatl was, as his name indicates, a feathered serpent, a flying reptile (much like a dragon), who was a boundary maker between earth and sky. He was also a creator deity, having contributed essentially to the creation of mankind. He also had anthropomorphic forms that allowed him to take the form of the deity at hand. Among the Aztecs the name Quetzalcoatl was also a priestly title; the two most important priests of the Aztec Templo Mayor were called "Quetzalcoatl Tlamacazqui." In the Aztec ritual calendar, different deities were associated with the cycle of year names: Quetzalcoatl was tied to the year Ce Acatl (One Reed), which correlates to the year 1519. Was it a coincidence that Hernan Cortes, a magistrate in Cuba at the time, selected the year 1519 to invade Mexico and trick the Aztecs into thinking he was the return of an Aztec god?

The earliest iconographic depiction of the deity Quetzalcoatl is believed to have been found on Stela 19, at the Olmec site of La Venta. It depicts a serpent rising up behind a person probably engaged in a shamanic ritual. This depiction is believed to have been made around 900 BCE. Although probably not an exact depiction of the same feathered serpent deity worshipped in Classic and Postclassic periods, it does show the continuity of the symbolism of feathered snakes in Mesoamerica. Coincidentally, feathered headdresses played a big part in the history of the ancients.

On the basis of the iconography of the feathered serpent deity at sites such as Teotihuacan, Xochicalco, Chichen Itza, Tula, and Tenochtitlan, combined with certain ethnohistorical sources, historian David Carrasco has argued that the preeminent function of the feathered serpent deity throughout Mesoamerican history was as the patron deity of the urban center and the god of culture and civilization. This would fit with the findings of this study, which finds that the site under study here was chosen to commemorate and define the territory of a worldwide scientific and spiritual philosophy that existed for thousands of years, of which the Preclassical Mesoamerican culture was a part. This should make the pyramids in Mesoamerica easier to understand. At the time of the invasion of Hernan Cortes and the Spanish Inquisition, Montezuma was chief of the Aztec empire. Montezuma was captured and killed shortly after the arrival of the conquistadores. The ancient knowledge bestowed upon the Aztecs was also evident in many ancient cultures, including the Portuguese and Celts.

The Geoglyphs

Google Earth – The Faram Research Foundation

Locations where the following geoglyphs were found

The lines composing the following geoglyphs were detected using higher magnification than is depicted in the photos. Some of the lines are visible in geoglyphs 2–5, and some are not. Much of what is presented here was destroyed after it was first made public.

Geoglyph 1: The main image at Medicine Hat

Image of Montezuma, chief of the Aztecs

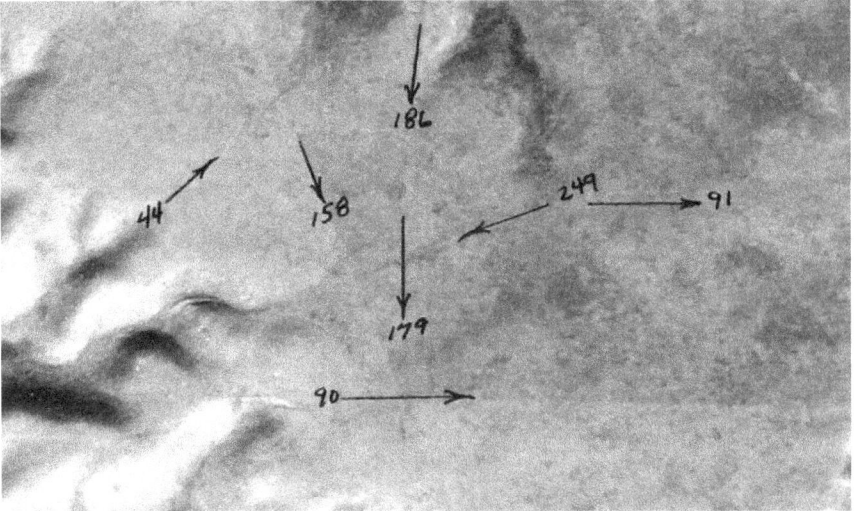

Geoglyph 2 - The lines on the ground are barely visible in these images.

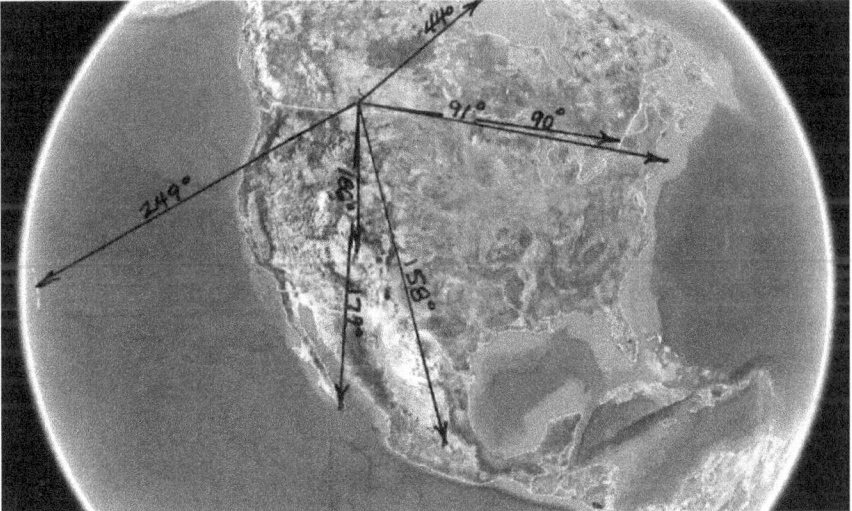

Geoglyph 2 radials

End points for the bearings displayed in the previous image:

044-Degree Radial - Western tip of Ireland
090-Degree Radial - Faram Tower, Maitland, Canada
091-Degree Radial - Southern tip of Cape Cod, Massachusetts, USA
158-Degree Radial - Matlalcueitl volcano, Mexico City, Mexico
179-Degree Radial - Southern tip of Baja California, Mexico
186-Degree Radial - Southern tip of the Grand Canyon
249-Degree Radial - Hawaiian Islands

Discussion of Glyph 2

The Maitland tower and associated docking facilities were built to monitor traffic on the Saint Lawrence Seaway during the Norse/Templar battles c1400 CE. (See *La Merica* – 2013) Noticing that both Hawaii and Cairo were mentioned in two of the geoglyphs got me to thinking that this was something larger than the traditional geoglyphic territories previously studied.

The Maitland (Faram) Tower, Maitland, Canada
See the book "La Merica" by Arthur Faram

Built by the Templars ca. 1400 CE, during their battle against the Norse.

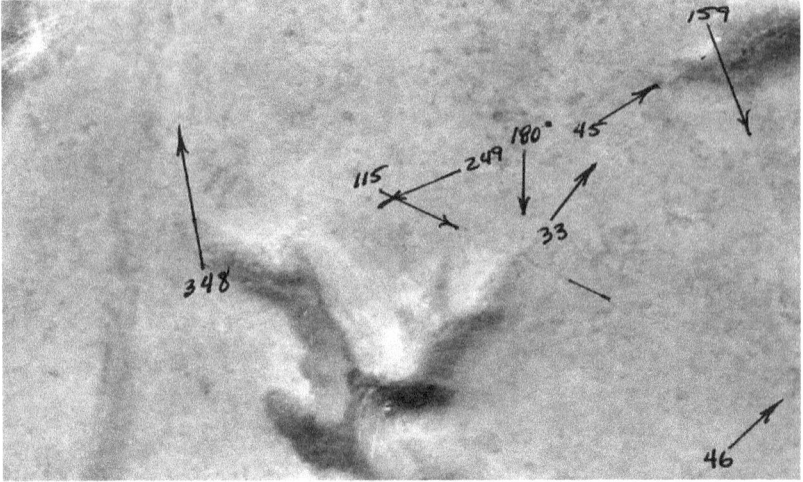

Google Earth – The Faram Research Foundation

Geoglyph 3

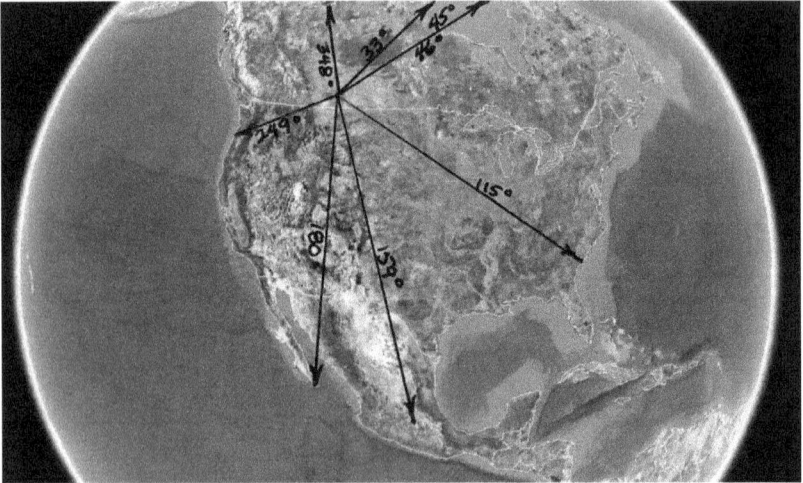

Google Earth – The Faram Research Foundation

Geoglyph 3 radials

End points for the bearings displayed in the previous image:

033-Degree Radial - Cairo, Egypt

045-Degree Radial - Southern tip of Britannia, France

046-Degree Radial - Southern tip of Ireland

115-Degree Radial - Tip of Cape Romain, South Carolina, USA

116-Degree Radial - Charleston Bay, South Carolina

159-Degree Radial - Iztaccihuate volcano, Mexico City

180-Degree Radial - Southern tip of Baja California

348-Degree Radial - West entrance to the Beaufort Sea

Now we have Cairo, Egypt, and Mexico City, Mexico, mentioned. This geoglyph no doubt is to outline a much larger territory. On any of these geoglyphs all you have to do to determine the territory is to connect the endpoints.

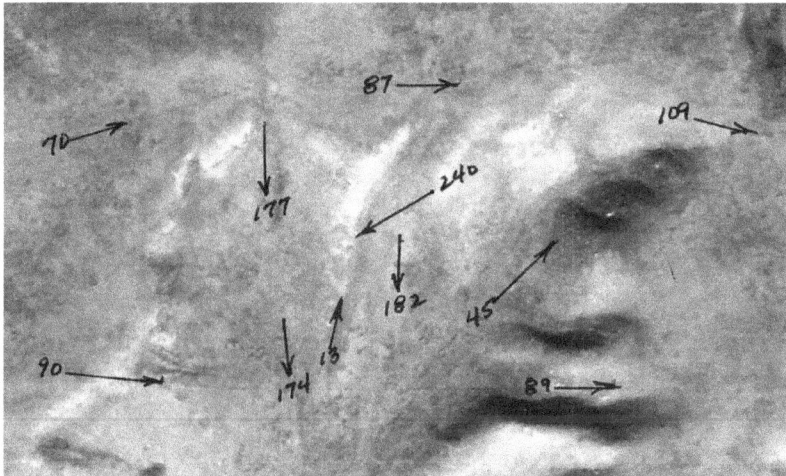

Google Earth – The Faram Research Foundation

Geoglyph 4

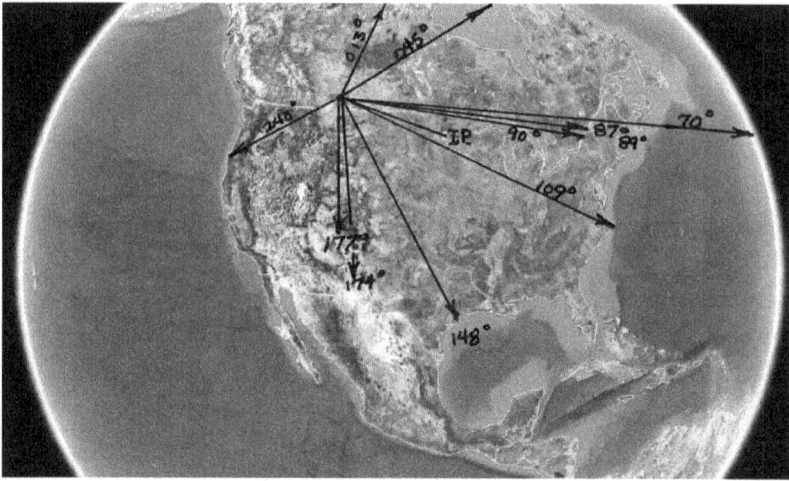

Google Earth – The Faram Research Foundation
Geoglyph 4 radials

End points for the bearings displayed in the previous image:

013-Degree Radial - Northern tip of Greenland
045-Degree Radial - Southern tip of Cornwall, UK
070-Degree Radial - Southern Canary Islands
087-Degree Radial - Junction of the Ottawa River and the Saint
Lawrence Seaway, Canada (the beginning of the route to central
North America)
089-Degree Radial - Entrance to the river at Portsmouth, New
Hampshire, USA
090-Degree Radial - Faram Tower, Maitland, Canada
109-Degree Radial - Southern end of Cape Hatteras, North Carolina,
USA
174-Degree Radial - Chaco Canyon, home of the Anasazi Indians
177-Degree Radial - Shiprock Mountain, New Mexico, USA, sacred
to Anasazi Indians
240-Degree Radial - Cape Blanco, Oregon, USA

Discussion of Glyph Photo 4

All but two of the radial end points are familiar and have been used for centuries in Celtic descriptions of their explorations in North America. However, there are two end points I have never seen outside of my own studies. These are the radials that refer to the Anasazi Indian territories in New Mexico and Colorado. Those two end points are the Chaco Canyon and the Shiprock locations. I have plotted out the geoglyphs located within the Anasazi area, and they share the same protocols as the geoglyphs mentioned in this study. It is now becoming obvious that this site was constructed for something more than the normal territorial survey marker. It is beginning to look like a description of a larger territory encompassing the western cultures that shared the same secret ideological concepts that have been passed from one secret society to another for over thirty-two thousand years. Please keep in mind that "secret" is not necessarily synonymous with "bad." Many societies chose secrecy in self-defense against the negativity of outside sources.

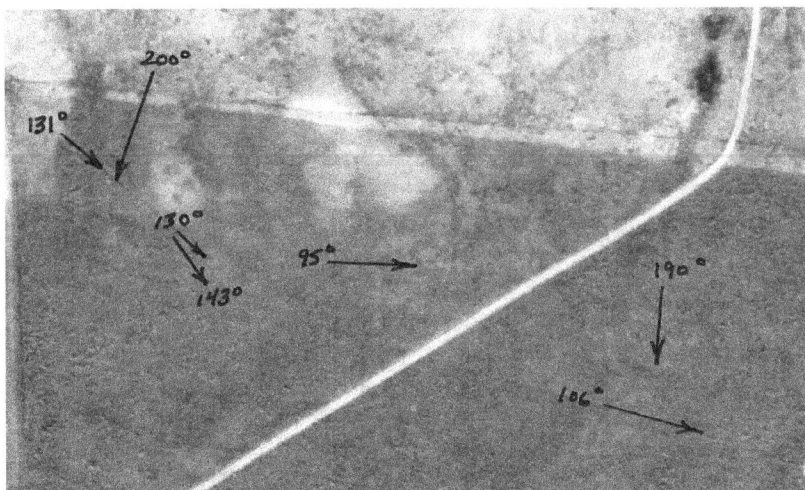

Google Earth – The Faram Research Foundation
Geoglyph 5

The lines on the earth are difficult to see due to the expansion needed to include all the bearings.

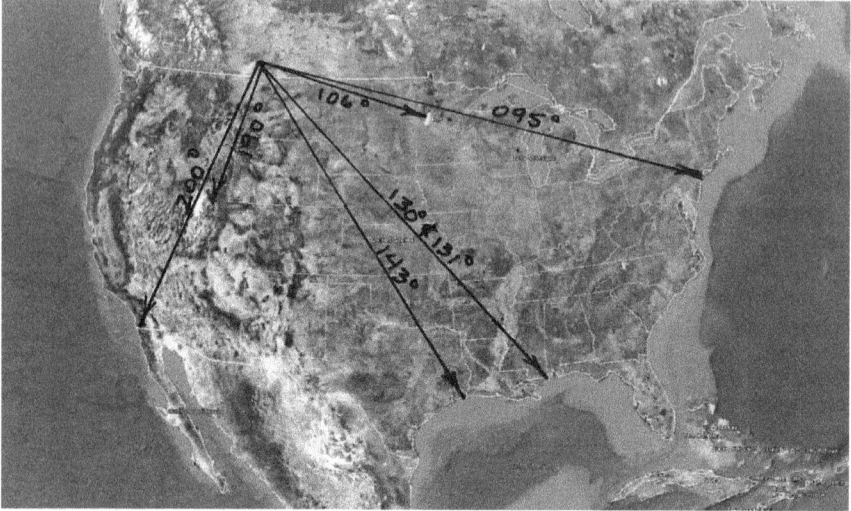

Google Earth – The Faram Research Foundation
Geoglyph 5 radials

End points for the bearings displayed in the above photo:

095-Degree Radial - South end of Long Island Sound, New York, USA
106-Degree Radial - Inspiration Peak, Minnesota, USA (major survey marker for the ancient territory that would become the United States)
130-Degree Radial - Pensacola Bay, Florida, USA
131-Degree Radial - Mobile Bay, Alabama, USA
143-Degree Radial - Sabine River entrance at Port Arthur, Texas, USA (leads to a major Norse geoglyph)
190-Degree Radial - Salt Lake City/The Great Salt Lake, Utah, USA
200-Degree Radial - Entrance to San Diego Bay, California, USA

Discussion of Glyph Photo 5

You will notice one of the radials in this collection of geoglyphs points to Inspiration Peak. Inspiration Peak is the most important survey marker in marking the ancient boundaries of the North American territory that eventually became the United States. As would be expected, all the pointers but one, Salt Lake City, clearly mark a point on the US boundary. The redundancy of the end points, and the location of these geoglyphs south of the other images, tells me that this group of geoglyphs was most likely added at a later time period than the geoglyphs north of here.

It is common for the builders of major geoglyphs to provide a clue to let the interpreter know that they are dealing with a genuine geoglyph created by man and not by a freak of nature. In the case of this geoglyph, that cross-check lies in the distance from this site to Cairo, Egypt, the eastern limit of the territory described, and the distance from the site to Hawaii, the western limit of the territory described. The distance from the site to Cairo is exactly twice as far as it is from the site to Hawaii (6,430 miles versus 3,215 miles).

Had the US boundary remained as set down by the ancients, the Badlands Guardian would still be within US territory. The following photo shows a line identified as the ancient North American territory by other geoglyphs. The treaty that was negotiated between the United States and the British after the American Revolution moved the boundary to its current position. This placed the geoglyph in Canada rather than in the United States.

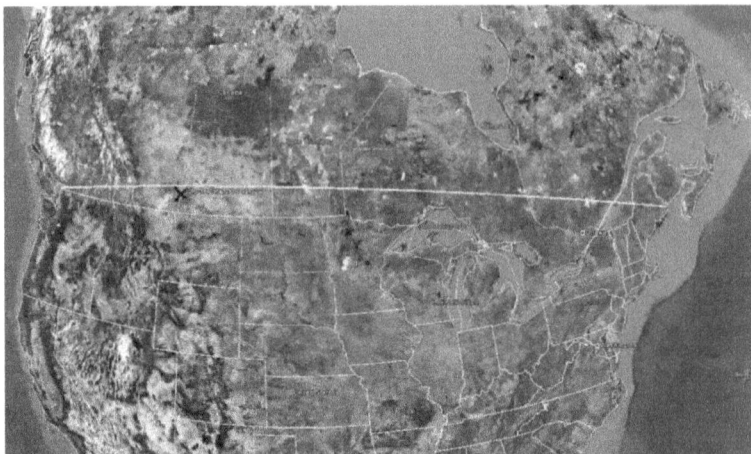

Google Earth – The Faram Research Foundation

**Main Geoglyph (Marked with the X) in Relation to Old
North American Boundary**

There are several elements that need to be considered in
order to come to a conclusion as to what these geoglyphs are about.
First, there is the definite regional identification of Mesoamerican
cultures, Olmec, Aztec, and Maya. In addition, the only deity
involved here was the feathered serpent, which was venerated by all
three cultures. Many believe that the Aztecs and Maya migrated
north at some point in their history.

395

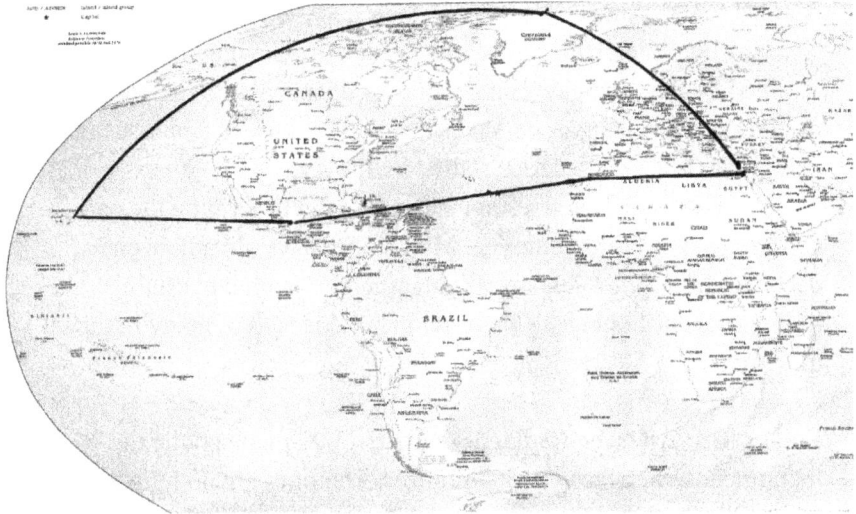

Google Earth – The Faram Research Foundation

The territory outlined by all the Medicine Hat geoglyphs

After plotting the outer boundaries of the territory, which is described by the linear geoglyphs, a pattern begins to emerge. Virtually all the end points described by the linear geoglyphs lie on the boundary of the territories inhabited by cultures who, down through the centuries, have been associated with the Celts or their predecessors, the Etruscans and Phoenicians. The territory described in the previous image correlates precisely with Celtic, Templar, and Portuguese territories outlined by other geoglyphs.

Secret societies all over the world have used these same protocols and end points for over thirty-two thousand years. These groups, particularly the Portuguese, were interacting and trading in the Americas for hundreds of years in secret prior to the voyage of Columbus.

The thirst for power by Hernan Cortes, along with the Spanish Inquisition and the Spanish search for gold in the Americas, destroyed the Mesoamerican cultures that had existed there for over two thousand years. Apparently, these secret cultures were appalled at the atrocities dispensed upon their allies, the Mesoamericans, and decided to construct a memorial to their departed brothers and sisters. This conclusion can be arrived at by reviewing the territory outlined by the Medicine Hat geoglyphs. It specifically makes note of two sacred volcanoes outside Mexico City and encompasses the precise area in Mesoamerica settled by the Aztecs.

This geoglyph does not stand alone in describing the early colonization of North America. Many more have already been decoded. In this new age of enlightenment, it is time to establish the truth about our heritage. This study is but one step of many in that direction.

Follow-Up: After the Badlands Guardian was made public the monument was defaced by a bulldozer. The lines are no longer sharp, and the line glyphs are now missing. See the following satellite images. Since the defacing, trees have been planted to disguise the tragedy.

Google Earth – The Faram Research Foundation
Medicine Hat Aztec chief before defacing

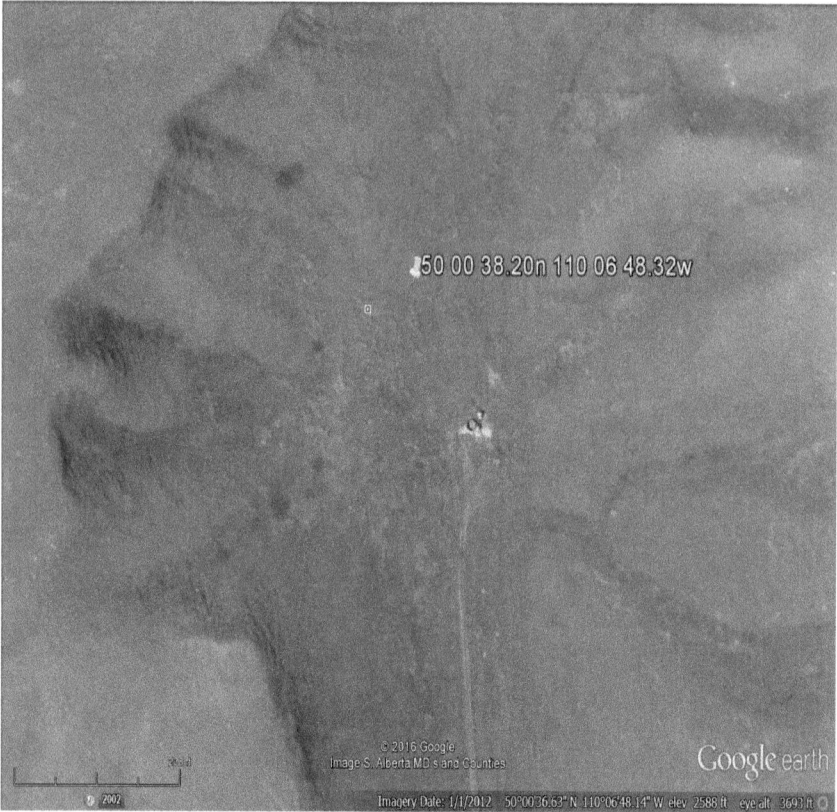

50 00 38.20n 110 06 48.32w

Medicine Hat Aztec chief after defacing

End Narrative K

Narrative L

The Tinitiqilaq Geoglyph, Greenland

Circa 1000 CE the Catholic Church imposed Catholicism on Norway. The Vikings of course were of Nordic origin. What most are not aware of is that the Vikings were recruited by and fought with the Celtic Danes in Zealand Denmark for three hundred years before this. The Celts of the time held to their Coptic beliefs. The Vikings had come to believe in Celtic spirituality and refused to convert to Catholicism. As a result they were banned from Norway. At this same time, the Danes and Norway were engaged in a mutually beneficial trade agreement named the Denmark–Norway Alliance. At this point the Vikings were banned from Norway and were given their own territory to include the area from the shores of Norway and Scotland west to Nova Scotia.

The Tinitiqilaq geoglyph was then built on a previously used sacred location in Greenland to designate the new territory given to the Vikings.

The Tinitiqilaq geoglyph, Greenland

Tinitiqilaq, Greenland, geoglyph, north half bearings

401

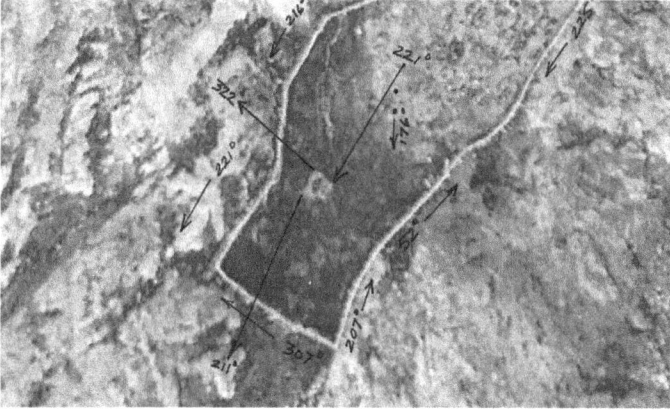

Google Earth – The Faram Research Foundation
Tinitiqilaq, Greenland, geoglyph, south half bearings

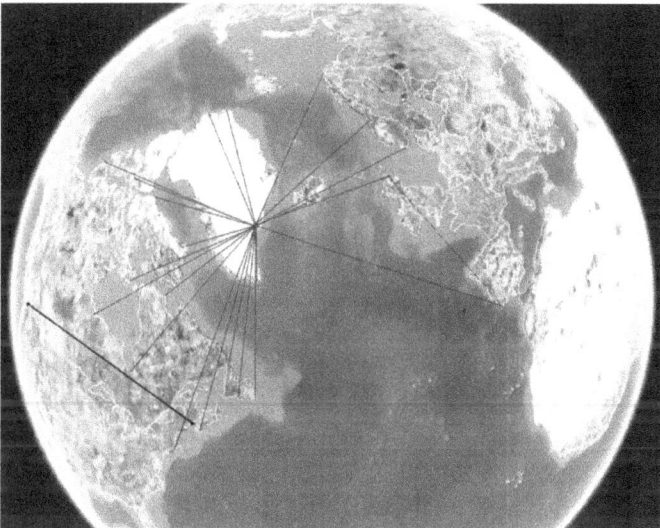

Google Earth – The Faram Research Foundation
Tinitiqilaq radials and Viking territory

The territory depicted by the Tinitiqilaq radial end points is the territory allotted to the Vikings by the Denmark–Norway Alliance ca. 1000 CE. In 1313 CE the little Ice Age occurred, which made it impossible for the Vikings' descendants to live that far north. This caused a mass migration to the southern latitudes.

Unfortunately for the Vikings, the Celts and Templars held claim to the land south of the heavy black line in the previous image. This caused the Celts and Templars, led by Sir Henry Sinclair, to set sail from Scotland in 1398 CE to reclaim their territory from the Norse. (See the book *La Merica*, 2013)

End Narrative N

Narrative M

The Guimar Pyramids, Canary Islands

Google Earth – The Faram Research Foundation
North American territory, ca. 1450 CE

The territory outlined above is the result of a coming together of the Newport Tower, Rhode Island, geoglyph, the decoding of the Kensington Runestone, and the location of Inspiration Peak, Minnesota. (See Narrative N.) Although the North American territory is made clear by the application of geoglyphology to these three locations, there was no prominent marker to validate this gift of North America to the Templars by the Portuguese.

In the early nineteenth century, Portugal was slated to turn the Canary Islands over to Spain. Their last action was to construct the Guimar pyramids to perminantly preserve and validate their deeding of North America to the Templars. The Portuguese and the Celts visited the Americas centuries before Europe became aware that the continents existed. The Portuguese and their predecessors, the Etruscans and Phoenicians, held claim to the Americas until they were split between the Templars, Spain, and the Portuguese, just before Columbus sailed to the Americas to place geoglyphs in the Carribean to claim the Carribean for Spain. (See Narrative O)

Guimar pyramids, Tenerife, Canary Islands, ca. 1822 CE

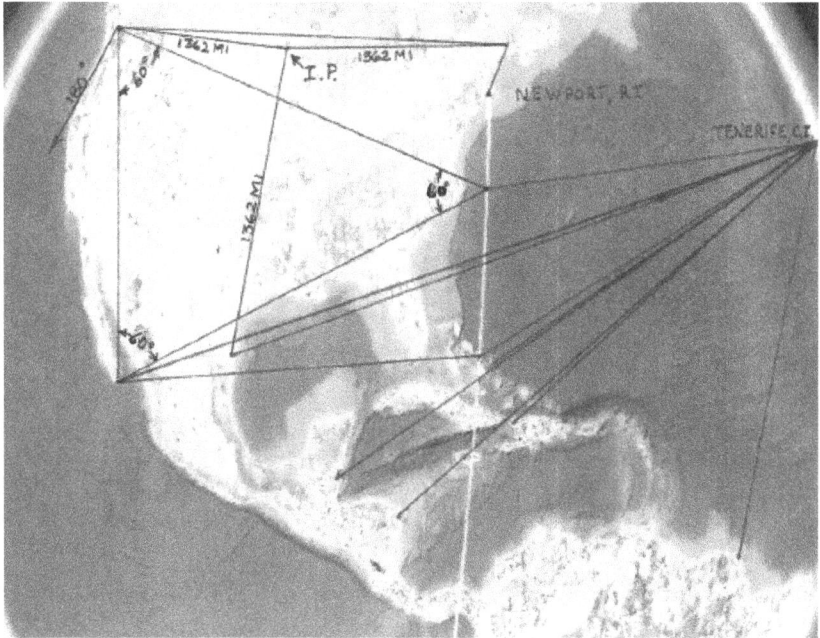

The Guimar pyramid radials confirming the US territory as it was when given to the Templars by the Portuguese c1450 CE

The southeast corner of the Templar territory was located in the Bahamas. The four red lines south of the Bahamas designate countries that were given their independence by Portugal ca. 1822. The Templar (United States) territory is designated by the lines north of the line running from Cat Island, Bahamas, to the tip of Baja California.

406

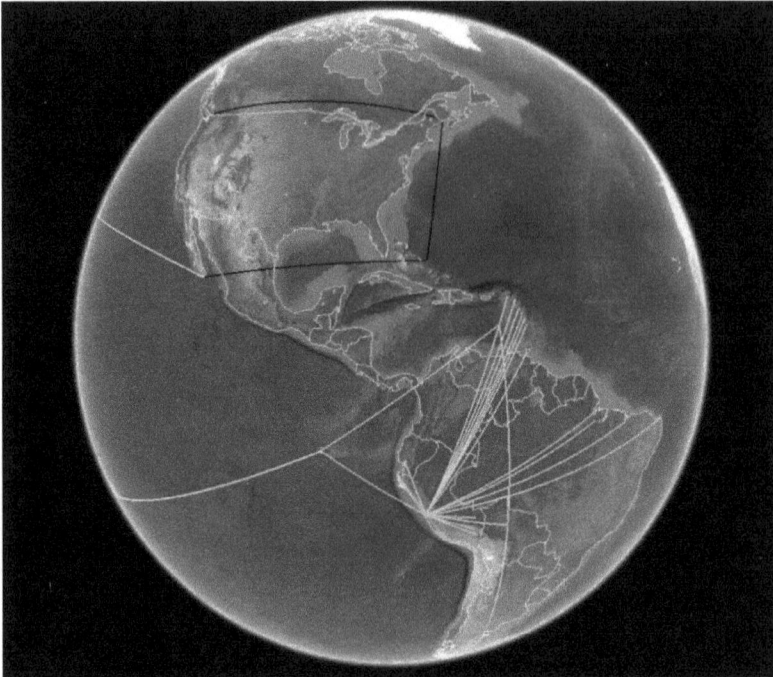

Google Earth – The Faram Research Foundation
The subdivision of the Americas

For many years, prior to Spain's claim to Mesoamerica, the Portuguese and Celts enjoyed free movement between Europe and the Americas. During the Moorish war (ca. 700–1492 CE), the Templars, Portugal, and Spain fought together to win back the Iberian Peninsula. It was during this collaboration that Spain learned about the Americas. Of course, they and the Church wanted a piece of the pie.

Immediately after the Moorish war ended in 1492 CE, Columbus was dispatched to place geoglyphs in the Caribbean to mark Spain's claim to Mesoamerica. The geoglyphically aligned territories seen in the previous image were the result. From top to bottom: Templar, Spanish, and Portuguese territories. (See narratives N, O, and G.)

End Narrative M

Narrative N

The Newport Tower and Kensington Runestone, United States

Google

Newport Tower, Rhode Island

"*I'm going to build my secrets into the geometry of these buildings, because I know that books can be burned but buildings not so easily.*"— Thomas Jefferson

The Newport Tower Story

The Newport Tower has been the subject of discussion and controversy since the colonists first arrived in the New World and discovered the structure on Rhode Island, United States. Early explorers noted that the tower existed during their early explorations of North America. However, that did not deter skeptics from claiming that the tower was constructed in colonial times. Documented research shows that the tower was most likely constructed in the fifteenth century, destroyed in the sixteenth century, and then rebuilt in the seventeenth century on the two hundredth anniversary of its original construction. The Newport Tower is an important North American landmark; however, it is Newport Island itself that has been an important focal point of knowledgeable civilizations around the world for thousands of years.

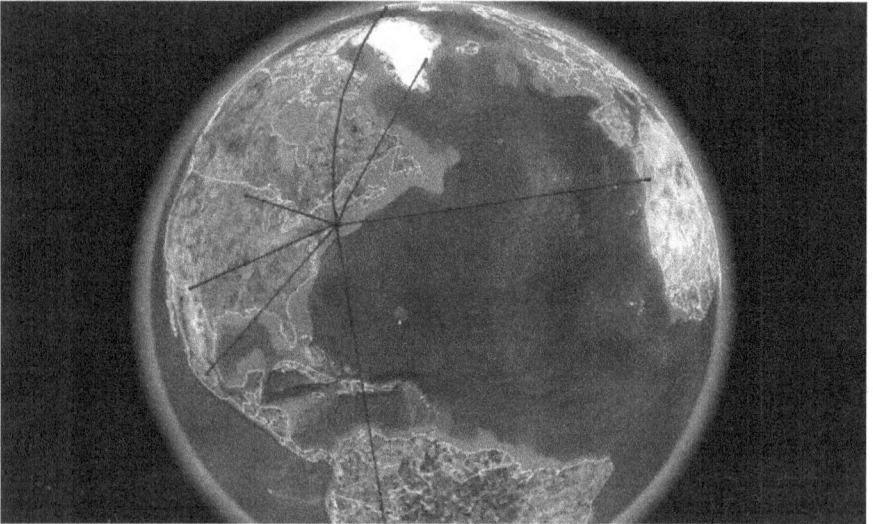

Google Earth – The Faram Research Foundation

Image showing known origination points of geoglyphs around the world that point to the Newport RI location

What follows are the origination points for the pointers displayed in the previous photo. Included are the approximate dates the pointers were created.

Gulfo de Cintra geoglyphs, Sahara, West Africa—ca. 7000 BCE
Inspiration Peak, Minnesota, USA—ca. 7000–3100 BCE

Cahuachi, Nazca, Peru—ca. 5 CE

Pyramids of China—ca. 100 BCE–400 CE

Tiniteqilaq geoglyph, Greenland—ca. 1100 CE

River geoglyph, El Paso, Texas, USA—ca. 1300 CE

Mexico City geoglyph—ca. 1325 CE

Kensington Runestone, Minnesota, USA—ca. 1473 CE

"Michoacan," Mexico, a geoglyphic mural by Diego Rivera—ca. 1925 CE

The Newport Tower

The Newport Tower has been carbon-dated as being over five hundred years old. The simple geometry associated with the tower is outlined below. The results of the carbon dating and details of the Newport Tower, the Kensington Runestone, and many more landmarks, geoglyphs, and monoliths can be found in the book *Ancient Signposts* (2011). As you will see, the Newport Tower and Inspiration Peak locations have been known and revered for thousands of years.

Purpose

Newport Tower was built by early inhabitants of North America for two reasons. The first was to point the way to Inspiration Peak, a place of special geographical importance. The second was to substantiate the builders' land claim to North America by using the unique geographical location of Newport, Rhode Island, and Inspiration Peak, Minnesota. The predecessors of the people that built the tower knew of Newport for over seven thousand years. This is substantiated by the 7000 year old Egyptian Gulfo de Cintra geoglyph in West Africa, and others, which point out the Newport Tower site.   There was a reason that North America held some special significance. Geoglyphs found around the world show that people were mapping out what would later be known as the United States as far back as the building of the Mayan pyramids. Mayan pyramids located in Central America outline the boundaries of what would eventually become the United States (see *Ancient Signposts*, 2011).

Geometry of the Newport Tower Mystery

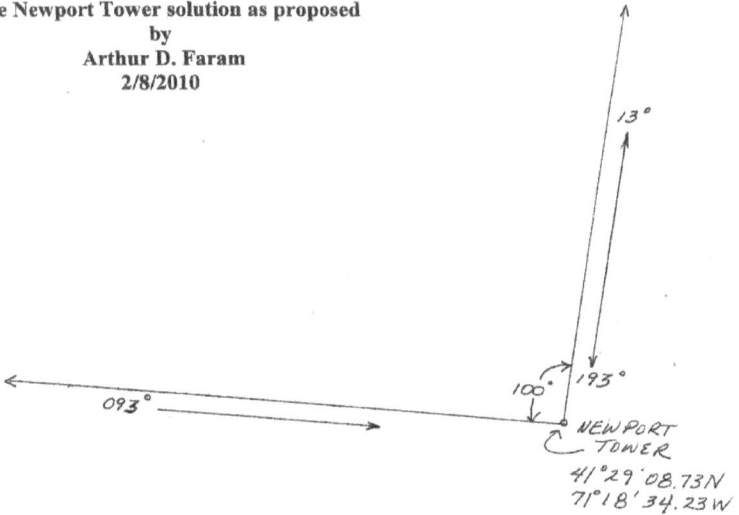

The Newport 13° radial

Something that should be remembered about the builders of the tower is that they placed little value on words. The builders, their predecessors, and their descendants, were men of numbers and symbols. You should also know that the builders and their predecessors never present a puzzle without setting up another solution to the same puzzle by some other method. This prevents the skepticism that has prevailed over the past centuries about the Newport Tower and other ancient artifacts for which no verification from another source has been found until now. It is a known fact that the Newport Tower is aligned along a 93/273-degree axis. In addition, there has always been a question as to why most European structures of non-secular origin have six legs, while this one has eight legs. It was decided that the eight legs might be a clue.

Was it possible that the eight legs on the tower were a symbol for eighty degrees? Navigators of this era oriented their maps and alignments to the east. As a result the solution was started by subtracting eighty degrees from the east orientation of ninety-three degrees. This obviously left a bearing of thirteen degrees. If this was correct, there now existed one angle and two sides, of undefined length, to a triangle. In order for the thirteen-degree radial to be significant, a geographical location along the thirteen-degree bearing would have to be found to define the length of that side of the triangle.

Google Earth – The Faram Research Foundation
La Haute-Côte-Nord
(48°23′13.48″ N, 68°49′52.19″ W)

While tracing the thirteen-degree bearing, it was noticed that the line went directly over a small island in the Saint Lawrence Seaway that the locals call La Haute-Côte-Nord. Loosely translated, La Haute-Côte-Nord means in French "the highest point on the north dimension." This appeared to be a vital clue. There now existed two sides, one length, and one angle of the triangle. In order to make a triangle, one more angle or side was needed. During previous research several other triangles were discovered. The angles of the information collected thus far at Newport coincided with angles in the previously identified triangles. Those angles were applied to the Newport Triangle to see if there was any significance to the previously identified information. Sure enough, there was a correlation. It was as if the other triangles were constructed to give the solution to the Newport Tower mystery.

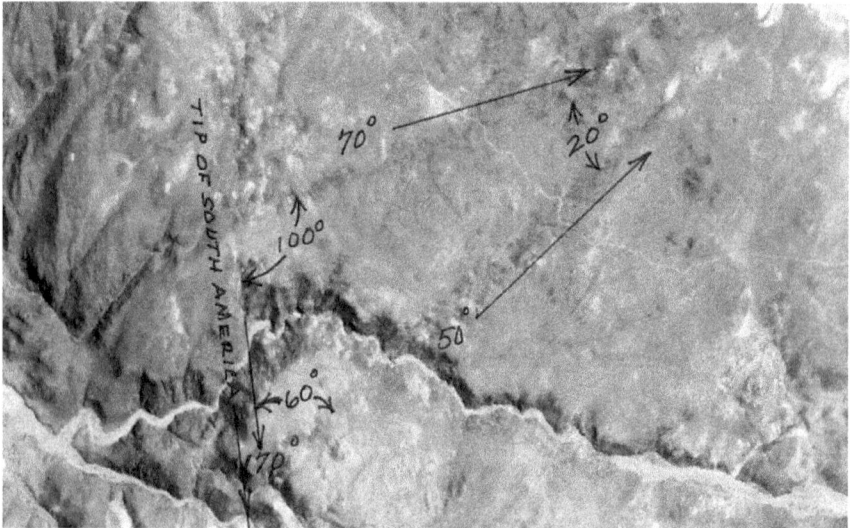

Google Earth – The Faram Research Foundation
The Copiapo, Chile, triangle

One of the triangles is located in Copiapo, Chile, and is just one of the many glyphs scattered around the globe as clues to substantiate the Newport Triangle solution. The importance of this triangle is that it provides the three angles that make up the Newport Triangle. This was just one more check to substantiate that the solution to the Newport Triangle is valid. This and other geoglyphs pertaining to the Newport Tower were discovered by following the directions provided by geoglyphs all over the world. This in itself proves the validity of geoglyphology.

The Copiapo triangle consists of three interior angles of twenty, sixty, and one hundred degrees. Since one hundred degrees was the one angle that had already been decoded from the Newport Tower, the other two angles were applied to the partially completed triangle to see what developed. The sides of the triangle were extended to the west, because to the east there was nothing but water. If a significant landmark existed at the point of the western vertex, a solution to the mystery of the Newport Tower might have been found. As hoped, there was a significant landmark situated right under the western vertex of the triangle. The name of that landmark is Inspiration Peak, and this triangle was named the Newport Triangle. The resulting triangle is in the next image.

The Newport Tower solution as proposed
by
Arthur D. Faram
2/8/2010

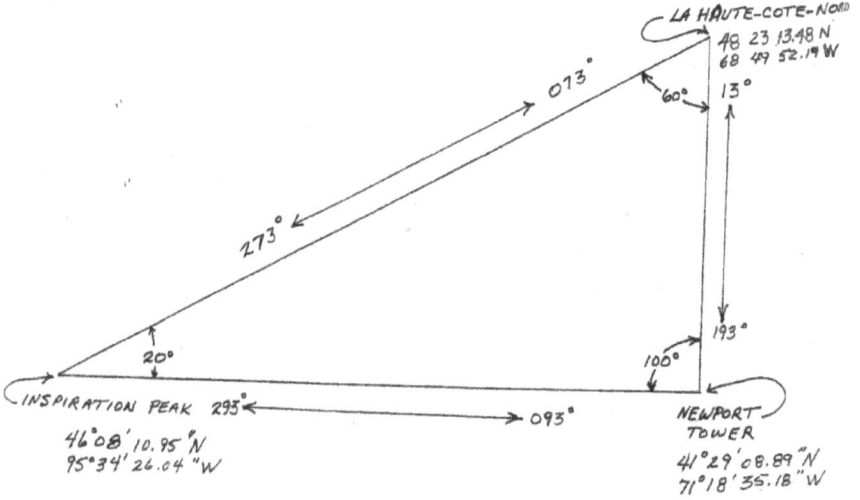

LA HAUTE-COTE-NORD
48 23 13.48 N
68 49 52.19 W

073
273
20°
60°
13°
100°
193°
093°

INSPIRATION PEAK 295
46°08'10.95"N
95°34'26.04"W

NEWPORT TOWER
41°29'08.89"N
71°18'35.18"W

NOTE: NOT TO SCALE

The Faram Research Foundation

The Newport Triangle

As hoped, there was a significant landmark situated right under the western vertex of the triangle. The name of that landmark is Inspiration Peak.

The Faram Research Foundation

Inspiration Peak, Minnesota, USA
(46°08′09.49″ N, 95°34′14.61″ W)

Inspiration Peak, like the Newport Tower location, has been known and surveyed for thousands of years. The knowledge of the significance of Inspiration Peak in ancient times is identified and verified by Stonehenge in England. Inspiration Peak was not only identified by the complex mathematics built into the Newport Tower but also by many other geoglyphs around the world, including Stonehenge. This also holds true for the site where the Newport Tower resides.

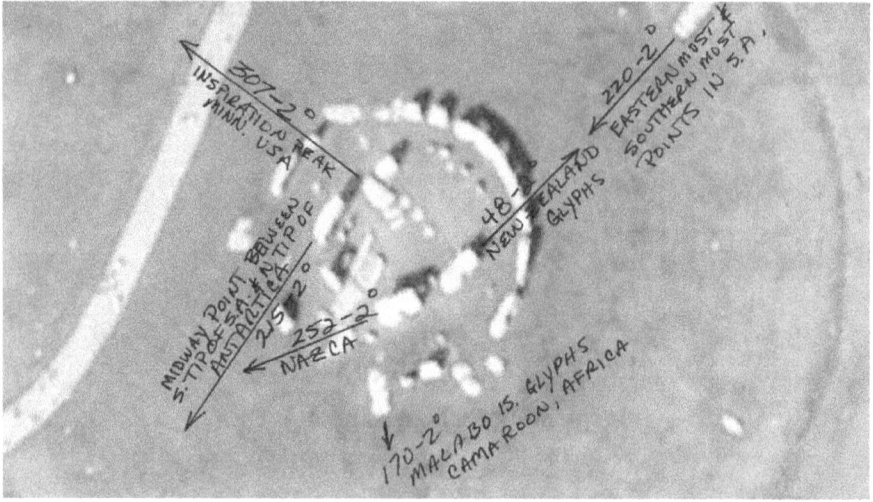

**Radials generated by Stonehenge, one of which points to
Inspiration Peak, Minnesota**

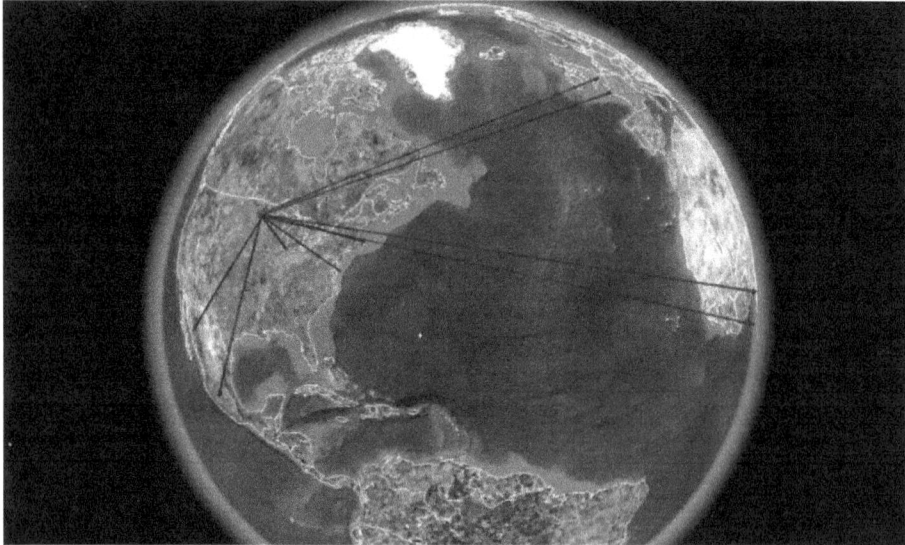

**Photo showing known origination points of geoglyphs that point
to the Inspiration Peak location**

Origination points for the pointers displayed in the previous image:

Stonehenge monolith, UK
Monte Alban Pyramid, Oaxaca, Mexico
Pigeon Point geoglyph, Minnesota, USA
Manchester, Ohio, geoglyph, USA
Kensington Runestone, Minnesota, USA
Twenty-Third Street NW geoglyph, Washington, DC, USA
Point du Raz geoglyphs, Bretagne, France
Malabo Island geoglyphs, Equatorial New Guinea, West Africa
Cape of Good Hope geoglyphs, south tip of Africa
Atanacio geoglyphs, Mexico
Newport Tower, Newport, Rhode Island, USA

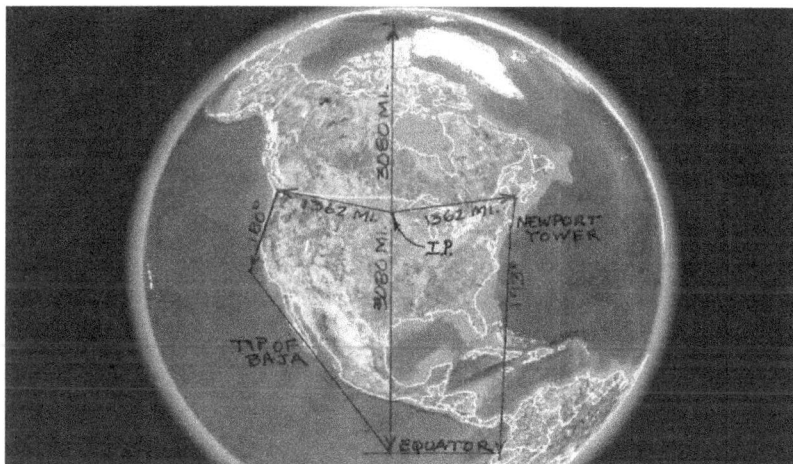

Google Earth – The Faram Research Foundation

Inspiration Peak, Minnesota, USA, the North American territory deeded to the Templars by the Portuguese, ca. 1400 CE. (Notice that Inspiration Peak is the geographic center of this territory.)

Inspiration Peak lies halfway between the equator and the North Pole. The peak lies 1,362 miles from ancient northwest, northeast, and southern geoglyphs that had an influence on the final boundaries of the United States. (More details can be found in *Ancient Signposts*, 2011.) For ancient cultures to be able to locate and survey this location and tie it to the Newport Tower location over seven thousand years ago boggles the mind. Newport Tower and Inspiration Peak are the most important of the markers found in North America. They are important because these two markers are able to combine to delineate the North American land claim prior to the gift of Mesoamerica to Spain ca. 1400 CE. After Spain inherited Mesoamerica, the Kensington Runestone was carved to realign the North American territory from consisting of North America and Mesoamerica to just North America. The differences in boundaries are presented in the image before and after this paragraph.

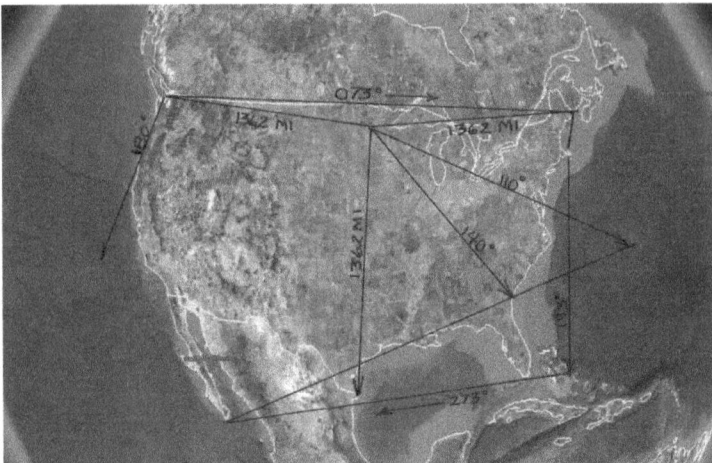

Google Earth – The Faram Research Foundation
Inspiration Peak, USA, revised North American territory, ca. 1400 CE

Using the geoglyphic data retrieved from the Kensington Runestone, Newport Tower, and Inspiration Peak, a picture of the revised North American (US) territory is made possible.

The Kensington Runestone was not needed until the Spanish/Mesoamerican revision presented itself. This revision placed the new boundary between the United States and Mexico as a line running from Cat Island in the Bahamas and the southern tip of Baja.

This alignment was agreed to between the Templars, Portugal, and Spain sometime during their alliance while ridding the Iberian Peninsula of the Moors. This revision allowed Hernan Cortes to invade Mexico in 1519 CE. Unfortunately Spain exceeded their boundaries and expanded into North and South America in search for gold. Before the invasion of Mexico, the Templars, later to become the Freemasons, owned the territory shown in the previous image.

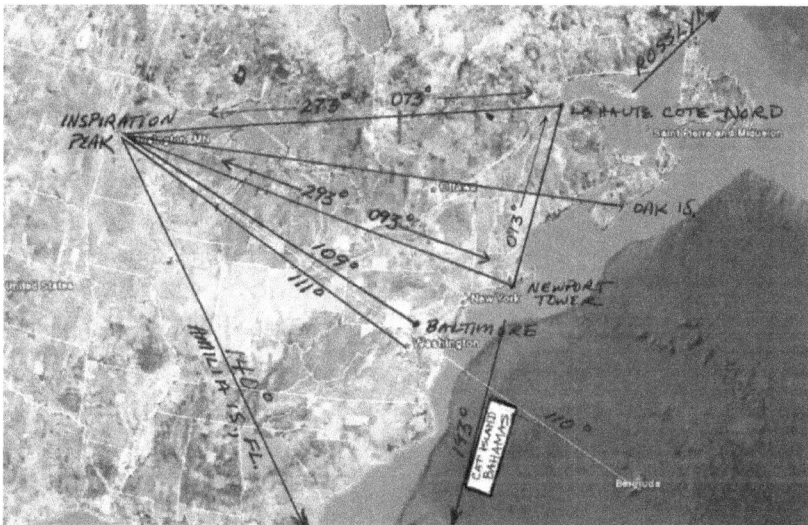

Google Earth – The Faram Research Foundation

Inspiration Peak radials as defined by the Kensington Runestone

In the previous image, all the bearings associated with solving of the Newport Tower and Kensington Runestone mysteries are depicted. The thirteen-degree bearing was the initial bearing that had to be discovered before the puzzles could be solved. The reciprocal of the thirteen-degree bearing is the 193-degree bearing, which was important in defining the Celts' original claim to North America.

In decoding the Kensington Runestone, which verified the math in the Newport Tower solution, the bearings of 110 and 140 were mentioned. Those two radial end points make up the line that runs to Baja California. Note that the 111 radial, which added together makes three, goes through the current capital of the United States. The number three is a sacred number to ancient societies. This could not have been a coincidence.

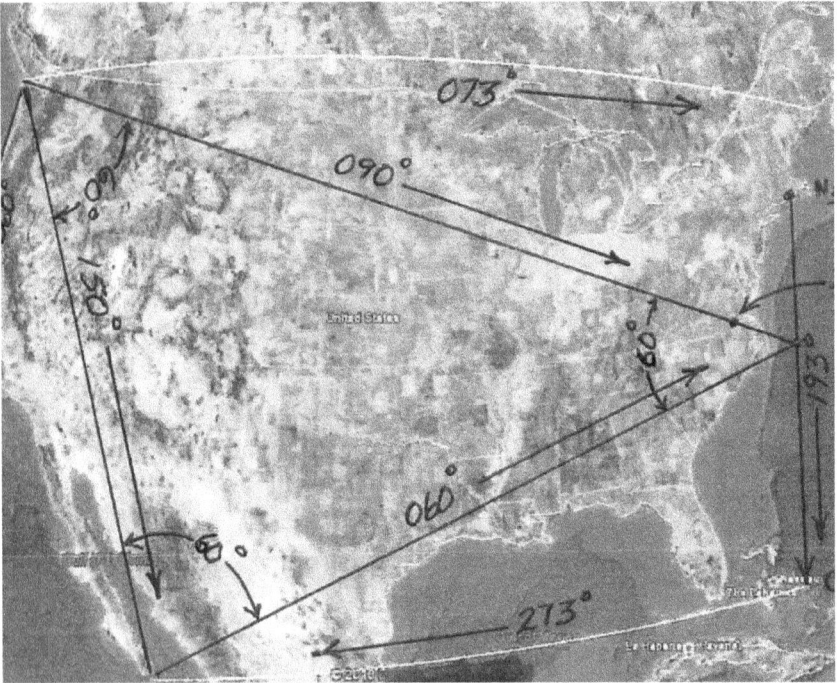

Google Earth – The Faram Research Foundation

Map of the North American land claim (The outside black and light colored lines.), ca. 1400 CE, also showing the Great Triangle

It is no coincidence that the SE corner of this land claim was where Columbus landed on his first voyage. It is clear that Spain was attempting to establish a land claim to the Gulf of Mexico and Mesoamerica. This is proved out by the geoglyphs found on several

Caribbean islands left by Columbus to claim the land for Spain. The original boundary between what is now the United States and Canada was established by the Stonehenge geoglyph.

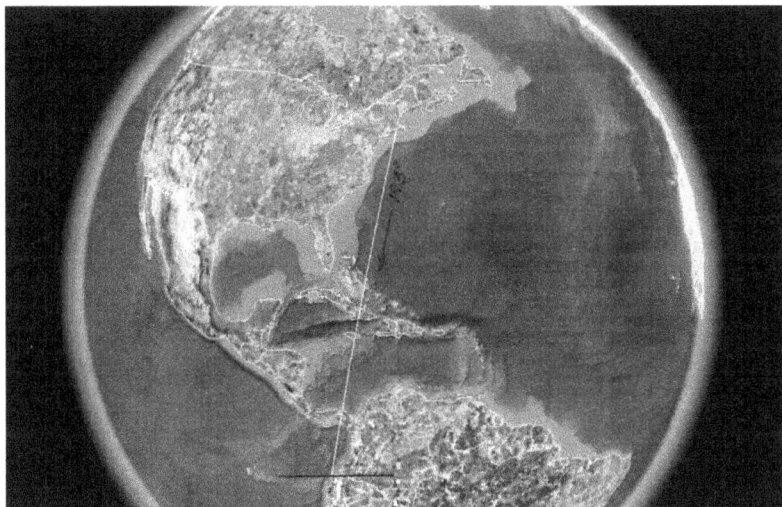

Google Earth – The Faram Research Foundation
The Newport Tower, 193-degree radial

Further confirmation that the 13/193-degree radial was not chosen at random is the fact that when extended to the south, it intersects exactly at where the equator crosses the coast of Ecuador. This point has been confirmed as an important marker to the ancients and is identified by numerous glyphs around the world. As you have seen previously, the 193-degree radial runs through Cat Island, previously named San Salvador.

The combination of mathematics, geometry, and survey skills necessary to accomplish such a perfect geometrical puzzle is phenomenal. By including two of the same bearings used in the solution of the Newport Triangle, the originators are not only showing their skill but, as usual, are providing a cross-check to verify to any investigator that they have the correct solution to the land claim. As stated before, the early colonizers of America always provide a way of verifying their work. By the time you finish reading the Kensington Runestone solution (linked below), you should be convinced that the Kensington Runestone, Newport Tower, and Inspiration Peak all complement and verify the credibility of each other. It is obvious that the evidence shows a time-consuming survey of North America. A prudent person would have to question who did it, when they did it, and why. The answers are astonishing but not surprising.

The Kensington Runestone

The Kensington Runestone

Runestone Introduction

The Kensington Runestone has been the subject of discussion and
controversy since its discovery in 1898 by a Swedish farmer named
Olof Ohman while he was clearing land for his farm near
Kensington, Minnesota (45°48′46.17″ N, 95°40′01.53″ W). Due to
inherent skepticism, and the fact that Olof was himself Swedish,

many people thought the stone was a forgery. This controversy has existed for over a hundred years up until this very time. Well, the controversy is over. There is now physical proof that the Runestone is authentic and plays a large role in American history. The Kensington Runestone, pictured above, is thirty-one inches high, sixteen inches wide, six inches thick, and weighs 202 pounds. On the face and one side are characters known as runes, a type of writing used in the Middle Ages only by inhabitants of northwestern Europe, such as the Norwegians, Celtic Danes, and Gotland Islanders.

As you saw in the Newport Tower presentation, the Newport Tower led us to two geographically and historically important points, Inspiration Peak and the Kensington Runestone. Newport Tower, Inspiration Peak, and the Kensington Runestone were important in outlining the territory given to the Celts/Templars by the Portuguese. (See *La Merica*, 2013.) There was a previous North American territory that existed prior to the Newport Tower being constructed. Based on the fact that the Inspiration Peak and Newport locations were identified by geoglyphs as far back as 7000 BCE, it is safe to assume that said territory existed prior to the Newport Tower being built. The Kensington Runestone was carved to designate the revision of the original territory. That revision came about through an agreement between the Templars and the Portuguese to deed Mesoamerica to Spain.

The Kensington Runestone Solution

Runestone front

Runestone side

Upon submitting the Runestone to a handwriting analysis, it was determined that the writing had been done by two different persons. The first five rows were done by one person, and the last four rows and side were done by a second person. The first tip-off is the slant of the work. If you check the slant in the pictures above, you will notice a distinct difference from one person's writing to the other. Another tip-off is the way the letters are formed. For example, the first person brings the right leg of his R all the way down to the baseline, while the second person stops short of the baseline. As is common when someone is attempting to copy another person's writing, the copier gets tired of trying to copy the other person's style, and toward the end of the first line and thereafter, he reverts back to his own style.

It is believed that the second person's writing was added to more clearly define the boundaries of the North American territory after an agreement to deed Mesoamerica to Spain. As is depicted in the Newport Tower solution, Mesoamerica was once part of a North America land claim.

Text (Nielsen interpretation)
With one slight variation from the Larsson rune rows, using the letter þ (representing "th" as in "think" or "this") instead of d, the inscription on the face (from which a few words may be missing due to spalling, particularly at the lower left corner where the surface is calcite rather than greywacke) reads:

" 8:göter:ok:22:norrmen:po:
??o:opþagelsefarþ:fro
vinlanþ:of:vest:vi:
haþe:läger:veþ:2:skylar:en:
þags:rise:norr:fro:þeno:sten:
vi:var:ok:fiske:en:þagh:äptir:
vi:kom:hem:fan:10:man:röþe:
af:bloþ:og:þeþ:AVM:
fräelse:af:illu:
"

Translation: Unlike the version in the infobox above, this is based on Richard Nielsen's 2001 translation of the text, which attempts specifically to put it into a medieval context, giving variant readings of some words:

8 Geats and 22 Norwegians on ?? acquisition expedition from Vinland far west. We had traps by 2 shelters one day's travel to the north from this stone. We were fishing one day. After we came home, found 10 men red with blood and dead. AVM (Ave Maria) Deliver from evils.

The lateral (or side) text reads:

" har:10:mans:we:hawet:at:se:
äptir:wore:skip:14:þagh:rise:
from:þeno:öh:ahr:1362:
"

Translation:

(I) have 10 men at the inland sea to look after our ship 14 days travel from this wealth/property. Year [of our Lord] 1362

Nielsen's translation of the Runestone

In order to discover how the Runestone and the tower were connected, it is necessary to study a translation of the Runestone by Dr. Richard Nielsen. As previously stated, the builders of the Newport Tower and creators of the Kensington Runestone had little use for words and instead place most of their emphasis on numbers, geometry, and symbols. Attention is directed to the numbers contained in the translation.

The number 1362, the last characters on the Runestone, rather than being a date, was found to be a code that validates the Runestone as genuine. Until the writing of this book, this information has been kept secret. But 1362 is the elevation above sea level of the location where the Runestone was found. This is the final proof that the Runestone is genuine. One would have to ask how they knew the elevation of the Runestones location. I would have to answer: Why not, it's from the same place where they were projecting lines over thousands of miles with precise accuracy.

Text (Nielsen interpretation)
With one slight variation from the Larsson rune rows, using the letter þ (representing "th" as in "think" or "this") instead of d, the inscription on the face (from which a few words may be missing due to spalling, particularly at the lower left corner where the surface is calcite rather than greywacke) reads:

" 8:gōter:ok:22:norrmen:po:
??o:opþagelsefarþ:fro
vinlanþ:of:vest:vi:
haþe:läger:veþ:2:skylar:en:
þags:rise:norr:fro:þeno:sten:
vi:var:ok:fiske:en:þagh:äptir:
vi:kom:hem:fan:10:man:rōþe:
af:bloþ:og:þeþ:AVM:
fräelse:af:illu:
"

— SUBTRACT 80 DEGREES FROM 093° ORIENTATION OF I.P. TO OBTAIN 13° STARTING POINT.

Translation: Unlike the version in the infobox above, this is based on Richard Nielsen's 2001 translation of the text, which attempts specifically to put it into a medieval context, giving variant readings of some words:

22° @ 2 MILES FROM RUNESTONE SPACER TO I.P.

8 Geats and 22 Norwegians on ?? acquisition expedition from Vinland far west. We had traps by 2 shelters one day's travel to the north from this stone. We were fishing one day. After we came home, found 10 men red with blood and dead. AVM (Ave Maria) Deliver from evils.

10° @ 22 MILES FROM RUNESTONE TO SPACER

The lateral (or side) text reads:

" har:10:mans:we:hawet:at:se:
äptir:wore:skip:14:þagh:rise:
from:þeno:ōh:ahr:1362:
"

Translation:

110° RADIAL TO BERMUDA   140° RADIAL TO EAST COAST MARKER

(I) have 10 men at the inland sea to look after our ship 14 days travel from this wealth/property. Year [of our Lord] 1362

DISTANCE FROM I.P. TO THREE CORNERS OF US.

Nielson translation decoded
by Arthur Faram

The previous image is the original translation by Dr. Nielsen. The decoding was performed by the Faram Research Foundation and led to discovery of the real reason that the Runestone was carved.

The Geometry of the Runestone

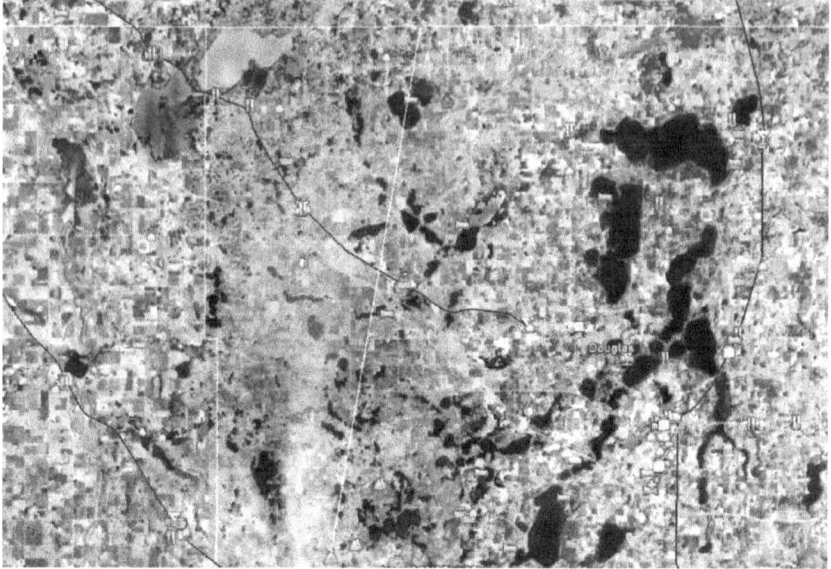

Google Earth – The Faram Research Foundation
Ten degrees at twenty-two miles

One solution derived from the numbers given on the Runestone was a heading of ten degrees at twenty-two miles. This was the measurement from where the Kensington Runestone was found to what we labeled as "the Spacer," mentioned below. Although this interpretation seemed to be headed in the right direction, toward Inspiration Peak, there were no indications that the line met any of the protocols of geoglyphology. Neither did any of the other combinations of numbers. Research was done to see if the method of measurement had changed from 1362 CE until now. Sure enough, Queen Elizabeth had changed the universal standard of measurement, the mile, from 5,000 feet to 5,280 feet after she became queen in 1592. That meant that twenty-two miles in old English miles would convert to 20.8 miles in new English miles. Curiously enough, most of the explorers' maps that have been discovered are dated in the sixteenth century. Could this change in

431

universal measurement have come about to mask all the measurements done before that?

Google Earth – The Faram Research Foundation
The Spacer

After converting the old English miles to new English miles, the figures ten degrees at 20.8 miles were used. This placed the end point on what became known as "the Spacer," shown above. It was called this because the measurements are so precise that when you land on the south end of the Spacer and begin your second leg from the south end, you will come up short of reaching the all-important Inspiration Peak by the same length as the spacer. The second leg of the connection must start on the north end of the Spacer. The Spacer is the line on the left side of the picture that looks like a runway. This is in reality a stone wall that someone has mowed around. This object may or may not be currently shown on Google Earth.

Notice the geometric symbols across the road from the Spacer.

Google Earth – The Faram Research Foundation

Inspiration Peak, twenty-two degrees at two miles

Now that the Spacer has come into play, one must follow the new direction in which the stone wall points at twenty-two degrees. The Kensington Runestone describes as this leg as twenty-two degrees at two miles in order to reach the main survey marker named Inspiration Peak. But remember, we are dealing in old English miles, so the real distance is 1.9 miles. The end of the last line drawn lands precisely where the west vertex of the Newport Triangle solution landed on Inspiration Peak.

The Campsite

The figures displayed above are the figures used to transition from the place where the Kensington Runestone was found to Inspiration Peak. However, locating Inspiration Peak was meaningless unless

433

you already knew the geometry associated with it. It appears that the first writer assumed that the reader would already know the geometry and would only need to locate Inspiration Peak in order to apply the mathematics. There was enough information in the first five lines of the text to locate the "traps and two shelters one day north from this spot." (This is referring to a campsite containing the stone wall pointing to Inspiration Peak. This campsite is depicted in the next two photos.) However, the second writer had a different agenda and wanted to make the complete solution available to whoever might find the stone. This would be a prudent move if the second writer assumed the details would be lost to time. But this was not the only reason for placing new information on the stone. Since the time that Inspiration Peak was surveyed, thousands of years before, things had changed that required a revision of the boundaries that had existed for millennia. The main reason for the revision was the deeding of Mesoamerica to Spain.

The critical addition to the Kensington Runestone was the number 1362. As you will see, the 110-degree radial and the 140-degree radial were also added and are also critical in solving the revised puzzle. The revised North American survey excluded Central America and retained Baja California. Unfortunately Baja California was later lost after the Mexican–American War.

The Stone Wall Pointer

Google Earth – The Faram Research Foundation

Campsite one day north of Kensington Runestone site

Note: This photo is presented so that you can see the geoglyphs on the ground before they were covered with lines in the next photo. These geoglyphs were plowed under after we naively posted them.

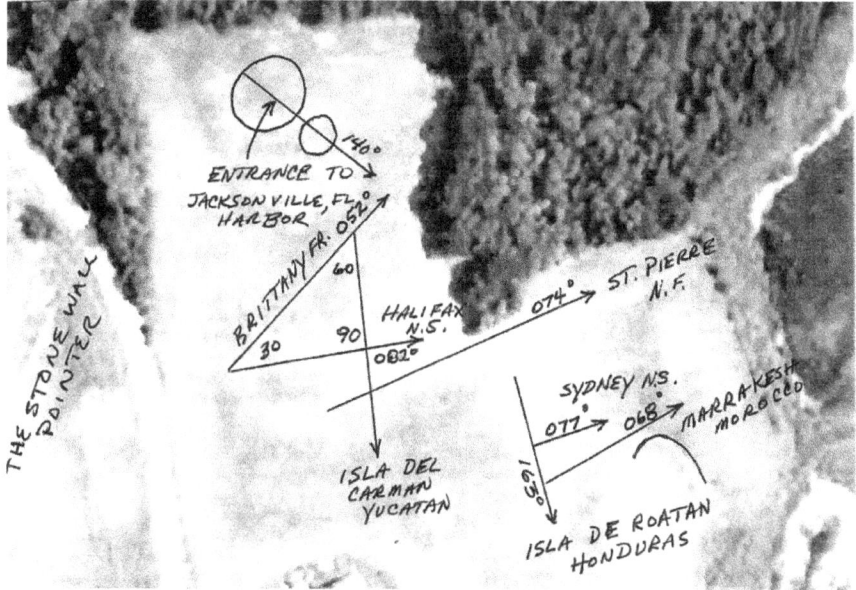

Campsite with geoglyphs and stone wall pointing to Inspiration Peak

This campsite is obviously the one mentioned in the first five lines on the Kensington Runestone. The stone wall here is oriented twenty-two degrees at two miles from Inspiration Peak. All that would be necessary from here is to follow the stone wall pointer, a common pointer in geoglyphology, to Inspiration Peak. The pre-Columbian geoglyphs confirm this was a campsite, as placing geoglyphs at your campsite to claim a territory or denote your travels was a common practice at the time. The radial end points shown in the photo are all known pre-Columbian geoglyphic locations. The lines that are generated by this geoglyph, unlike most, do not seem to form an organized territorial boundary. However, the end points are geoglyph end points used consistently by other geoglyphs around the world.

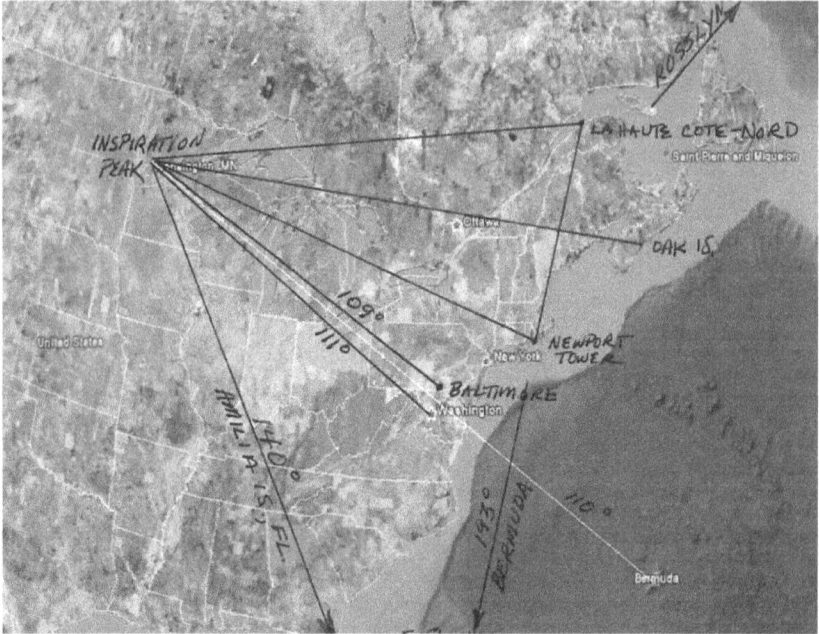

Inspiration Peak 110- and 140-degree radials as defined by the Kensington Runestone.

The other lines are added for relationship purposes.

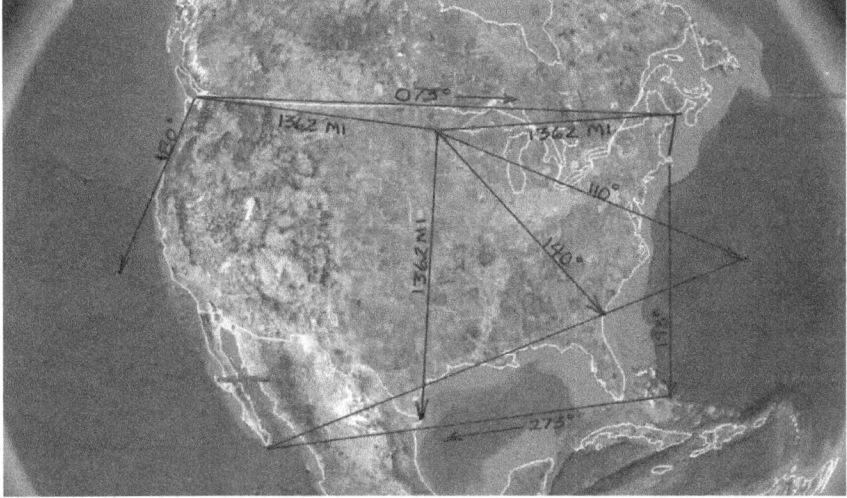

Google Earth – The Faram Research Foundation

The revised North American territorial boundaries as described by the Newport Tower, Inspiration Peak, and the Kensington Runestone

Notice that by running a line from Bermuda, the termination point of the 110 degree radial, through Amelia Island, the termination point of the 140 degree radial you have a line that terminates at the tip of Baja California, the new boundary of the North American territory. There were further revisions of the United States boundary after the Mexican–American War.

Geoglyphs at the End of the Three Radial End Points from Inspiration Peak

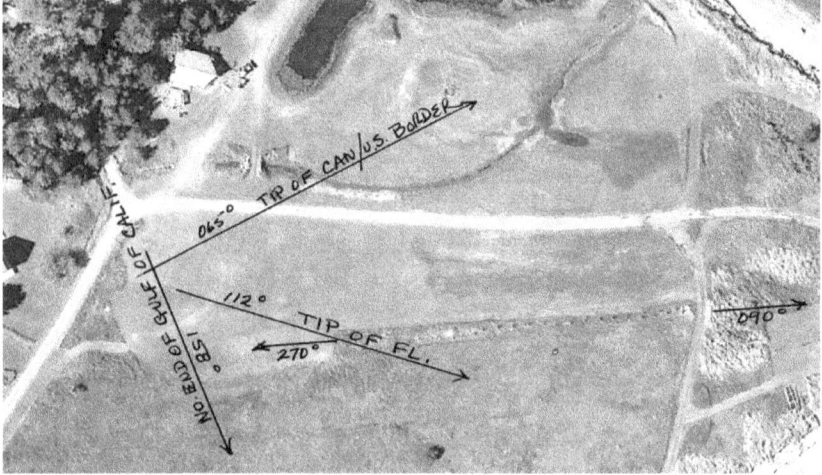

Google Earth – The Faram Research Foundation

The northwest end point and associated square geoglyph

(Geoglyph was destroyed by landowner after being published)

Depicted above is the termination point of the northwest radial from Inspiration Peak. The associated square geoglyph is a survey marker validating the northeast corner of the northern territory (later to become the United States). This geoglyph is on Stuart Island, the last island before Vancouver Island, Canada. Based on protocols used in constructing the four geoglyphs depicted here, it is believed that the geoglyphs were made by the same group of people that revised the North American land claim. It is apparent that they wanted there to be no mistake as to the territory they claimed and, as would be proved later, were willing to fight for. Unfortunately the landowner has since destroyed this survey marker.

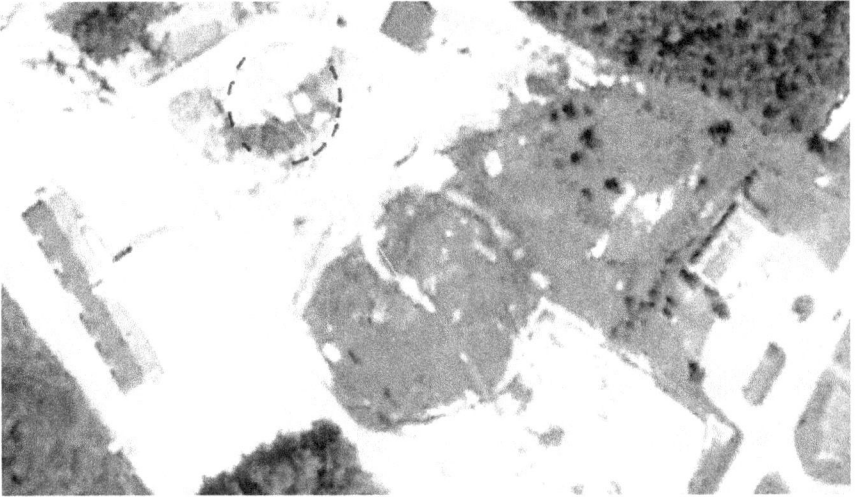

The northeast end point and associated geoglyph

(This geoglyph was destroyed after being published)

Depicted above is the termination point of the northeast radial from Inspiration Peak. Unfortunately the owners of this property have not taken very good care of this geoglyph. Amazingly, this geoglyph points directly to the island of La Haute-Côte-Nord, the island in the Saint Lawrence Seaway that provides the first clue as the termination point of the thirteen-degree radial from the Newport Tower. This geoglyph is located at the original northern boundary of the State of Maine and the northern territory. The land north of here was added to the United States later. Unfortunately this geoglyph has also been destroyed by the land owner.

The Texas end point of the Inspiration Peak southern 1362 radial.

(Still visible)

This geoglyph requires some explanation. This southern radial extended to within thirty miles of the Rio Grande. Up until the Mexican–American War, there had always been a dispute as to where the southern boundary of the United States ended. After Spain took over Mexico, they claimed that the point where the southern 1,362-mile-long radial ended, the Nueces River, was the southern boundary of the United States. The United States claimed that the Rio Grande was the boundary between the United States and Mexico. This dispute was not settled until the Mexican–American War.

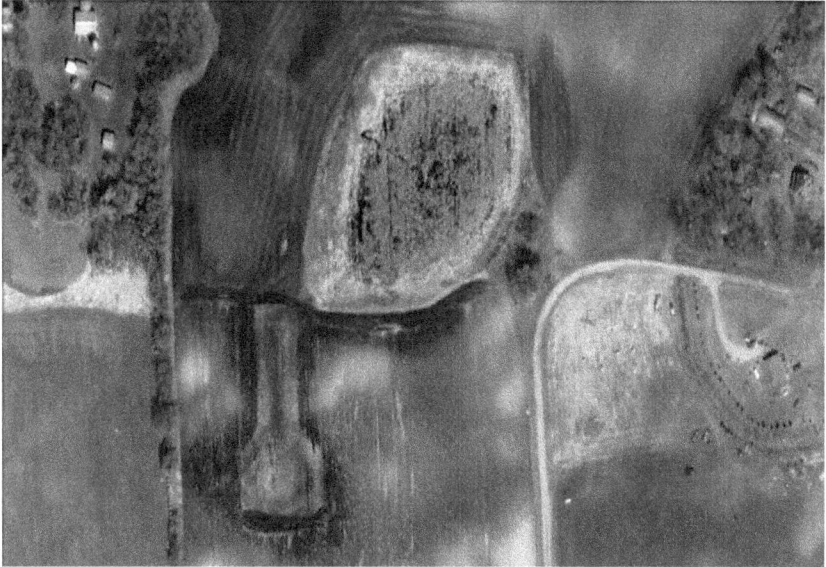

The Inspiration Peak all-seeing eye

The preceding photo shows the glyph of the "all-seeing eye," which is seen in Egyptian hieroglyphics, Masonic icons, and on the US one-dollar bill. This glyph and the key next to it are of raised earth so that they will stand the test of time. This and similar glyphs are located at numerous locations around the United States as survey markers and reminders of European visitations in ancient times. The key glyph to the left of the eye is oriented at 360 degrees true and points to Inspiration Peak.

End Narrative N

Narrative O

The Columbus Secrets

Christopher Columbus, 1451-1506 CE

The name Christopher Columbus is the Anglicization of the Latin name Christophorus Columbus. His name in Italian is Cristoforo Colombo, and in Spanish Cristóbal Colón. After reading this chapter, I am certain you will agree that the story of Columbus is not at all what we have been told. This chapter is not written to infer that Columbus did not travel to America; there is plenty of historical evidence to establish that fact. This chapter will validate that by the time Columbus made his voyage, the Templars and Celts owned the North American territory mentioned throughout this book, and that Spain acquired knowledge of this fact while fighting with Portugal and the Templars during the Moorish war, which ended in 1492. This chapter will also prove that Spain had plans to conquer Mesoamerica even before Columbus began his voyage. Based on this information, the story that Cortes invaded Mesoamerica on his own, without permission from Spain, is most likely not true.

The Quest for Support

In 1485, Columbus presented his plans to King John II of Portugal to cross the Atlantic. Columbus proposed that the king equip him with three sturdy ships and grant him one year's time to sail out into the Atlantic, search for a western route to the Orient, and return. Columbus also requested that he be made "Great Admiral of the Ocean," appointed governor of any and all lands he discovered, and given one tenth of all revenue from those lands. The king submitted Columbus's proposal to his experts, who rejected it. It was their considered opinion that Columbus's estimation of a travel distance of 2,400 miles (3,860 km) was, in fact, far too low. The true reason for the denial was that Portugal did not want their colonies in South America discovered.

In 1488, Columbus appealed to the court of Portugal once again, and once again, John II gave him an audience. King John again showed no interest in Columbus's far-fetched project. Columbus traveled from Portugal to both Genoa and Venice, but he did not receive encouragement from either. Columbus had also dispatched his brother Bartholomew to the court of Henry VII of England to inquire whether the English crown might sponsor his expedition, but he was also without success.

Columbus then sought an audience with the monarchs Ferdinand II of Aragon and Isabella I of Castile, Spain. Isabella had united many kingdoms in the Iberian Peninsula by marrying and ruling together with Ferdinand. On May 1, 1486, Columbus received permission to see Queen Isabella. Columbus presented his plans to the queen, who in turn referred it to a committee. After the passing of much time, the experts of Spain, like their counterparts in Portugal, replied that Columbus had grossly underestimated the distance to

Asia. They pronounced the idea impractical and advised their royal highnesses to pass on the proposed venture.

However, to keep Columbus from taking his ideas elsewhere, the Spanish monarchs gave him an annual allowance of twelve thousand maravedis, and in 1489, they furnished him with a letter ordering all cities and towns under their domain to provide him food and lodging at no cost. This was a full six years prior to Columbus's departure for the New World. In reality this was a contingency plan by the Vatican, Spanish, and Portuguese. They now knew that Columbus was very serious about crossing the Atlantic. If he was successful, he would discover the Portuguese, Mayan, Aztec, and Templar colonies already in the Americas. The Portuguese and Spanish needed a tactic to delay his departure until they had finished their war against the Moors (Muslims). Once the war was over, they could divert their resources to protecting their interests in the Americas.

On January 2, 1492, the last Muslim leader, Muhammad XII, known as Boabdil to the Spanish, surrendered complete control of Granada to Ferdinand and Isabella, los Reyes Católicos ("the Catholic Monarchs"). The reconquest (reconquista) of Iberia was complete.

On the evening of August 3, 1492, Columbus departed from Palos de la Frontera with three ships: a larger carrack, the *Santa María* (a Galician ship), and two smaller caravels, the *Pinta* (meaning painted) and the *Santa Clara*, nicknamed the *Niña* (meaning little girl) after her owner, Juan Niño of Moguer. The monarchs forced the Palos inhabitants to contribute to the expedition.

The *Santa María* was owned by Juan de la Cosa and captained by Columbus. The *Pinta* and the *Niña* were piloted by the Pinzón brothers, Martín Alonso and Vicente Yáñez. The *Santa María* was not only a Galician (Celtic) ship owned by de la Cosa; de la Cosa is also responsible for printing the now-famous Juan de la Cosa map. The map was printed ca. 1500 and shows twenty-five ancient geoglyphic survey markers that currently exist on the North and South American continents. These geoglyphs would have taken centuries to explore and construct. Could both the North and South American continents have been explored from coast to coast in the eight years between the voyage of Columbus and the printing of the map? I think you already know the answer. A photo of each of the geoglyphs can be seen in the book *Ancient Signposts* (2011).

The Pinzón Brothers

The Pinzón brothers were Spanish sailors, explorers, and fishermen, natives of Palos de la Frontera, Huelva, Spain. All three were Marisco Muslims, according to Christian scholar Jerald Dirks. Martín Alonso, Francisco Martín, and Vicente Yañez Pinzón participated in Christopher Columbus's first expedition to the New World and in other voyages of discovery and exploration in the late fifteenth and early sixteenth centuries.

The brothers were sailors of great prestige along the previously Muslim-held coast of Huelva. Huelva is located in Spain near the border with Portugal. Thanks to their many commercial voyages and voyages along the coast, the Pinzóns were famous, well off, and well respected in the maritime community. The strategic position of Huelva was established by the historic Atlantic port of Palos, from which expeditions had set forth to the African coasts as well as in the previous wars against Portugal, organized on many occasions by the Pinzón family.

Martín Alonso and Vicente Yáñez, captains of the caravels the *Pinta* and the *Niña*, are the best known of the brothers, but the third brother, the lesser-known Francisco Martín, was aboard the *Pinta* as its master.

Although they sometimes quarreled with Columbus, on several occasions the Pinzón brothers were instrumental in preventing mutiny against him, particularly during the first voyage. On October 6, Martín intervened in a dispute between Columbus and his crew by proposing an altered course (which Columbus eventually accepted) and thus calming the simmering unrest. A few days later, on the night of October 9, 1492, the brothers were forced to intercede once again, and this time they proposed the compromise that if no land was sighted during the next three days, the expedition would return to Spain. On the third day, land was in fact sighted by Juan Rodríguez Bermejo (also known as Rodrigo de Triana). Could it be a coincidence that the Pinzón brothers knew exactly what correction to make in order to land on the first island outside the southeast corner of the Templar territory, a territory ceded to the Templars by Portugal, Spain's ally? Could it have been a coincidence that the Pinzón brothers knew exactly when they would sight land? It is clear that either the Pinzón brothers or Juan de la Cosa had already been to the Americas many times. De la Cosa, being a Celtic Galician, was most likely the one with the navigational knowledge of the Americas. Not only did de la Cosa travel with many famous explorers, but his name implies that he may have had some secret navigation device that we no longer know about. As I mentioned before, people of that time were named after something peculiar to that person. Juan de la Cosa is Spanish for "John of the Thing." I have always wondered what "the thing" referred to.

Why would the monarchs of Spain and the king of Portugal choose three Muslim brothers to accompany Columbus to the Americas? After all, hadn't the two countries just spent seven hundred years getting rid of Muslim control, and weren't the Pinzón brothers the architects of wars against Portugal? The obvious answer is that they had many reasons to persecute the Pinzóns, but instead they used this, and the Pinzóns' knowledge of the Americas, against them in directing Columbus to the uncolonized and unclaimed parts of the Americas. (Actually, the Caribbean had already been claimed by the Mayans, as indicated by the Chichen Itza pyramid geoglyphs, but that is another story.)

The First Voyage of Christopher Columbus
After departure, Columbus first sailed to the Canary Islands, which belonged to Castile (an eastern extension of Galicia), where he

restocked the provisions and made repairs. After stopping over in Gran Canaria, he departed from San Sebastián de la Gomera on September 6 for what turned out to be a five-week voyage across the ocean. A lookout on the *Pinta*, Rodrigo de Triana (also known as Juan Rodríguez Bermeo), spotted land about two o'clock on the morning of October 12 and immediately alerted Columbus by firing a small cannon. Columbus later maintained that he himself had already seen a light on the land a few hours earlier, thereby claiming for himself the lifetime pension promised by Ferdinand and Isabella to the first person to sight land.

Google

The first voyage of Columbus

(Please note that the preceding map, and documentation from the voyage, verifies that the *Pinta* left the other two ships at some point near Cuba [dotted line]. Also notice the jagged lines on the route that exist between Hispaniola and the island of Tortue. This information is vital to the following story.)

448

While performing research on Columbus, I ran across a story that I had never heard before. Until the writing of this chapter, I just placed it in the back of my mind because of the lack of validation. Now that I have obtained a definitive map of the first voyage of Columbus, and Wikipedia has updated their information, I am inclined to believe that the story is true. The story asserted that one of the ships, the *Pinta*, captained by one of the Pinzón brothers, mysteriously departed the convoy at Cuba and was not seen again until forty-five days later, after Columbus had supposedly began his trip home without the *Pinta*. The story indicated that the *Pinta* mysteriously joined Columbus near an island off the coast of Hispaniola.

The story also said that when the *Pinta* arrived back in Spain, it was loaded with a cargo of gold. This is not hard to believe after reading that Montezuma, twenty-seven years later, sent Hernan Cortes, while an official in Cuba, a circular piece of gold three feet wide. This was accompanied by a circular piece of silver three feet wide, along with much more gold. This was payment to keep Spain from invading Mesoamerica. Why did Montezuma think Spain was going to invade Mexico? This question is answered by one of the geoglyphs that Columbus and the Pinzón brothers placed during their first voyage to the Americas. All that payment of gold did was intensify the appetite of Cortes, who, supposedly against orders from Spain, invaded Mesoamerica in 1519. Thus began the quest for gold and the Spanish Inquisition in the Americas.

It should be noted that the Spanish Inquisition was sponsored by the Vatican and that a priest accompanied every Spanish expedition in order to protect the interests of the Church. An exception to the harsh treatment of the natives was the Catholic Jesuit order, who protected the American Indians from slavery whenever possible.

The "Exploration"

The Wikipedia article on Christopher Columbus explains,

> Columbus explored the northeast coast of Cuba, where he landed on October 28. On November 22, Martín Alonso Pinzon took the *Pinta* on an unauthorized expedition to places unknown. Columbus, for his part, continued to the western tip of Hispaniola, where he landed on December 5 at what is now Mole Saint-Nicolas bay.
>
> There the *Santa María* allegedly ran aground on Christmas Day, 1492, twenty days after it arrived, and had to be abandoned. The native chief in the area, Guacanagari, gave Columbus permission to leave some of his men behind. Columbus left thirty-nine men behind and founded the settlement of La Navidad, Haiti. When he departed Haiti, he sailed along its northern coast, with a single ship, until he encountered the *Pinta* on January 6, 1493.

Did the *Santa María* really run aground, or was it left behind by the Pinzón brothers, with a crew of thirty-nine men, to collect more gold after Columbus returned to Spain? Based on the documented information, a picture is emerging of what transpired during the Columbus expedition. From the documentation available, and the history of Columbus in his later life, it appears that he was but a pawn in a plan by Spain to gather gold and occupy Mesoamerica.

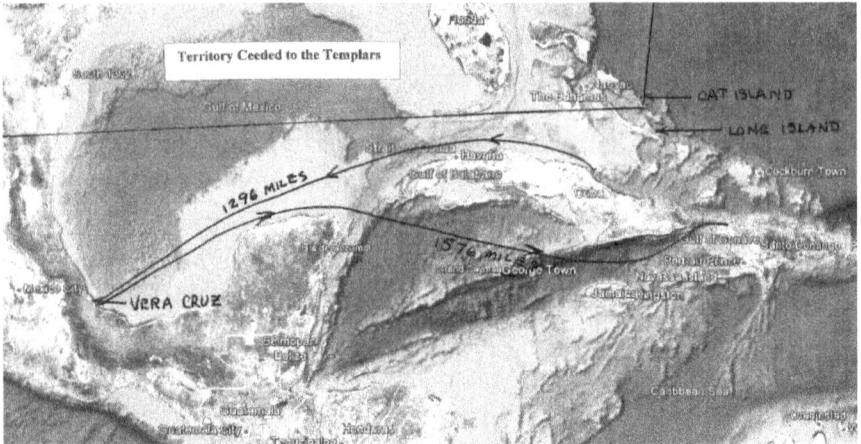

Presumed route of the *Pinta* during its absence

The preceding map depicts the probable route of the *Pinta* prior to rejoining Columbus at Hispaniola. The fact that the two ships were able to locate each other at all in such a vast ocean is inconceivable. The only way that this could have happened was for the Pinzón brothers to have known the area and agreed to meet at an easily recognized point, such as between the island of Tortue and the island of Hispaniola. The *Pinta* was missing from November 22, 1492, until January 6, 1493, a period of forty-five days. Allowing for a speed of only five knots, the *Pinta* could have traveled 5,400 miles during that period of time.

It is most likely that the *Pinta* traveled to Vera Cruz, Mexico, to obtain gold for Spain. If this is true, it would have been logical for the *Pinta* to have left the other two ships at the northernmost point in the voyage, while off the coast of Cuba. The distance from that point to Vera Cruz is 1,296 miles. The distance from Vera Cruz to Hispaniola is 1,576 miles. Based on this mileage, the sailing time from Cuba to Vera Cruz and back to Hispaniola would be approximately twenty-four days. Based on the forty-five days that the *Pinta* was absent, this leaves twenty-one days unaccounted for. Assuming that the *Pinta* did go to Vera Cruz, which this author has many reasons to believe, a portion of the twenty-one days would have been used in resupply, negotiations, and loading. During our research it was learned that Vera Cruz, Mexico, and Lisbon, Portugal, are two of the oldest cities on the Atlantic. I find it interesting that both countries play a part in this story.

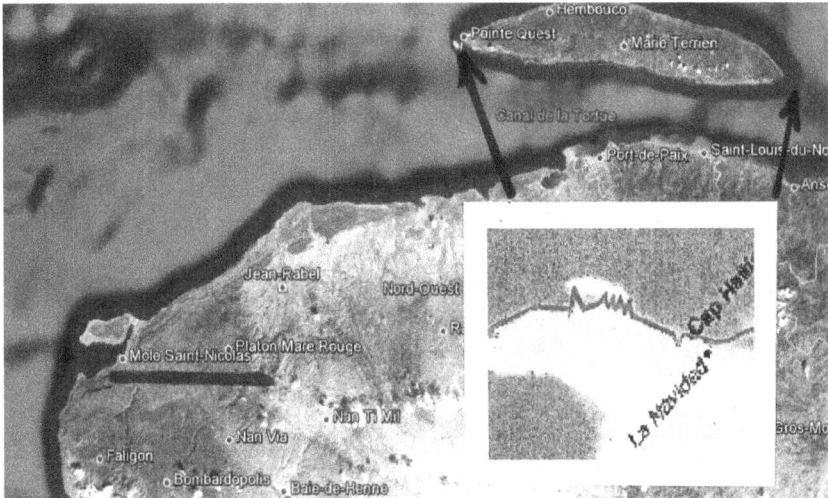

Google Earth – The Faram Research Foundation
Mole-Saint-Nicolas, Haiti

The Pinzón brothers most likely had agreed to meet between the islands of Tortue and Hispaniola. The *Pinta* most likely passed by the bay where Columbus was waiting and proceeded to the agreed meeting place. When the captain of the *Pinta* found no one waiting, he would have dropped anchor at the east end of the island and waited for Columbus and his brother.

The preceding photo is provided to show two things: the bay where Columbus was waiting, and the zigzag pattern (called tacking in nautical terminology) taken by the *Niña* after leaving the bay. Tacking like this in such confined quarters is very dangerous unless you already know the depth of the water. This type of maneuver would be used if there were limited visibility, such as a light fog, and you were looking for another ship. The visibility to the horizon from the deck of a ship is twelve miles. The distance between the two land masses here is only four miles. This would preclude the need for tacking unless the visibility was diminished and you were looking for another ship. It should also be noticed that as soon as the two ships joined up, there was no more tacking and they began their voyage home.

The Columbus Geoglyphs

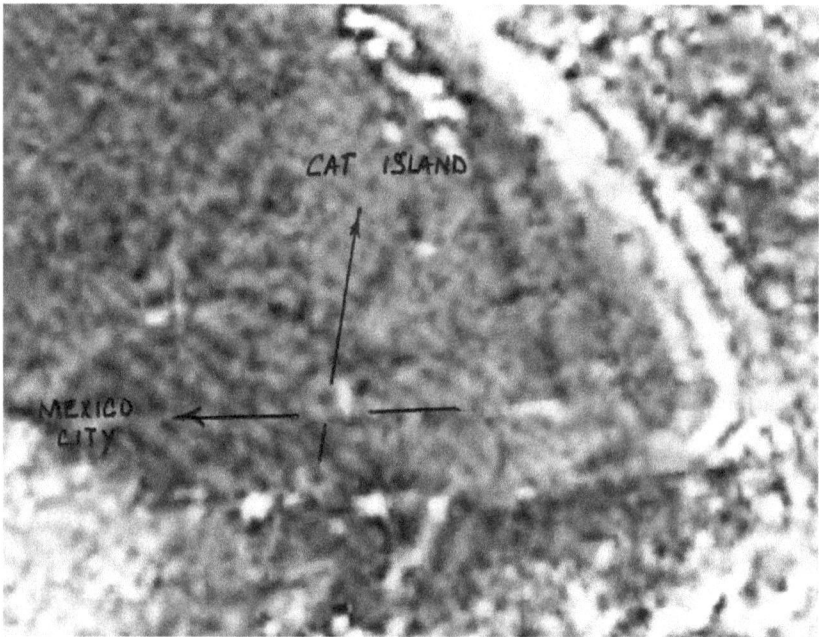

Google Earth – The Faram Research Foundation

Geoglyph 1 (two circles) constructed by the Columbus expedition.

(The location is not disclosed to protect the site.)

The preceding geoglyph shows one of many geoglyphs that Columbus placed in the Caribbean to claim the territory for Spain. The radial extending to Mexico City is based on the white line on the right side of the photo. The geoglyph also shows a line projecting to the southeast corner of the Templar territory. Using the standard protocol of running a line through the center of the two circles located at the bottom left of the photo; the line terminates precisely at Cat Island. Cat Island is the southeast corner of the territory given to the Templars by Portugal and the first landing spot of Columbus.

This, along with a second Columbus geoglyph shown below, proves that Spain knew about and had plans to colonize the Caribbean and Mesoamerica prior to Columbus's departure on his first voyage.

This is but another validation of the origins of the United States of America, which has been the subject of this book.

Google Earth – The Faram Research Foundation

Geoglyph 2 constructed by the Columbus expedition.

(The location is not disclosed to protect the site.)

Geoglyph 2 is a more defined geoglyph and is located more than 250 miles from geoglyph 1. Each side of these stone structures constitutes a bearing pointing to a place that meets the protocols of the ancients and outlines the new territory claimed by Spain. This geoglyph, as are all geoglyphs, is confirmed as legitimate by one of the bearings pointing to a cardinal point of the compass, in this case 360 degrees. The final verification stems from the fact that one of the radials points directly to geoglyph 1.

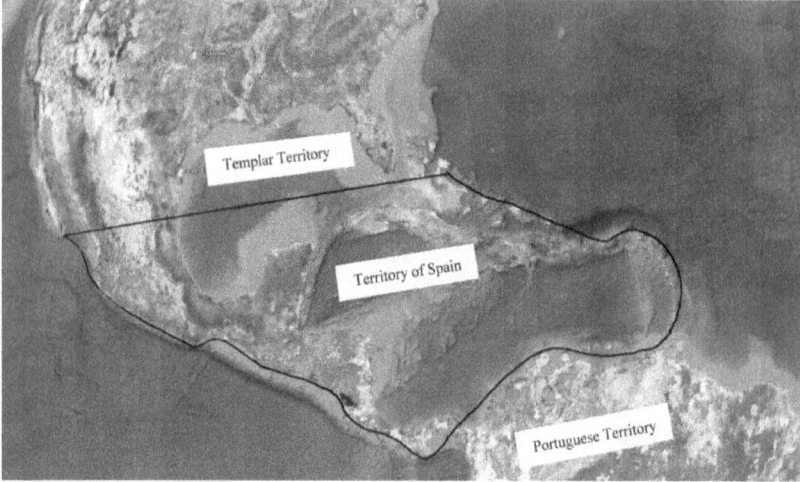

Google Earth – The Faram Research Foundation

**The territory claimed by Spain on the first voyage
of Columbus, as defined by geoglyphs 1 and 2**

Based on the information now available, it would appear that Spain had two objectives when they sent Columbus to the New World. One was to geoglyphically establish their claim to the Caribbean and the surrounding territory. The second was to bring back gold to Spain to help eliminate the deficit that they had acquired during the seven-hundred-year-long war against the Moors. The Portuguese most likely did not participate in this adventure, since they already had substantial colonization in eastern South America (Brazil) by this time. Spain had other motives. They were now aware of the vast hoard of gold brought back to Spain by the Pinzón brothers from the Aztecs. Spain and the Vatican wanted more gold and all the land that they could conquer. Notice on the following map that none of the voyages of Columbus encroach upon the territory ceded to the Templars by Portugal, or on Brazil, which was colonized by Portugal.

The Vatican also had motives to participate in the planning of this expedition. During the seven-hundred-year war with the Muslims, the influence of the Catholic Church had been decimated. The Vatican's control had also been compromised by the split of Europe into two camps consisting of Eastern Europe and Western Europe. The Orthodox churches prevailed in the eastern half of Europe, and the western half was involved in a dispute for control of the Church between the Vatican and the royal families of France. Both Spain and the Vatican needed to restore their wealth and prestige. To protect the Vatican's interests, a priest accompanied each expedition that the conquistadores made to the Americas.

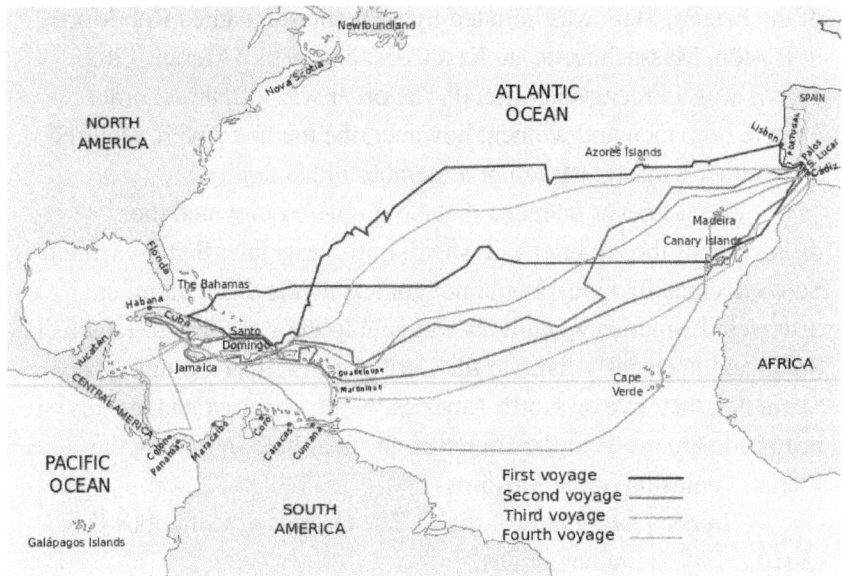

Google

The four voyages of Columbus

Between 1492 and 1503, Columbus completed four round-trip voyages between Spain and the Americas, all of them under the sponsorship of the crown of Spain. These voyages marked the beginning of the massive exploitation and colonization of Central and South America and are thus of enormous significance in Western history. Columbus always insisted, in the face of mounting evidence to the contrary, that the lands he visited during those voyages were part of the Asian continent, as previously described by Marco Polo and other European travelers. Columbus's refusal to accept that the lands he had visited and thought he had claimed for Spain were not part of Asia might explain in part why the American continents were named after the Templar term "La Merica" (the Western Star) and not after Columbus. The lack of knowledge by Columbus of where he had been further confirms that the Pinzón brothers and Juan de la Cosa were the driving forces during the expedition and were responsible for the building of the geoglyphs.

Coincidentally, in 1850 a Freemason order named "the Order of the Eastern Star" was initiated by a Freemason named Rob Morris in Boston, Massachusetts, an East Coast city in "La Merica." Rob Morris was a Freemason official. The order was a fraternal order open to both men and women; however, the members were required to be either a master Mason or a member of his family.

It was never intended that Columbus be crowned the discoverer of the Americas. It wasn't until years later that the United States decided that they would not contest myths that Columbus discovered America. Columbus was sent to the Americas to establish Spain and Portugal's claim to the Caribbean. Neither Columbus nor Spain had their eye on North America. North America had already been ceded to the Templars in return for their help in ridding the Iberian Peninsula of the Muslims.

In her *Times Online* article "The Origins of Columbus Day" (2010), Katy Steinmetz writes,

> Columbus Day was the brainchild of New York state senator Timothy Sullivan, an archetypal Tammany Hall man who greased the wheels of New York City's notoriously corrupt political machine during the late nineteenth century and early twentieth century. His bill to set Columbus Day

aside passed by a vote of eighty-six to thirty-five in 1909, and the initial reaction from those hardworking Americans of yore wasn't great. People labeled it superfluous and called for its repeal.

Sullivan's power was so great there is no doubt he could accomplish the feat of getting this bill through Congress. Sullivan began life selling newspapers as a young boy from Ireland. During his rise to fame, he was deeply involved in the criminal element in New York. Once he achieved his political success, he protected the people with whom he had risen to power. Sullivan served in the New York State Assembly, the New York Senate, and the US Congress.

Sullivan forced the bill on reluctant New York lawmakers, and they in turn forced it on other states. An objector wrote of the day, "Its occurrence interferes sadly with the conduct of business in the season which should be the busiest, but once we have a holiday we must keep it. Luckily there are no other new holidays in sight at present."

Geoglyphs that make up the three North American territories:

Original North American territory
Stonehenge, ca. 3100 BCE
Newport Tower location, prior to 7000 BCE
Inspiration Peak, prior to 7000 BCE

Revised North American territory
Stonehenge, ca. 3100 BCE
Newport Tower location, prior to 7000 BCE
Inspiration Peak, prior to 7000 BCE
Kensington Runestone, ca. 1362–1492 CE

Spanish Territory
Various geoglyphs placed around the Caribbean along the route of
Columbus's first voyage, 1492 CE

Portuguese Territory
Caral, Peru, geoglyphs, ca. 3000 BCE

End Narrative O

Narrative P

An Introduction to Geoglyphology

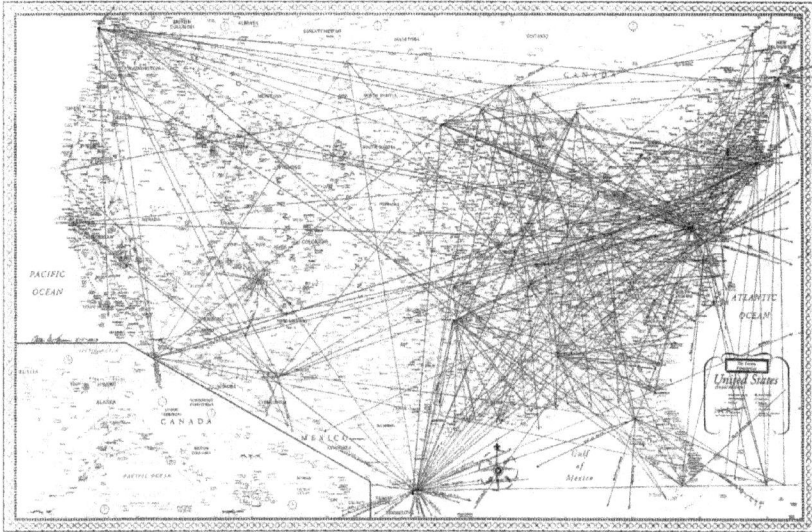

The Faram Research Foundation
Map of just a few of the geoglyphs in the United States

Much of the information mentioned in this book was obtained through the ancient science of geoglyphology. Being so, it seemed logical that a short chapter on how to read the many geoglyphs you will encounter should be one of the first considerations.

Research has shown that ancient civilizations have passed down a secret science named geoglyphology for millennia. There exists a legacy of geoglyphs, "geo" meaning earth and "glyph" meaning writing, on the shores and highlands of land masses around the world. A well-known example of a geoglyphic survey marker is Stonehenge in England. Stonehenge has been known for centuries, as have earlier monoliths, for the many astronomical alignments that were designed into their construction. This phenomenon of astronomical alignment is presented in most megalithic and geoglyphic structures around the world and has recently been accepted as a legitimate science named archaeoastronomy. Until now the geoglyphic attributes of these structures have been overlooked and known only to a few people in secret societies.

Since the practice of geoglyphology is to mark a claimed territory, the practice would inherently require some degree of secrecy. Most of these survey markers are so large and so spread out that they remain hidden unless someone who knows of their existence points them out. By being so large, they are for the most part immune to tampering and remain hidden until the builder needs to prove their prior claim to a given territory. The ability to create survey markers that span continents and are accurate to within two hundred feet indicates a degree of sophistication currently being ignored, and in some cases destroyed, by academia worldwide. The fact that geoglyphs are being destroyed as soon as they are made public is in itself proof of their importance.

Until now the majority of the information available to the archeologist has been gleaned from information recovered at a dig site. During our research we realized that a great majority of the ancient architectural, monolithic, and geoglyphic structures built around the world had something more to offer. There exists a commonality in the structures and associated geoglyphs that shows they were aligned in such a manner that the study of their linear alignment unveils a much larger story. Studying these attributes immensely expands the data available to the archeologist, historian, and the related disciplines.

Extensive research on these geoglyphs, which exist on every continent and many islands around the world, has shown that no matter when or where they were constructed, they all tie into a worldwide network of persons or entities of common beliefs and culture. These cultures have progressed, prospered, and suffered setbacks for millennia. However, the secret of geoglyphology has been perpetuated for millennia, through all the apocalypses.

These geoglyphs range in age from before the thirty-two-thousand-year-old Bosnian pyramids to geoglyphs in the United States as late as one hundred years ago.

Data recovered from geoglyphs can include obtaining the geographical range of the culture being studied, the level of sophistication that existed in relation to their understanding of mathematics and geometry, their knowledge of world geography, the discovery of other archeological sites that were unknown prior to the studies, and the dating of the culture itself by the data collected at the offsite locations.

What makes up a geoglyph?

Glyph: A glyph can be any earthly design that is used to convey a message, whether it is a petroglyph, hieroglyph, or geoglyph.

Geoglyph: A geoglyph is a glyph that occurs on the ground.

Bearing: A bearing refers to the direction of a line formed by a geoglyph that points in relation to magnetic north. Magnetic north can be used at the geoglyph site because it has not been distorted by magnetic deviations that exist between the starting point and the destination. A true or direct line is used once you depart the origination point in order to overcome any magnetic deviation along the way. Magnetic deviation exists all over the world and renders the magnetic heading of a compass useless over long distances because of the error occurring naturally from the magnetism of the earth. A true heading is the shortest distance between two points without having to consider magnetic deviation. True headings can be scribed on a globe, derived from celestial navigation, GPS, and computer software These methods produce true headings that are not distorted by magnetic deviation. It was learned, through the efforts of Google Earth, that all the bearings used in ancient geoglyphs proved to be true radials, after extending the magnetic bearings measured at the source.

Radials: Radials are bearings after they leave the source. At the source, magnetic bearings and true headings are the same, because no distortion has taken place by moving away from the source. Once a direction away from the source is plotted, it must be plotted on a true course, not a magnetic course, in order to avoid magnetic deviation.

For the most part, geoglyphs are so large that they can only be recognized from the air. The civilizations that placed these geoglyphs must have had mathematical capabilities well beyond anything we are taught. Even knowing where some sites exist, it is difficult to find some except from the air. The Nazca Lines are a prime example. The glyphs take on several forms. Some take the form of a triangle, another might be one or more circles, and another might be one or more lines touching or crossing each other. No matter what shape a glyph takes, any line can be a pointer to a place important to the creator of that glyph.

Spherical Geometry

The geoglyphical data presented here represents the use of spherical geometry. In spherical geometry all lines are curved along the surface, and no lines are parallel. It is difficult to grasp the concept that two parallel headings can cross. That is because we are used to thinking in terms of plane geometry on a flat plane. However, this changes when you draw lines on a sphere. In dealing with a sphere, you enter the realm of spherical geometry.

Spherical geometry is the study of figures on the surface of a sphere, as opposed to the type of geometry studied in plane geometry or solid geometry. In spherical geometry, straight lines are great circles. One of the characteristics of spherical geometry is that any two lines will always cross in two places. There are also no parallel lines. The angle between two lines in spherical geometry is the angle between the planes of the corresponding great circles, and a spherical triangle is defined by its three angles.

In the field of geoglyphology, we are plotting lines in a spherical world and then displaying the results on a flat plane. That is why the field of geoglyphology could not have been proposed without the advent of software that computes using spherical geometry and then displaying it on a flat plane. This type of precise mapping precludes the plotting of these bearings on a flat map. Maps become distorted when converted from a sphere to a flat map. Any lines that are depicted here on a flat, nonsatellite map were first plotted using the Google software and then drawn on the flat map after the end points were determined. Even then, the proper curvature is missing.

Geoglyphological Protocols
What follows is a description of the various ways in which the initial bearings can be shown in a geoglyph.

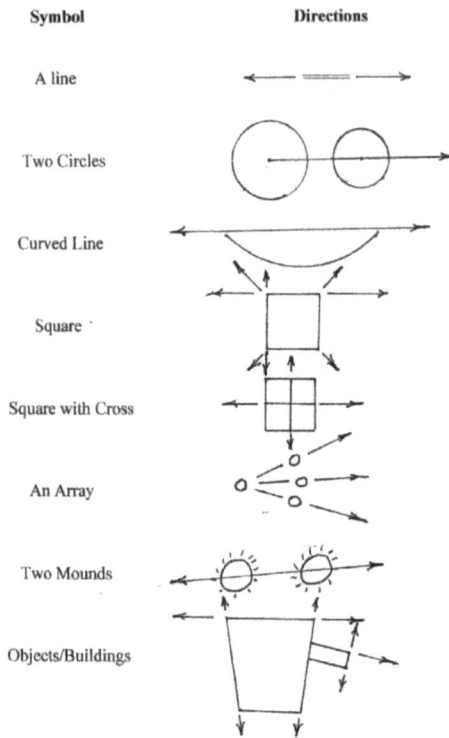

Symbol	Directions

A line

Two Circles

Curved Line

Square

Square with Cross

An Array

Two Mounds

Objects/Buildings

The preceding diagram outlined the various ways that a geoglyphic bearing can be generated. Any geoglyph can be composed of several of these methods of generating a line. The last figure in the previous illustration is especially significant. Many cultures incorporated the bearings that would designate their territory into their buildings. Ancient buildings with nonparallel walls are most likely a sign that the building is a territorial geoglyph.

After applying the protocols in the previous illustration to determine the applicable bearings, the protocols illustrated in the following diagram are applied to determine the end point of the extended bearing. An extended bearing is known as a radial.

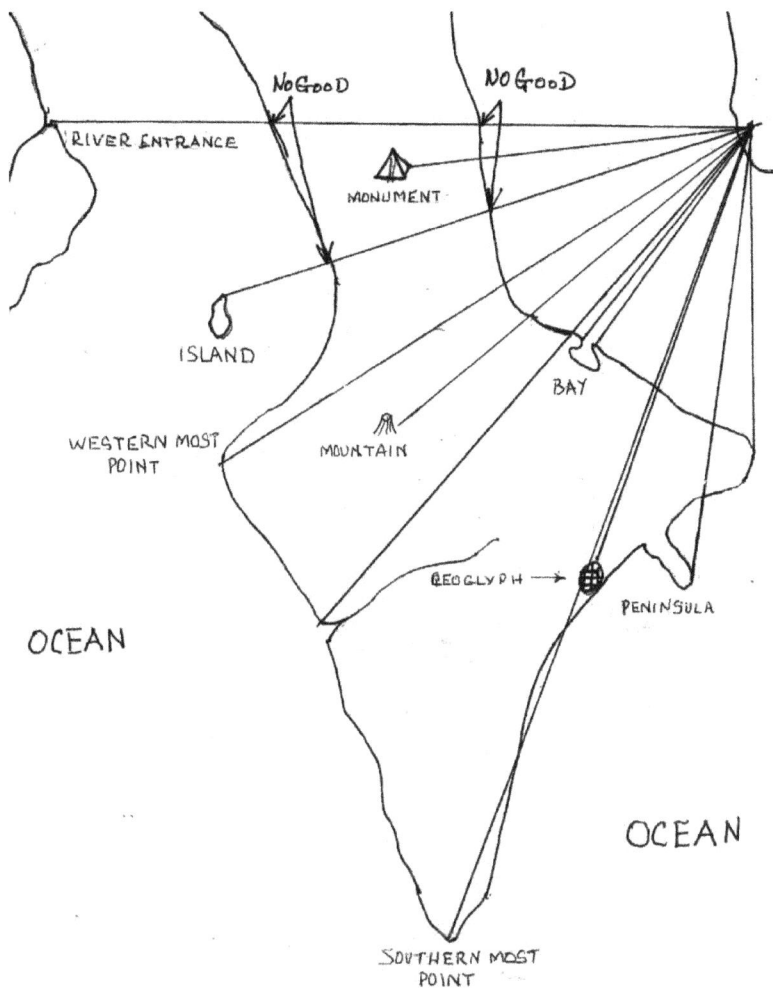

The protocols used to determine the end point of a radial can be:

    1. The entrance to a river.
    2. The entrance to a bay.
    3. The tip of a peninsula.

4. The easternmost, westernmost, northernmost, or southernmost point on a continent.

5. An island.

6. Another major geoglyph or group of geoglyphs.

7. A major monolith or ancient monument.

8. A volcano.

9. The highest mountain in a mountain range.

10. A prominent geographical point on a river or shoreline.

Please keep in mind that each of the geoglyphological surveys in the book meet these protocols. Although the scale may prohibit the end points being shown, they do terminate at a point meeting one of the previously mentioned protocols.

Once the bearings are established for a geoglyph, the bearings are extended in the form of radials (true bearings) to determine if and where they intersect with an object that meets the ancient protocols established millennia ago. In order for an extended radial to be considered legitimate, the radial must intersect at a specific point meeting the protocols set down by the ancients. (See previous illustration.) These points verify that the radial is legitimate and indicate the end point of the radial.

After some study it was discovered that many mediums were used to construct geoglyphs. These included the arrangement of stones; the planting of different colors of flora; the sterilizing of the ground; the scraping of the earth to reveal a different color underneath (Nazca); the changing of natural geological features by modifying or supplementing those features; aligning the walls of structures (Caral, Peru), monoliths (Stonehenge), and pyramids (worldwide); creating stone and earth mounds; and more. For instance, the edges of the mounds of the Mississippian Indians (Mound culture) in the central United States have been proven to be geoglyphic territorial pointers. Two or more circular mounds side by side can also be a pointer when a line is drawn through their center points.

Ancient archeological locations, many previously unknown, have been identified through geoglyphology. The accuracy of the calculations of the ancient peoples is incredible. The GPS accuracy of modern software programs is seldom more accurate than the orientations by the ancients. By calculating the bearing at the source, one can follow the extended radial for sometimes thousands of miles and locate a related geoglyph with little or no error. Many of the termination points are used many times over by geoglyphs from different points around the world. This fact alone validates that there was once a worldwide culture. The percentage of success in locating a verifiable end point of each of the extended radials of any one glyph was variable but ran in the range of 90–100 percent. Much of the lack of success in finding an end point for an extended geoglyphological bearing was attributed to urbanization, overgrowth, and vandalism at the ancient end point.

Surprisingly, based on the glyphs that were found, there seems to be an incredible amount of durability built into the geoglyphs. It appears that the meteorological conditions at any given site were considered in determining the materials used. At sites where rain and wind seldom occurred, most glyphs were made of earth. At locations that endured rain and wind, stones and rock were used.

Research results indicate that geoglyphology holds great promise in expanding our understanding of the civilizations that have preceded us. Through the tireless efforts of many devoted archaeologists, and new methods of discovery, the world is on the cusp of a new awakening. To some this new paradigm change will be quite uncomfortable.

The result of plotting ancient geoglyphs has revealed the following:

1. Geoglyphs have been incorporated into the architecture of many ancient complexes.

2. Geoglyphs can hasten and enhance the discovery of critical information not otherwise available to the scientist at a newly discovered site.

3. Geoglyphs can indicate at least the minimum range of the geographic dispersal of a civilization or culture.

4. Geoglyphs can uncover a hidden sophistication in a society that may have gone unnoticed from data gathered at a dig site.

5. Geoglyphs can reveal other sites related to the initially discovered site that may have never otherwise have been discovered.

6. Studies have proven that geoglyphology can be of immense importance to archaeology and the related disciplines.

End Narrative P

Narrative Q

The Sterling Castle, Scotland, Geoglyphs. Perfection in Geoglyphology

Google

Entryway to Sterling Castle, Scotland

"King Arthur's Knot" (geoglyph), Sterling Castle, Scotland

Google Earth – The Faram Research Foundation

Sterling Castle geoglyph bearings

As is the case in many of the more important geoglyphs, there is a built-in error factor to prevent the uninitiated from decoding the puzzle. In this case, there is a two-degree error factored into the bearings. Two degrees must be subtracted from the readings on each bearing in order to obtain the correct directions. It is difficult to recognize one of these types of geoglyphs unless you have experience and know the points used for millennia around the world.

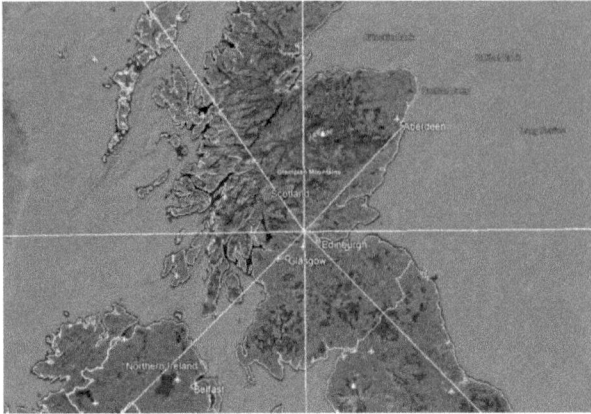

Sterling Castle geoglyph radials

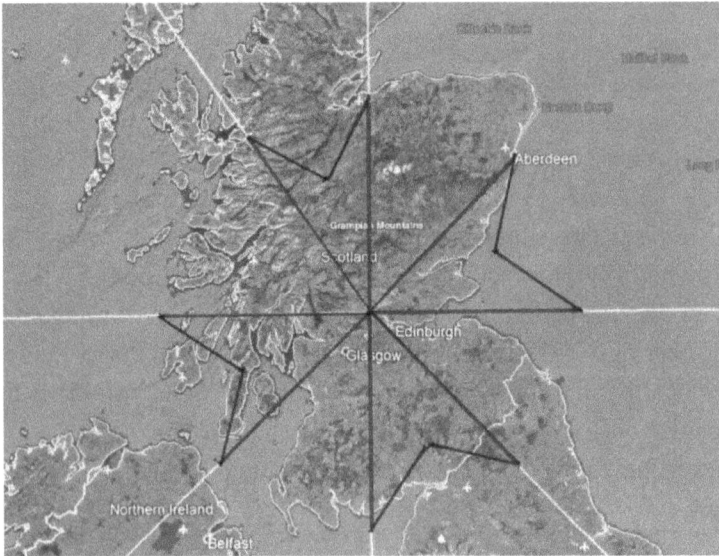

The Maltese Cross is suggested by the Aberdeen end point

473

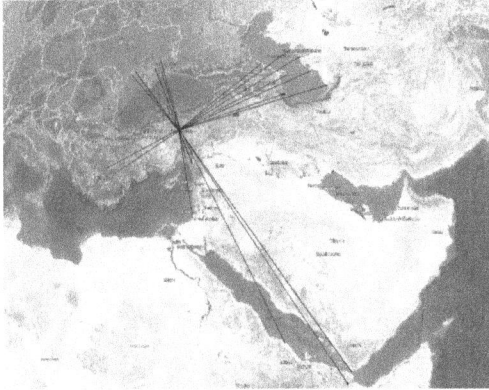

A similar cross pattern at Kultepe, Turkey, ca. 2000 BCE.

Many others exist around the world.

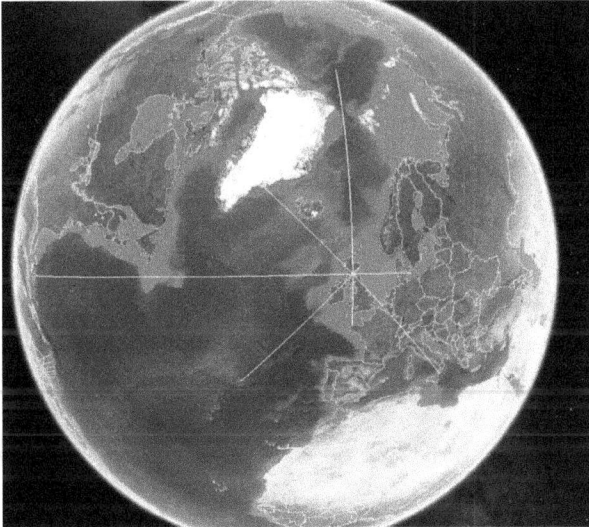

Sterling Castle radial end points

In the previous image notice the line intersecting with the westernmost radial. This line originates at the Newport Tower location. This is discussed on the next page.

Details of the Termination Points Related to the Sterling Castle Geoglyphs

Before we proceed, it should be remembered that the site and end points of all the major geoglyphs around the world were established thousands of years ago. Therefore the date of the structure on any given site may be more recent and may not coincide with the date that the site was first used. In this case, and with many other ancient geoglyphs, the original end-point structures may have been replaced with more modern structures or geoglyphs. The end points' existence does not depend on when the geoglyph was constructed. Many sites and end points have been used repeatedly down through time.

Google Earth – The Faram Research Foundation

The end points of the Newport Tower 193-degree radial and the Stewart Castle 272, minus two, degree radial

The southern orientation of the Newport Tower is 193 degrees. By extending the 193 bearing south, you see that it intersects at two important places: Cat Island Bahamas, previously called San Salvador Island, and the intersection of the equator with the west coast of Ecuador. San Salvador Island (Cat Island) is the place where Columbus first landed. (See narrative O.)

The Newport Tower location is an important site that helps define the original North American territory that eventually became the United States. (See narrative N.)

In Columbus's time Cat Island was named San Salvador Island. At some point the name was switched to Cat Island. As is indicated on the map, the island west of Cat Island is named Little San Salvador. It was not an accident that Columbus landed on this particular island. As is illustrated by the radial extending from King Arthur's Knot and the important 193 degree bearing from the Newport Tower location, this island has been important for many centuries.

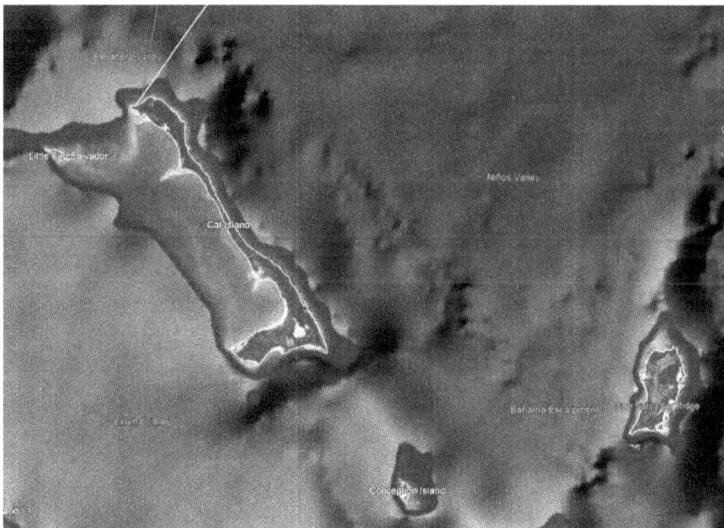

Google Earth – The Faram Research Foundation
Cat Island (San Salvador), Bahamas

Google Earth – The Faram Research Foundation

The 092-2 radial, Moan Lighthouse, Zealand, Denmark. It is little known that Zealand was inhabited by the Celts until ca. 1398 CE.

Sacred sites were established thousands of years ago and were used and re-used repeatedly down through time. The structure, or geoglyph, which currently resides on a site, does not necessarily reflect previous uses of the site. Lighthouses and antennas are the favorite modern replacements for old geoglyphs.

It has been suggested that the error component in the older geoglyphs could be the result of the shifting of the magnetic pole. This is not a correct assumption since geoglyphs are aligned on true headings rather than magnetic headings. However, magnetic headings can be assigned at the origination point to assist in

477

calculating the true headings destination. At the origination point both the true and magnetic heading are the same.

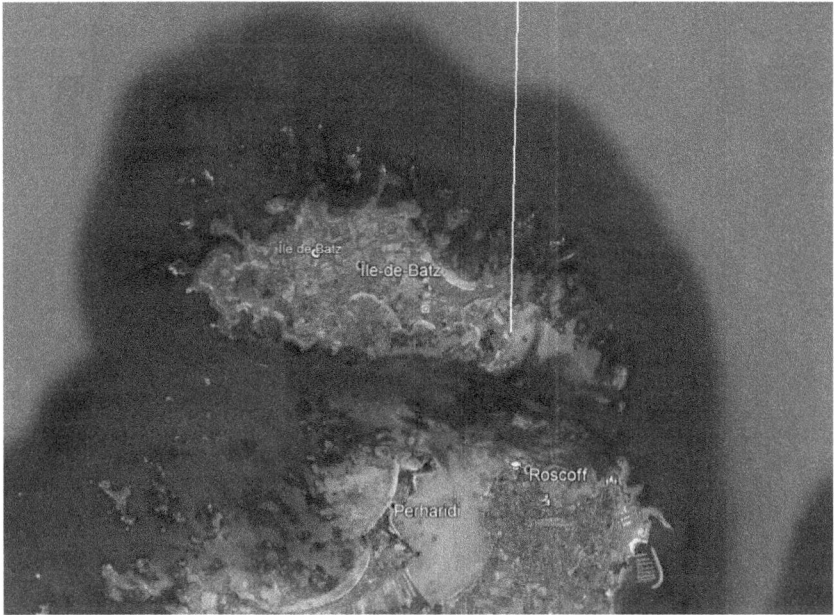

Google Earth – The Faram Research Foundation
182-2 radial, tip of Batz Island, Britannia, France

Google Earth – The Faram Research Foundation
047-2 Radial, Aberdeen, Scotland

The 229-2 degree radial at Point Arnel Lighthouse, Azores.
Notice the four-pointed cross and the eight-sided walls.

138-2 radial, Torre Faro (Lighthouse), east tip of Sicily. With four-pointed cross.

The 327-2 radial points out the Viking Tiniteqilaq, Greenland, geoglyph

This geoglyph was laid down to outline the territory given to the Vikings by the Denmark–Norway Alliance after the Vikings were banned from Norway ca. 1000 CE. Don't forget that the site can be much older than the geoglyph that currently exists there. Many geoglyph locations have been used over and over for thousands of years. (See Narrative L.)

End Narrative Q

References

All images in this book are presumed to be the property of the person or entity notated, in the public domain, in the expired copyright category, or are property of the author. All geoglyph maps were constructed using the Google Earth application.

Publications:

Algaze, Guillermo. *The Uruk World System: The Dynamics of Expansion of Early Man*

Anderson, Fred. *Ancient History Encyclopedia*, February 24, 2017.

Ball, Martin, and Nicole Muller, *The Celtic Languages*. Routledge, 2003

Bitel, Lisa M. *Land of Women: Tales of Sex and Gender from Early Ireland.* Cornell University Press, 1996, p. 212.

Case, H. "Beakers: Deconstruction and After." *Proceedings of the Prehistoric Society* 59 (1993)

Childe, Vere Gordan. *The Bronze Age.* 1930.

Clay, Berle R. *Circles and Ovals, Two Types of Adena Ritual Space.* Southeastern Archaeology.

Collis, John. *The Celts: Origins, Myths and Inventions.* Stroud: Tempus Publishing, 2003

Cooper, L. D. *Cracking the Freemason's Code.* Chapter 4. Rider, 2006

Cooper, Robert Dafoe, Stephen. "Rosicrucians and Freemasonry." *Masonic Dictionary*.

Crowhurst, Howard. *Carnac, the Alignments*. 2012.

Cunliffe, Barry, and John T. Koch, eds. *Celtic from the West*. David Brown Co., 2012.

Cunliffe, Barry. *Facing the Ocean*. Oxford University Press, 2004.

Cunliffe, Barry. *The Celts: A Very Short Introduction*. Oxford, 2003.

Doyle, John Andrew. *English Colonies in America*. Vol. 4 of *The Middle Colonies*. 1907.

"Meeting of Frontiers." *The Russian Colonization of Alaska*.

"Pre-Columbian Civilizations." *Encyclopedia Britannica*.

Faram, Arthur. *Ancient Signposts*. Foundation Press, 2011.

Faram, Arthur, *La Merica*. Foundation Press, 2014.

Fountain, Henry. "Archaeological Site in Peru Is Called Oldest City in Americas." *New York Times*, April 27, 2001.

George, Andrew, trans. *The Epic of Gilgamesh*. Penguin Classics, 2003.

Glassner, Jean-Jacques. *The Invention of Cuneiform: Writing in Sumer*. 2003, p. 31.

Hall, Manly P. *The Secret Teachings of All Ages: An Encyclopedic Outline of Masonic, Hermetic, Qabbalistic and Rosicrucian Symbolical Philosophy*. Courier Corporation, 2010.

Griffin, David Ray. *Spirituality and Society*. SUNY, 1988.

Haak, et al. *Neolithic Mitochondrial Haplogroup H Genomes and the Genetic Origins of Europeans.*

Hanegraaff, Wouter J. *New Age Religion and Western Culture. Esotericism in the Mirror of Secular Thought*, Leiden/New York/Koln: Brill, 1996.

Heath, Richard. *Sacred Number and the Lords of Time*: *The Stone Age Invention of Science and Religion.* 1st ed. 2014.

Holloway, April. "The Mystery of the Carnac Stones." *Ancient Origins* (September 15, 2013).

Hoelle, Jeffrey. "Postcards from the Amazon: Massive Clues of Amazon Area's Past." *San Angelo Standard Times*, July 31, 2010

Houtman, Dick, and Stef Aupers. "The Spiritual Turn and the Decline of Tradition: The Spread of Post-Christian Spirituality in Fourteen Western Countries, 1981–2000." *Journal for the Scientific Study of Religion* (2007).

Jacobsen, Thorkild, ed. "The Sumerian King List." *Oriental Institute of the University of Chicago, Assyriological Studies*, no. 11 (1939).

Jacobsen, Thorkild. *The Harps That Once…: Sumerian Poetry in Translation.* 1976.

———. *Treasures of Darkness: A History of Mesopotamian Religion.* 1976.

Jacobs, James Q. *Understanding Chavin and the Origins of Andean Civilization.*

James, Simon. *Exploring the World of the Celts*. London: Thames & Hudson, 1993, p. 21.

Kapuscinski, Afton N., and Kevin S. Masters. "The Current Status of Measures of Spirituality: A Critical Review of Scale Development." *Psychology of Religion and Spirituality* (2010).

Kennedy, Maeve. "Ancient DNA Study Shows Arrival of Beaker Folk Changed Britain Forever." *The Guardian Online*, February 2018.

King, Richard. *Orientalism and Religion: Post-Colonial Theory, India and "The Mystic East."* Routledge, 2002.

Koch, J. T. *Celtic Culture: A Historical Encyclopedia*. ABC-CLIO, 2006.

Leick, Gwendolyn. *Mesopotamia, the Invention of the City*. Penguin, 2003.

Leyburn, James Graham. *The Scotch-Irish: A Social History*. 1989.

Lyon, David Murray. *History of the Lodge of Edinburgh (Mary's Chapel)*. Preface. No. 1. Blackwood, 1873.

MacCulloch, J. A. *The Religion of the Ancient Celts*. Morrison & Gibb, 1911

Maisels, Charles Keith. *The Near East: Archaeology in the "Cradle of Civilization."* 1993.

Maisels, Charles Keith. *Early Civilizations of the Old World: The Formative Histories of Egypt, the Levant, Mesopotamia, India and China*. 2001.

McMahan, David L. *The Making of Buddhist Modernism*. Oxford
University Press, 2008.

Morgan, Diane. *Essential Islam: A Comprehensive Guide to Belief and
Practice*. ABC-CLIO, 2010.

Morris Brent. The Complete Idiot's Guide to Freemasonry. Alpha/Penguin
Books, 2006

Nazarova, Irina. *Caral—Cradle of American Civilization*. Peru, January,
2000.

Needham, S. "Transforming Beaker Culture in North-West Europe:
Processes of Fusion and Fission." *Proceedings of the Prehistoric
Society* 71 (2005): 171–217.

Ottman, Doug. *Defining Religion and Spirituality*. 2013.

Paloutzian, Raymond F., and Crystal L. Park, eds. *Handbook of the
Psychology of Religion and Spirituality*. 2nd ed. April 30, 2013.

Peet, Stephen D. *The Mound Builders*. 1892.

Rambachan, Anatanand. *The Limits of Scripture: Vivekananda's
Reinterpretation of the Vedas*. University of Hawaii Press, 1994.

Randall, E. O. *The Serpent Mound Adams County, Ohio*. 1905.

Rankin, David. *Celts and the Classical World*. Routledge, 1996

Rowell, Charles. *Devil's Head*. 2017.

Roy, Sumita. *Aldous Huxley and Indian Thought*. Sterling Publishers Pvt.
Ltd, 2003

Schneiders, Sandra M. "Spirituality in the Academy." *Theological Studies* (1989).

Sharf, Robert H. *Buddhist Modernism and the Rhetoric of Meditative Experience*. 1995.

Sheldrake, Philip. *Spirituality and History: Questions of Interpretation and Method*. Maryknoll, NY: Orbis Books, 1998.

Sheldrake, Philip. *A Brief History of Spirituality*. Wiley-Blackwell, 2007.

Simmons, Victoria. *Celtic Culture: A Historical Encyclopedia*, 2006.

Stevenson, David. *The Origins of Freemasonry*. Cambridge University Press, 1988

Shady Solis, Ruth, Jonathan Haas, and Winifred Creamer. "Dating Caral, a Preceramic Site in the Supe Valley on the Central Coast of Peru." *Science* (27 April 2001): 723–726

Science News. "Peru Holds Oldest New World City."

San Jose State University. *Origin of the Etruscans*.

Squire and Davis. *Ancient Monuments of the Mississippi Valley*.

Sutherland, A. "Hiram Abiff." AncientPages.com, January 27, 2019.

The Duke of Barcelos. *Templar Survival in Portugal*.

Tierney, J. J. "The Celtic Ethnography of Posidonius." *Proceedings of the Royal Irish Academy* 60 (1960C): 189–275.

Tuveson, Ernest Lee. *Redeemer Nation: The Idea of America's Millennial Role*. University of Chicago Press, 1980.

University of Chicago Press, *Mesopotamian Civilization*. 2nd ed. 2005.

Versluis, Arthur. *American Gurus: From Transcendentalism to New Age Religion*. Oxford University Press, 2014.

Waaijman, Kees. *Spirituality: Forms, Foundations, Methods*. Peeters Publishers, 2002.

Wallace-Murphy, Tim, and Merilyn Hopkins. *The Secret History of the Templars in America*. 2004.

Windle, Bertram. *Remains of the Prehistoric Age in England*.

Wong, Yuk-Lin Renita, and Jana Vinsky. "Speaking from the Margins: A Critical Reflection on the 'Spiritual-but-not-Religious' Discourse in Social Work." *British Journal of Social Work* 39, no. 7 (2009): 1343–59.

Wolkstein, Diane, and Samuel Noah Kramer. *Inanna: Queen of Heaven and Earth: Her Stories and Hymns from Sumer*. New York: Harper & Row, 1983.

Wolter, Scott. *The Hooked X*. North Star Press, Minnesota 2009

Zestermann, Adolph. *Memoir on the European Colonization of America in Ante-Historic Times*.

Websites

https://www.academia.edu/35664479/geoglyphology _A_ new_tool_for_the_Archaeologist

http://ancientamerica.com/geoglyphography-an-ancient-science-

rediscovered/

https://www.ancient-origins.net/geoglyphology

https://internationalresearchsociety.wordpress.com/2012/09/14/a-study-of-

the-ancient-geoglyphs-located-at-medicine-hat-canada/

http://www.livescience.com/50698-nazca-lines-images.html

http://www.whodiscoveredit.com/who-discovered-alaska.html

http://www.thefaramfoundation.com/medicinehatcanada.htm

http://www.yonaguni.ws

http://www.thekensingtonrunestone.com

http://www.thefaramfoundation.com

http://www.dandebat.dk/eng-dk-historie10.htm

http://www.gosanangelo.com